C000077500

The Speed Handbook

POST-CONTEMPORARY INTERVENTIONS

Series Editors: Stanley Fish and Fredric Jameson

THE
SPEED
HANDBOOK

Velocity, Pleasure, Modernism

Enda Duffy

DUKE UNIVERSITY PRESS   DURHAM AND LONDON   2009

© 2009 Duke University Press
All rights reserved.
Printed in the United States of
America on acid-free paper ∞
Designed by Amy Ruth Buchanan
Typeset in Monotype Fournier by
Tseng Information Systems, Inc.
Library of Congress Cataloging-in-
Publication data appear on the last
printed page of this book.

To Maurizia

CONTENTS ⟶

The Adrenaline Aesthetic: Speed as Culture

I think that cars today are the equivalent of the great Gothic cathedrals.
— Roland Barthes, quoted in Modris Ekstein, *Rites of Spring*

La prothese organique est devenue une prothese de l'esprit.
— Christophe Tison, *L'Ere du vite*

Speed, claimed Aldous Huxley, is the only new pleasure invented by modernity. This book argues two propositions: first, that access to new speeds, whether on a roller-coaster, airplane, but especially with the automobile, has been the most empowering and excruciating new experience for people everywhere in twentieth-century modernity; and second, that this experience should be thought of as political.

First, two images. Both are British, that is, from the place where the dread of forgetting about the nation's past domination of so much of the world's space, in the British Empire, makes markers of the new order of space and speed stand out all the more. The first: from Piccadilly Circus, beginning of the twenty-first century. Lurid neon facade, awash in the logos of multinational cash: McDonalds, Sanyo, Sony, Carlsberg. These front what bills itself as the world's first virtual reality theme park. Within, intensive, half-finished construction — the raw materials of escalators and air vents exposed amid dust and plaster — seems aggressively apt: here the physical space is of no consequence, and Richard Rogers's techno-architectural logic of leaving pipes exposed, as in the Lloyd's tower, is fulfilled when the guts of the building's systems are simply left unfinished. Four escalators later, one stands in a windowless, multileveled, cacophonous, thoroughly disorienting space, every centimeter packed with video games, virtual reality apparatuses, slot machines, and a bumper car carousel, with young, poor, multiethnic Londoners, all shifting gears, staring at screens, shouting, concentrating, screaming. The noise is searing: beyond the base notes of techno and house sound the beeping, whining, ringing, and pulsing of the banks of machines. Light is mostly the televisual vividness of flickering machines. For a pound coin, you get to sit on a pillion, hold a steering wheel, and imagine yourself in a grand prix race along a corniche road displayed on a screen. The pixel-printed road curves and swerves before you — frantically — your mudguard scratches the TV curb guard with a spray of TV sparks, you swerve to pass imaginary competitors, pensioners driving RVs at the legal speed limit, you careen around vast, steep corners, your pillion seat inclining at the rate of your imagined incline, your adrenaline rises and subsides, your hands sweat, joining the sweat of others who held this steering wheel before you, you face another curve, this one thousands of feet above a pixel-pointillist ocean — and you swerve toward the curb guard — your right headlight crashes against it, crumpling it — your car leaps backward against the rock face on the other side — your competitors are zooming up out of the horizon behind you, and your car leaps backward, front crushed, flips over, and you sigh — and the screen blanks pink and gives you a score: the game's over.

Now for the second image: Princess Diana's fatal crash. "The car was doing 196 kph — and the driver was drunk," the *Guardian* of London announced on the Monday after the horrific accident in the short-pillared underpass by the Seine at the Pont d'Alma in Paris.[1] The infamous paparazzi again and again snapped photos centimeters from the princess's face as (one rumor said) she waved her broken hand and spoke her last words: "Leave me alone." While all over the world the next morning people viewed TV images of the gruesomely crushed car, followed by lingering shots of the pillar that the car had hit, even the world's most exploitative media agreed almost at once not to publish those most telling photos of all, those (as near as was possible) of the crash itself. Media polemics focused on two issues: the fate of Britain's monarchy and the horrors of media intrusion into private lives, thus participating in what seemed close to a tacit collusion never to say the obvious thing, which was that this was a crash, a traffic accident. Diana was the "people's princess" precisely because, even if her status, wealth, and way of life were fabulously beyond those of ordinary people, she had nevertheless lost her life in a way that everyone stands a chance of losing it every day — in a car crash. Read in this way, her death marked the confrontation of a figure whose glamour derived from the remnants of an archaic and feudal order thoroughly imbued with fantasy, and a characteristic, familiar modern event, wholly imbued with fear. In the reporting of the accident, royalty, the feudal fantasy element, could be faced and considered, but the fearful mundane quality of the car accident had to be held sacred—a last taboo of the fear of speed. In the weeks after the crash, the British Road Safety Association launched a new campaign: "We all drive a bit too fast sometimes. Slow down. Speed kills."

The Adrenaline Aesthetic

Remember the two claims: first, speed is the single new pleasure invented by modernity. Second, the experience of speed is political.

By speed, I simply mean the sensation you get when you drive at a speed you are not used to. As you think of how pervasive and central a phenomenon speed is in modern culture, you might dwell on countless examples like my opening ones. First, video games. These games, like the earliest films, subsist in large part as homage to the car chase. In the game where you are the out-of-control speeder, the screen is your car windscreen, you accelerate as the sparks fly, you hear the tear of your tires as you sideswipe slow drivers, you imagine the torque effect at the hairpin bends, you overtake runaway trains at two hundred miles per hour, and you crash in flames: game over. Consider the thin line from this cheap thrill to that of the celebrity car crash. In the case of Princess Di—or Princess Grace, or Isadora Duncan, or James Dean—it was as if the masses were moved that one so exalted could not escape such an ordinary fate. It is ordinary: about forty thousand people (as the "safety" articles point out) were killed in car crashes on U.S. roads alone each year since Diana died. The figure for Britain is around three thousand. "Slow down, speed kills."

What is striking about these examples is that even though each is a simulation, a representation of real events, they all still have the power to make the heart race: each can excite or terrify. The video game car chase uses simulation to make a game: the crash that killed Diana exists for almost all of us as no more than a media spectacle, a representation of what occurred. Yet their power derives from their success at awakening our own memories of real experiences. The argument of this book is this: that a series of new human-scaled and immediately vastly popular technological inventions of the beginning of the twentieth century, centrally and most importantly the motorcar, offered to masses of people that rarest of things: a wholly new experience, the experience of moving at what appeared to be great speeds, and the sensation of controlling that movement. This, literally, was the moment at which individual people were allowed to feel modernity in their bones: to feel its power as a physical sensation, through their sensing of speed. It's an amazing moment of breakthrough because they were *not* here being offered something itself quite rare but more comprehensible: a new kind of "cultural turn." Modestly, technology had trumped culture, offering not the *frisson* of new kinds of telling, but an actual new experience. This experience — of speed — could in the first instance be *felt*: it did not need to represent itself. Still, it could be represented, and such representations, as the record of experiences, make up the fragments of evidence considered in any study in the history of speed.

It was Aldous Huxley who made the claim, in the course of his brilliant occasional writing, that speed is the only new pleasure invented by modernity; but in doing so, he went further, implicitly reckoning speed to be modernity's only newly invented experience. It is a commonplace to assert that the pace of life has accelerated in the last hundred years, and to speculate that inventions in the realm of technology — the elevator, the escalator, the zipper, the moving pavement — have brought this about. When this phenomenon has been taken seriously, this has generally been read as an affront. This is the attitude that entered cultural theory with the pioneering sociologist Georg Simmel's famous early-twentieth-century discourse on the new urbanism, "Metropolis and Mental Life." Simmel's is essentially a moralistic approach: his enthusiasm for speed as a generator of alert intelligence is undercut by his fear that the populace counteracted overstimulation by shielding themselves with the "blasé attitude." I propose to counter it with Huxley's notion of speed as pleasure, the only new pleasure. At the distance of a century, it must be possible at last to outline a grammar of this pleasure. The time has come to describe its thrills and excitements. We can annotate, too, the curious appetites speed promises to sate and the incitements through which it arouses them. We can delineate the fears that accompany the fulfillment of this as every desire. Above all, since we are delineating the embracing of a *new* pleasure, we have a rare opportunity to historicize a subjective sensation: to describe a key moment in what Fredric Jameson called for in *The Political Unconscious*, a history of the senses.[2]

Here I stake my claim. With some of the turn-of-the-century speed inventions, particularly the motorcar, the increased regime of speed in modernity, which, with its time clocks, schedules, and Taylorist efficiencies, was becoming more and more onerous, was repackaged as a sensation and a pleasure to be put at the disposal of the individual consumer. Speed, which had been manifested as more intense and tighter social control, was rerouted into the excessive speed of individual pleasure. As machines designed to achieve this, cars and related technologies turned out to be thoroughly characteristic modernist artifacts: they too delivered defamiliarizing shocks, stunning their users with the shock of the new. Their shocks were, however, directly physical rather than intellectual or aesthetic. The machine shocks were visceral, and this made them immediately pleasurable, touching the body, potentially addictive. Insinuating themselves into everyday life unassumingly, as if by stealth, they were immediately, enthusiastically taken up. After all, as a counterpoint to much in modernist culture that was apparently new but turned out merely to offer variations on older themes, they offered the only truly new pleasure of modernity.

Of what did this pleasure consist? What do you feel when you are driving at, say, 120 or 140 miles per hour? (Today we need to increase the rate of speed incredibly to appreciate what those first drivers felt.) As with any pleasure, speed's thrill is polymorphous and resists being pinned down. Further, the ease with which one adapts to it makes appreciation of speed as a pleasure less likely, as this familiarity—except in the case where the pleasure is rehashed and retreaded as addiction—runs counter to desire. What we need to recapture is the excitement of those who drove the first cars or saw one raise the dust on a village street, for whom twenty-five miles an hour was intensely fast. For a brief moment, roughly the first quarter of the twentieth century, the thrill of velocity at any speed was vividly palpable. To those first granted the new experience of speed, the automobile appeared to enliven people by speeding them up. The automobile was the promise, through technology, of an experience lived at a new level of intensity. In offering the new sensation of hurtling through space at speed, it gave the car's driver a striking new level of personal power, both over the most minute manipulation of the new sensation and over its effect on others—most starkly, after the first car crash, the power of life or death.

It also made demands: that the individual rapidly improvise new powers of alertness and seeing, that she revise her established sense of space and distance, that she match her own response time, her sense of her self-control of her own energy, to the acceleration of the car. The conjunction of subject body and speed machine offered early inklings of cyborg subjectivity. It granted the machine-close subject a newly intense rush of adrenaline. As drivers, people were expected to demonstrate levels of concentration and instantaneousness of reaction rarely demanded of them in the rest of their lives. They were given a sense of excitement, a thrill, which was unprecedented. And they had to experience, engage with, and overcome a fear—of losing control or causing an accident—which was new in its immediacy and sense of responsibility. It was with the polymorphous perversity of this new pleasure that cultural representations had to contend.

The car was modernist mobile architecture; it offered a new pleasure to the masses. With it, a major realignment of the economy of pleasure and pain, duty and desire, through which the modernist persona was imagined was bound to occur. In brief, what took place was a cultural, psychic, and medical reconceptualization of the human organism: it would henceforth be valorized for its capacity for energy. The vehicle as prosthesis takes over some of the powers of locomotion of the body, then demands of it new intensities of sensory perception. Terms from the fields of locomotion, engineering, and electricity—"drive," "sparkle," "stress," "energy," "dynamism"—become the currency through which to judge the body as a suitable unit in modernist life's speeded-up traffic. Bodies came to be judged as speed machines, not only by Taylorist utilitarianism, which demanded that human bodies as motors be maximally efficient in every movement, but in the ways that people thought of their *own* well-being as energetic machines. In French, speed is *la vitesse*: with the advent of the new speed technologies, the very notion of life as the capacity for energetic movement, long the basis of scientific accounts for living organisms, took on a new valence. Human well-being was recast more vehemently as the capacity for active movement and the management of the organism's energy.

All kinds of cultural forces rushed in to understand this cyborgization. First there was a resurgent nostalgia for the unprostheticized fast human body: the Olympic Games were revived in 1896, corresponding to the moment of the invention of the mass-producible motorcar. (In 1896 Karl Benz patented the first internal combustion flat engine; in the United States Ransom Olds began to build cars on a production line in 1902.) In medicine, adrenaline was isolated in 1900 by Jokichi Takamine and Keizo Uenaka, two Japanese scientists working in the United States, and was conceptualized at once in terms of human response time, velocity, and drive. The numerous high modernist literary treatments of anomie and boredom—almost invariably, of pedestrian *flâneurs*—may be read in part as laments about the horrors of slowness and, by extension, as incitements to speed's prospect of vitality. Think of the almost unbearable languor of T. S. Eliot's *The Love Song of J. Alfred Prufrock* ("Let us go then, you and I, . . .") or the dreary dawdlings continually being lamented in Conrad's *Heart of Darkness*, an account of the excruciating slowness of inefficient transport, as told by an engineer. More strikingly, the driver's need for new levels of visual alertness for seeing in motion, for enjoying a shock-punctuated gaze, was matched by a full-scale invention in the realm of representation — the moving image. As you might guess, from the start movies specialized in car chase scenes. These and many other developments can be recouped for the cultural critic as efforts to rethink and reeducate the newly prostheticized citizen enjoying — albeit anxiously — the new speed pleasure. To comprehend the totality of what was at stake here, however, we need to extend our field of vision beyond the adventures of the morphed subject to take in the social milieu in which these new speeds were not only invented but offered as a newly pleasurable experience, a kind of social gift, to individuals. We need, in short, a politics of speed. And because any new pleasure turns out to displace and cast into upheaval the possibilities of acknowledged, existing pleasures — including aesthetic pleasure — this politics of speed turns out to be closely bound up with the politics of representation itself.

Speed politics, in the first instance, was a politics of access: this newly intense experience was offered to citizens based on their ability to pay, on their gender, proximity to centers of production, consumption, and power. Next, it was a matter of national control. Everywhere speed came to be monitored and patrolled by governments as traffic police. New national regulatory systems, with driver's licenses, speed limits, traffic signs, and checkpoints, were rapidly set in place. Fundamentally, however, the narratives of access to speed and its control need to be thought of in terms of how the access to all resources and pleasures has been organized in modernity. Since the mid-nineteenth century the story of access has been told as the matter of consumption, the desire for and possession of commodities. The story of national control has been one of the state's control of its land space, its territory, and the flow of traffic — in goods, people, workers — thereupon. In both these realms, the rush to speed was profoundly disruptive.

First, consumption. Note that speed arrived as a gift to individuals at precisely the moment when commodity culture also took over: when a market economy saturated by commodities had become the governing fact of everyday life in the West. Already by World War I it was clear that the automobile was the most characteristic and most desired commodity of all in this new age of mass consumerism. However—and crucially—the car, while offering itself as the ultimate fetish of the commodity age, went beyond the commodity form to embody something more: it offered not the mere pleasure of ownership but, more, the possibility of the new pleasure of the experience of speed. Note that in Marx's terms the commodity has been theorized as offering a spectral, illusory pleasure; its fetishistic power resides in its potency as a *mis*representation (but a representation, a spectacle nevertheless) of a real relation which it hides. The automobile as glamorous commodity offered all this, but as a technology, it offered more: the possibility of the *new* physical sensation—a pleasure possibility outside the realm of the illusory if spectacular fetish of the commodity. Enter into a prosthetic relation with the machine, it promised, and (for a price) experience a new pleasure. The implicit conception of nature, and of social order of authentic relations between people based on a natural order, on which Marx had built his theory of commodification was undermined radically at this moment when technology allowed people to feel modernity in their bones. This was a key moment in the history of the commodity—a history that has more ruptures and turns than have yet been theorized.

Second, consider how the arrival of the new speed experience transformed their sense of space—and how that matters as a political fact. Clearly, when one drove at new speed, distances were foreshortened and space condensed. Consider that the promise of speed pleasure appeared at the moment when the age of empire was at its height, but just when awareness was dawning that it would soon effectively be over. The new offer of speed as pleasure participated in this political and cultural turn to the extent that it exemplified a move away from projecting desire onto the faraway exotic locale, and onto personal effort and intensity experienced on one's own body. In the late Victorian period, the boy's adventure novels spawned with the rise of pulp fiction were likely to be imperial romances, as in the tales of H. Rider Haggard and Rudyard Kipling. By the twenties, the new heroes were more likely to be race car drivers or adventurers who endured massive hardship to break some record of endurance, rather than colonial explorers. Pleasure as heterotopic fantasy was being replaced by pleasure in the sensation of personal strenuousness. Territoriality mattered less than mobility, and speed was envisioned not only as pleasure but as a measure of extraordinary personal power.

I am not claiming that the new pleasure of speed somehow short-circuited or transcended either commodity fetishism or the dominant epistemic mind-set of the age of empire. *Au contraire*, it worked through both to effect a more intense colonization — an endocolonization[3] — of the subject-citizen's sensorium and body. In doing so, it radically altered the terms of both. The fetish of the commodity and the mirage of the heterotopic colony are, no doubt, related structurally: both are object worlds outside the viewer subject, and into which she supposedly longs to project herself — working to do so through the offers and variously theorized logics we call desire. Commodification and imperialism alike work on a logics of distance — the very sense of spatial distance that the new thrill of speed uses but operates to nullify. Nearly all accounts of modernist culture in one way or another speak of how modernist art works to show us that the object world as perceived by the subject is in fact illusory, a mirage, a simulation, an element of the "society of the spectacle." The works do this, the accounts go, by shocking us, defamiliarizing our aesthetic sensibilities into the default mode of an epiphany. What these critical narratives still maintain, however, is the story of critical distance: that is, they assume that in the final instance modernist art demands a contemplative (and hence slowed-down) encounter. The new experience of speed as individual pleasure, however, refuses distance. This speed gives us pleasure as sensation, not as the contemplation made possible by critical distance. Thus, too, it does not need desire. What it needs — and what has not yet been given it — is what I am calling adrenaline aesthetics. This would be a new grammar of culture which overrides the imperatives of Western models of representation and aesthetic reception in modernity at least since Kant: a protocol which subsumes aesthetics under rationality by adhering to a model of critical distance and rational contemplation. Refusing this, adrenaline aesthetics works to delineate a pleasure that is effected first on the body and its sensorium.

How to explicitly show speed and its dramatic intensities, then, may have been a problem that much high modernist cultural production would tackle only tenuously, with suspicion. Popular culture, however — and especially new forms such as film — flooded in to pick up the slack. Attuned to people's everyday experiences, these forms signaled the thrills as well as the anxieties characteristic of the new speed culture. Sifting through the myriad signals from these forms about the nature of the speed experience, we can read the protocols by which elements of this experience came to be organized. We can outline a grammar of this pleasure. This in turn provides a basis for examining its politics. This politics, conceived in the most comprehensive sense, begins with the idea that speed was modernism's greatest shock: the only one that, in altogether refusing critical distance, might refuse (even as it completely fulfills) the mirage offerings of the standard subject-other protocols of the Western post-Cartesian consciousness.[4] In particular, it may transform their twentieth-century popular equivalents, the well-groomed narratives of consumer desire (the subject's desire to own the commodity) and dreams of empire (the subject's desire to possess the exotic other space). If speed is modernity's only new pleasure, then speed-in-culture had modernism's greatest potential to be truly new. If modernist art was propelled into strangeness by a logistics of innovations, Pound's dictum to "make it new," then a newness that was visceral in turn offered a model and a spur for newness in the realm of culture.

If much modernism is about human movement — as in the figures of the ship in Conrad, the *flâneur* and *flâneuse* heroes and heroines of Joyce and Woolf, the ramp-ascending villa inhabitants of Le Corbusier, and the stair-descending nudes of Fernand Léger — and in the organization of this movement in traffic, and if the rate of this traffic is in its speed, then speed itself becomes the very narrative heft of much modernist artistic production. In this sense, much high modernist culture gave us speed without knowing it. Therefore, to formulate a totalizing politics of the new speed pleasure, we must attend both to the myriad details of speed thrills provided by the popular, and to the big-picture purlieus of high culture. In each high modernist experimental form, the death of distance is hidden in plain sight, and speed as a way of life, a way of living, and a way of being has come true. As speed took over the texts and images of modernism, it did not make them more strange but rather helped them clarify. To trace this clarification and to show how speed infiltrated modernism is the purpose of this book. I trace how an angst at the idea of static spaces and the nostalgia for home was fostered in early mass popular culture. I explore how people were incited to desire a new pleasure which they could not really have known of in advance, and how the already familiar mechanisms of consumer desire were harnessed in the service of advocating this novel experience. I consider how anxieties about the onslaught of new speeds were countered and dispelled, and how the very ways in which culture had taught people to imagine space as pleasurable were recast in favor of experiencing rapid movement. I describe how the new protocols of speed looking were developed and explored, as a key example of how a new sensory experience was fostered, celebrated, and thrilled to. I delineate how fear of the crash, the accident, the end of speed, was exacerbated and repressed at once, in a nerve-wracking psychic conflict which served mostly to underline the realness of the speed experience and the gravity of its effects on the human body. Speed, as the only new pleasure of modernity, had its incitements, its rules, its practices, and its terrors improvised for it in a few years — the modernist moment.

To show how the infiltration of speed into modernist representations made simpler and more self-evident the energies which often we think of as having made modernist art strange and obscure, let us consider, as opening exhibits, three artworks of speed culture. One is proto-modernist, one the product of a new technology of representation, and one avowedly modernist: a painting, a photograph, and a lithograph. In these images, from 1860, 1908, and 1915, the viewer identifies with a subject who, ever more resolutely, is snatched by speed. In the first, the unseen subject experiences the speed passively, and the landscape, through transference as pathetic fallacy, is transformed to match her mood. In the second, an intense drama makes for gyrating dynamism as the subject wrestles with speed. In the third, the subject, half in joke, *is* speed. From proto-impressionism to an image produced by a technology of fast seeing to proto-surrealism, speed seeps into modernism and wipes the blur out of its art.

First, consider J. M. W. Turner's *Rain, Steam, and Speed: The Great Western Railway* (1844) (figure 1). In the early nineteenth century, the railway introduced unprecedented speeds, but it offered them to the vast majority of people as passive experience — as passengers borne along — and as spectacle. Luckily, we need not guess at the extraordinary sense of material instability and the prospect of the dissolution of matter altogether that was inspired, in its first viewers, by the train's speed: it is recorded majestically by Turner here. Showing speed through flux and blur presages many later experiments. Turner's stunning flux-imbued impressionism *avant la lettre* makes technology seem spectral and ominous. But speed's power is acknowledged as awe-inspiringly impressive: it literally vaporizes the landscape through which it cuts. Nature becomes diaphonous when speed out-natures it. This spectral, magically transformed landscape is effective as speed spectacle because in its vague comfort, it corresponds to the helplessness with which Victorians experienced this speed: passively, as passengers. This passivity, in turn, prompted them to fantasize about the roles of the train drivers, as in Emile Zola's novel about a murderous engine-

FIGURE 1. J. M. W. Turner, *Rain, Steam, and Speed: The Great Western Railway*, 1844. Reproduced by permission of the National Gallery, London.

man, *La bête humaine* (The Human Beast) of 1890, and to compulsively render their passivity before speed as spectacle, in new genres such as travel posters, the "decorated-shed" architecture of the grandiose new railway stations, from the Stazione Centrale in Milan to New York's Grand Central, and paintings from those of Turner to Monet's *Gare Saint Lazare* series of 1876–77. Once speed is offered as the spectacle of a locomotive, varieties of impressionism interpose themselves as the enabling form of the image. This vagueness is nevertheless an easeful blur, corresponding to a degree to the flashing landscape seen from the carriage window. This softening of visual focus offers an implicit assurance that although speed may radically alter the world around her, or at least her perception of it, it will not disturb the essentially static equilibrium of the viewer-subject as passenger herself.

Next, consider Jacques-Henri Lartigue's photograph of a racing car driver at the wheel, titled *Nov. 9, Road from Nice to Peira-Cava*, taken in 1908 (figure 2). Whereas Turner evokes rail speed through a swirl of diaphanous cloud, in Lartigue's photo the sense of a whorl of swirling dust results from the inadequacy of the camera lens and shutter mechanism to capture completely the details of the speeding object; it is a technological inadequacy that the photographer paradoxically deploys to great effect. Turner's whole image evokes nebulousness; here, instead, as with many early photographs of movement, the pinpointed center is in focus, defining a point of concentration which makes the margin's grainy vagueness encircle a fixed center point. Turner's evocation of the passive speed experienced by a passenger found its visual counterpoint in the steam billowing from the locomotive's engine to merge with the clouds; Lartigue's image demands that the viewer identify with the racing driver, and feel with him, that the power point of his speed is in the engine in front of him in his car. The pleasure we take with him in his speed's intensity is undercut by the glint of his goggles, the flash of his eye. Look more: this eye's flash resonates as a glance of fear. We too fear that that near-panicked eye might not be able to capture the exact curve of that twisting road as readily as can the camera's technologized eye. This image turns out to be fully concentrated, focused on the driver as a point of pleasure, desire and, fear, whereas Turner's is open, diffusely dreaming of speed as a utopian flight in the way dreamers before the Wright brothers did — as a means to merge with the clouds. Turner's perspective beckons to the heavens; Lartigue's lens turns downward toward the earth. The modernist reality Lartigue captures is earthier, and he shows lots of earth to represent speed. The lesson of its concentrated focus on the driver's eye is the same lesson of many images of cars since: the need for a new personal regimen of alertness, if only for the driver-speeder's management of fear.

So we come to the final exhibit, Francis Picabia's *Portrait of a Young American Woman in a State of Nudity*. It is a lithograph reproduced in the avant-garde journal *291* in July 1915 (figure 3). Here the fear has turned to laughter. The presumptive human subject is not struggling with speed, not prostheticized, but wholly technologized. With the nude morphed into a spark plug, floating upright in total blankness, not only has technology completely replaced the tenderness of the body, but all impressionist blur, whether of sky or earth, is erased when the sentient body is acknowledged as the spark plug which makes speed possible. By being the spark that enables speed and that will experience its energy, this subject can emerge from the blur that has up to now either suggested her passivity (as in Turner)

FIGURE 2. J.-H. Lartigue, *Nov. 9, Road from Nice to Peira-Cava.*
Courtesy of Friends of J.-H. Lartigue, Paris.

or her anxious struggle (as in Lartigue). She is now wholly divorced from landscape, freed from any sense of a relation to space, place, and geography. This is why the white blankness of the background, emphasized by the thin line marking the frame, is key here. The accession to speed's energy renounces real time at the same moment as it sheds physical space: that is the meaning of the avowal of the capitalized "FOR-EVER." This image seems culled from a catalog: we are unremittingly in the world of consumer components, too, with the implication that the human body must pass through this state—that is, be commodified to access the spark of speed's energy. All this is a joke here on the Western tradition of the nude, of the separation of the technological and the human, on women's bodies, on Americans, on car parts—but a joke that is thoroughly profound. The artist has intuited a

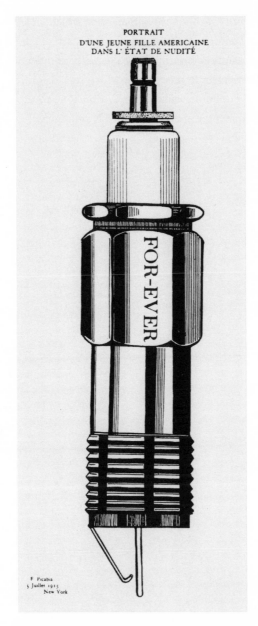

FIGURE 3. Francis Picabia, *Portrait of a Young American Woman in a State of Nudity*, 1915. Lithograph. Reproduced in the avant-garde journal *291*, nos. 5–6 (July–August 1915). Courtesy of the artist's estate.

supreme subjectivity for the speed moment, in which, in letting our bodies be technological components, we achieve the spark of speed as the power and pleasure of the self. Impressionist obscurity is overcome, and speed, in this high modernism (a modernism which forbids critical distance), is the evident secret of human subjectivity. Adrenaline aesthetics has worked itself out. The moment of modernist speed is announced.

Speed Theory

All revolution is movement, but all movement is not revolution.

—Paul Virilio, *Speed and Politics*

Consider speed. Specifically, imagine again the intense new thrill felt by those who at the dawn of the twentieth century drove a car fast for the first time. This is how Aldous Huxley describes it in his essay "Wanted, a New Pleasure" (1931):

> Speed, it seems to me, provides the one genuinely modern pleasure. True, men have always enjoyed speed; but their enjoyment has been limited, until very recent times, by the capacities of the horse, whose maximum velocity is not much more than thirty miles per hour. Now thirty miles an hour on a horse feels very much faster than sixty miles an hour in a train or a hundred in an airplane. The train is too large and steady, the airplane too remote from stationary surroundings, to give their passengers a very intense sensation of speed. The automobile is sufficiently small and sufficiently near the ground to be able to compete, as an intoxicating speed-purveyor, with the galloping horse. The inebriating effects of speed are noticeable on horseback at about twenty miles an hour, in a car at about sixty. When the car has passed seventy-two, or thereabouts, one begins to feel an unprecedented sensation, a sensation which no man in the days of horses ever felt. It grows intenser with every increase in velocity. I myself have never traveled at much more than eighty miles an hour in a car; but those who drunk a stronger beverage of this strange intoxicant tell me that new marvels await anyone who has the opportunity of passing the hundred mark. . . . Two hundred miles an hour must be absolute torture.[1]

You can sense Huxley's quaking with doubt about his proposition even as he wrote it, but you sense too that he knew his idea was too brilliant and audacious to let drop. As he sees it, despite vast changes through the centuries, people's experience of pleasure has remained remarkably the same. To claim that, with the car, the technological advances that had been a hallmark of the industrial revolution had finally brought to individual human subjects a new pleasure that they could tangibly experience—that it would give each of them a thrill which had never before been felt—is to posit a fundamental and truly wondrous kind of revolution. It also begs a host of questions. Why did it happen now? Was it a pleasure that was rationed, and who had access to it? How is it connected to the effects of other technological advances that were such a feature of that historical moment: the bicycle, the phonograph, the telephone, the airplane, the movie camera, even mass electrification and electric light? How does it jibe with the shocking changes in art, literature, and, soon, film that burst on the scene at the same time, the diverse experiments we now call modernism? If people's pleasure was radically revised, how did this impact the old, familiar pleasures? Finally, was the pleasure policed, and how did it matter to communities and even nations as well as individuals? Which is to say, what exactly are the politics of this new pleasure? Speed, as pleasure and as politics, would shake things up; here we begin the exploration of how and why.

To think of speed as a pleasure is to think of it strategically. It forces us to think of speed sensationally, that is, how it feeds our sensations, our senses, working on our bodies to produce physical as well as psychic and psychological effects. Centrally, it makes us attend to the way speeding changes how we experience space. Speed in modernity has, most frequently, been thought of as a matter of conquering time: the regime of clock time, timetables, clocking in, schedules, being on time, meeting deadlines, going faster. This is the modern urban regimen described by Georg Simmel in "The Metropolis and Mental Life."[2] It is the aspect of speed that modernity forces on us; it is the part of speed that is onerous. It is the speed of modern stress that the Austrian novelist Elfriede Jelinek had in mind when she said of New York, "I'm just afraid that the speed and noise would make me mad as soon as I set foot on land."[3] When we think of the thrill of speed as pleasure, however, as, for example, in driving a car at a hundred miles per hour, then we think of traversing space more quickly. If speed's nastiness is about beating time, speed's pleasure seduces by recasting our relation to space. To understand the politics of speed, why it came to be granted first to the rich and then to masses of people in the early twentieth century, how it was rationed and policed, how it was represented as a thrill to be desired, then we must theorize it as part of a revolutionary change in the ways in which space was reorganized in modernity, and in the ways in which people willingly embraced such changes. In terms of the history of the organization of the world's space, the salient fact in or around 1900 was that this was the moment of greatest expansion of the Western empires: the age of empire, in which a small group of Western nations ruled over vast swaths of territory and controlled the sea routes of the globe. At the same historical moment, the first cars were mass-produced: technological speed would first be offered as individual pleasure to masses of people in the West. The age of empire and the age of speed coincide; how to trace their relation?

Speed is not only a pleasure that has a politics; speed, it turns out, *is* politics: the expression of a new order of the organization of global space. My key proposition in this chapter is this: that masses of Westerners were granted access for the first time to the experience of speeds made possible by technology at the moment when empire was at its height, but more importantly, at that paradigm-shattering moment when it became clear that the whole world had at last been mapped and conquered, and that global space was finite. Until this time, in the age of empire as exploration, it had suited Western ideologies to encourage dreams of exotic "other" spaces, spaces to be enjoyed, mapped, and conquered. This had been the basis for a long-standing Western conception of space as a dualist entity, with the known home close at hand, and the exotic and potentially infinite space of exotic and threatening otherness far away. When the sources of such other-continent dreamscapes ran out, attention turned inward to the excitement of movement for its own sake: Western culture turned to speed. Fantasies of movement as adventure and exploration aimed at discovering uncharted lands were replaced by fantasies of the rate of movement for its own sake: fantasies of speed. The dream machine of the earlier travel had been the ship; of the new speed, the race car. Books like *Robinson Crusoe* had distilled the lies and dreams of the older ways of thinking about space; it remains to be seen what text or film will become the classic of the new. Speed, as the achievement of the technologies of Western modernity, was offered as personal sensation to individuals as a means to experience space in a new way, at the very moment when there was no more new world space left to organize. The new mass availability of speed as technology's tangible pleasure, and the organization of the world's territory known as empire, are deeply related.

This, then, is a global context for speed's pleasure. We can theorize it not just as a novel phenomenon experienced by people everywhere in this century, but as a new experience attached to the dynamic realignment of global space in modernity. To read speed in these terms is to grasp technology as a deep form of ideology: not merely as a cause that had cultural effects but as a force that at this moment not only infiltrated people's consciousness and their unconscious but offered people a wholly new sensation. We can trace the connection between the developing grammar of this sensation and the shifts taking place at the same moment in the global reordering of space. First, however, I hope to prove this (on the face of it, unlikely) collusion between the state's culture of empire and the mass-culture phenomenon of the speeding car.

To understand the modernist collusion between politics and sensation, it is useful to consider some theoretical work in geography, cultural studies, and critical theory, on issues of place, space, and the importance of territory, from the "new geography" to theory's "spatial turn." This work shares an attention not just to space but to movement and to the rates of movement, that is, speed. Speed issues, even speeding automobiles, crop up at crux moments in key essays by the thinker who taught cultural studies how to read starred spaces, Michel Foucault; in the work of Henri Lefebvre, who pioneered the study of spaces in materialist critical theory; and in that of Fredric Jameson, who first combined these materialist and culturalist perspectives for English-speaking audiences. Recent writing in the field of architecture has also become obsessed with speed. Each of these theorists of the reorganizations of space in modernity theorizes flows, traffic, movement, and speed, often, as it were, without knowing it. It took the arch-theorist of speed in modernity, Paul Virilio, to point up the force of speed in the West's reorganization of space. Each, likewise, places the matter of empire at the heart of his discussion of spatial reorganization. We will turn first to the work of David Harvey, a follower most directly of Lefebvre, and the leader of the "new geography," to see how his explanation of the end of the "spatial fix" in late-empire politics and economics becomes a rationale for the turn to speed in Western culture. We will then go on to consider how the theorist's fascination with speed might be read: we will formulate some rules for speed reading.

Speed Theory: Theory's "Spatial Turn" and Speed

On July 4, 1907, the *Paris Herald* quoted an American spectator at a race in Trouville as saying, "No one who did not see the race can in the least imagine the ecstasy of exquisite sensation that permeates one's being when a machine flashed by at that frightful speed. . . . You realize the awful danger. You sympathize in the keenness of the delight."[4] Compare this for a moment with the shock provoked by the high art of the modernist period. Could the shock that was elicited by the best high modernist art be an analogy to the shock of the new technological speed? Not quite; the visceral shock of the speed experience and the aesthetic-intellectual account of an encounter with an artwork occupy different registers. Nevertheless, to take speed into account is to revamp debates about how high modernist art reacted to the apparently shocking, cacophonous, disorienting social forces of modernity. The shock tactics of modernist prose, poetry, music, and art have been read convincingly as an education in high capitalist stresses, by theorists such as the architect Manfredo Tafuri,[5] or as attempts to register or "map" the confusions of dislocated social forces, as Fredric Jameson suggests in an essay we will consider in a moment, "Cognitive Mapping."[6] Once speed has been taken into account, the modernist artwork can be read as a specific—if sometimes quaint, even cumbersome—version of an energy-manipulating technology itself.

Modernist literature, from Eliot's *Prufrock* to Joyce's *Ulysses*, Woolf's *Mrs. Dalloway*, and Kafka's *The Trial*, as well as Walter Benjamin's *The Arcades Project*, returns obsessively to the figure of the city pedestrian, the *flâneur*, at the very moment when the car was taking over the city. (Robert Musil's modernist magnum opus, *The Man without Qualities*, opens with Viennese pedestrians as wittily blasé witnesses of a car crash.) In the years in question, only the Futurists were celebrating speed explicitly; here, while casting a cold eye on their bombast and politics, we will reread some other modernisms in the light of the speed-representing strategies they explicitly espoused. By making their heroes and heroines flâneurs in radically fragmented texts, Joyce, Woolf, and the rest came to terms in the early twentieth century with a new sense of urban space. By the end of the century, the theorists had caught up with them and were fascinated by shifts in the organization and perception of space as well. Focusing on speed as the basis for a modernist revolution in spatial perception, I want to carry forward the project of developing a materialist theory of space already elaborated by critics of the postmodern moment, from Edward Soja and David Harvey to Fredric Jameson. These thinkers, retheorizing twentieth-century culture and social life in political terms, reassessed how obscurity, a defining attribute in the century's cultural productions, can be read in the light of the tectonic shifts and strategic trajectories of globally rampant capitalism. All focus on material space. Each also turns out to be preoccupied with movement and the rate of movement, speed.

Speed has had a fugitive, supremely fragmented existence among some of the crucial academic disciplines of the twentieth century. The stresses of speed and speed's repetitiveness have, at important moments, such as Freud's investigation of "shell shock" and war traumas after World War I, been crucial issues for psychoanalysis. The most important and advanced branches of theoretical physics in both the nineteenth and twentieth centuries have been concerned, respectively, with dynamics, as in the second law of thermodynamics, and energy, as in Einstein's theory of relativity. Speed has been an explicit concern of mechanical engineering, in solving problems of faster engines, and of the new science of traffic engineering, in the planning of efficient road traffic flows. The effects of speed vision have concerned the makers of camera machinery at least since Etienne-Jules Marey. Kinesis, or kinesthetics, has been the express area of study of dance and dance theory. Despite this dispersal, however, speed has entered the field of vision of cultural and materialist theorists only recently. Why has theory avoided kinesis, velocity, speed? Materialists have had a difficult time theorizing technological advances. They are tempted to see them as perverse undercutters of labor power: capitalist tools. Forces as nebulous as "speed" seem impossibly elusive for deterministic accounts of social progress, especially for materialist critics who value their rigorous engagement with history. Jameson staked out the long view and stressed an engagement with time rather than space as the prerequisite for materialist analysis with his imperative to "always historicize!"[7] Yet materialist critics of culture, including Jameson himself, have also subsumed questions of history into those of spatial organization and perception.

Contemporary critiques of spatial materiality are often "theories against the state"; haunted by the idea of the modern state, they are anxious about whether it should be thought of in ideological (that is, as "community") or in spatial (that is, as "territory") terms. Theory's spatial turn repays geography's and cultural studies' debt to anthropology and to sociology, disciplines in which a search for culturally definable "places" in the morass of abstracted space is integral. Sociology influenced cultural studies through the importance of Gramsci's and Althusser's concepts of ideology, where the crucial ideology was that of the state—in Althusser's terms, the original ideological state apparatus. The state may be an "imagined community," but this community is held together by the belief that common identities are tied to a fixed territory, a demarcated space whose borders are controlled. With the state as a space upheld by an ideology of place, attention to space entered materialist theory through the back door of discussions of ideology. The resurgence of spatial theory in architecture, urban theory, the "new geography," and materialist criticism generally is, however, I suggest, only secondarily concerned with space per se; centrally, it is concerned with velocities of movement—of goods, people, money, and power—that is, with speed. As postmodern materialist critics attempt to return a materialist basis to a critical theory that has, in the hands of post-Gramscians such as Ernesto Laclau and Chantal Mouffe, been drained of almost all its materiality and become almost wholly a theory of influences and the potential to counteract them, they appear to see at last that that crucial ideology of modernity, nationalism, is not merely an effect or an ideological mirage producing imagined communities but rather an ideology based by analogy on the well-known capitalist conceptions of ownership and possession, applied to the most basic of material entities, space itself. Just as the good capitalist measures her success in the possession of money, goods, and land, so too the state will act to possess, in the first instance, the land that validates it. This state ownership of the territory will in turn be taken advantage of by capital in search of possibilities for expansion and new profit. In contrast to, yet in conjunction with, this stasis of fixed territory on which nationalism depends, movement and speed become qualities of capitalism. For both capital and its critics, therefore, the issue is how to overcome the static space of the state and to take advantage of—or, in the critic's case, to theorize—a dynamic global movement. Thinking space, materialist critics are doing nothing more than following the insight of Marx, who, in a famous phrase in *Capital*, described how capital desired to "annihilate space with time."[8] This is the most concisely political definition of speed yet available.

The turn to space and its cartographies is not limited to the materialist strand of contemporary criticism, however; the chronotope, the slice of space with all its possibilities that one can imagine inserted like a wedge into the relentless cause-and-effect chain of history, has also been an obsession of cultural criticism. The brilliant forensic scientist of the telling microspaces of modernity has been Michel Foucault, whose genealogies have cast an eye over warrens—the mental hospital, the prison, the disease-ravaged human body, read as real estate on which various institutional developers had intense designs. One revealing early lecture where Foucault maps his future interests, unsurprisingly, dwells on a cornucopia of dissonant and tantalizing spaces. Foucault has an acute feel for how power shows its face as perverse pleasure in a place. It is fascinating to discover already there a subtext centered on movement and velocity, built into his project from the beginning.

In his brief essay "Of Other Spaces," the text of a lecture delivered in 1967 and, according to a note appended to the English translation, "not part of the official corpus of his work,"[9] he begins strongly, "The present epoch will perhaps be above all the epoch of space," and goes on: "Our epoch is one in which space takes the form of relations among sites." He sketches the feudal order of the arrangement of territory, where a hierarchy of spaces—from sacred to profane, for example, each elaborately showcasing badges of power—made for a rigid, clearly demarcated order; cathedral and palace faced each other at the heart of the town. He turns then to the more devious disorganization of spaces in our own time, based, he claims, on relations between sites. At this point, he comes close to describing modern spatiality as not merely opposed to the older stasis, but wholly dynamic, a result of the management of movement. Tellingly, he raises the phantom of the automobile:

> Moreover, the importance of the site as a problem of contemporary technical work is well known: the storage of data . . . in the memory of a machine; the circulation of discrete elements with a random output (*automobile traffic* is a simple case or indeed the sounds of a telephone line), the identification of marked or coded elements inside a set that may be randomly distributed or may be arranged according to single or multiple classifications.[10]

Traffic flows, as in the car or the telephone's data here, emerge as Foucault's examples of "relations between sites," which, he claims, characterize the modern management of territory. He decided later that the "problem of the human site is . . . knowing what . . . type of circulation . . . of human elements should be adopted in a given situation to achieve a given end."

Here suddenly, however, Foucault invokes Gaston Bachelard, whose *The Poetics of Space* (1958) is an evocative existential meditation on the auratic qualities that imbue human spaces.[11] While he professes to be interested in the "external," that is, real, actually existing spaces, rather than the dynamics of "internal," or spaces of the mind, spirit, or imagination, and to maintaining the importance of the *relations* between them, he shifts his focus to concrete static spaces rather than the dynamics of traffic. The "heterotopias" — spaces of otherness — he then describes have the qualities of what the architect Charles Moore would later describe as "memory palaces";[12] they range from boarding schools and penal institutions to brothels and honeymoon hotels, cinemas, Oriental carpets and gardens, museums and hammams. The evocative quality of Foucault's readings of each results because of the spaces' equivocal and marginal qualities: few are central places of the world's business, but side attractions concocted for entertainment, incarceration, repose. Foucault then presents five principles, all to do with the relation of these spaces to others (they "juxtapose in a single real place several sites . . . themselves incompatible," and so on).[13] Unsurprisingly, therefore, this trove of examples begins and ends with spaces of transportation, the train ("an extraordinary bundle of relations") and the boat. Issues of traffic frame his wistful evocation of delirious perverse spaces. When he talks of boats as heterotopias, his project to discover the precise nature of the *dynamic* relation between sites is palpable:

> If we think, after all, that the boat . . . is a floating piece of space, a place without a place, that exists by itself, that is closed in on itself and at the same time is given over to the infinity of the sea and that, from port to port, from tack to tack, from brothel to brothel, it goes as far as the colonies in search of the most precious treasures they conceal in their gardens, you will understand how the boat has not only been for our civilization from the sixteenth century to the present the greatest instrument of economic development . . . but has simultaneously been the greatest reserve of the imagination. The ship is the heterotopia *par excellence*. In civilizations without boats, dreams dry up, espionage takes the place of adventure, and the police take the place of pirates.

Ships, from Columbus's sailing vessels to the *Titanic*, have most vividly exemplified modernity's union of speed, adventure, accidentality, and commerce; the twentieth century, nevertheless, has seen their eclipse in relation to other forms of transport, and since 1900 there has been a ferocious stripping from the ship of its aura. Here Foucault, magnificently echoing the poetic cadences of Bachelard, betrays his actual interest, not just in those prison-house worlds whose denizens experience otherness as society's refusal to allow them to move, but rather in spaces, even if they are archaic ones, of movement and speed.

One fascination of Foucault's marginal spaces, as explored in his subsequent work or sketched in this essay-manifesto, is precisely that in all of such spaces—honeymoon suite, prison, mental hospital, boarding school—movement, traffic, and circulation are controlled, forbidden, denied. Jean Baudrillard, polemical in *Forget Foucault*, accuses his fellow intellectual of pitching his lance at windmills whose importance had subsided before he deplored them: Baudrillard compares Foucault to the revolutionaries who stormed the Bastille only to discover that the prison was empty. The lure of nostalgic retrospection does color "Of Other Spaces" (who regrets, for example, that "espionage has replaced adventure"?), but Baudrillard's counterassertion, that all concrete real space has now, where it matters, given way to simulation, replaces Foucault's focus on institutions of the past with a nostalgia-in-advance for an unrealized future. Baudrillard thereby misses the way in which Foucault's spaces interest us because they are *slow*: that is, because they limit movement and control it with different rates of permitted speed. They are places of locks and keys, where guards practice arcane experiments in social engineering. A call for a logics of movement, an intellectual project to understand traffic between sites and the rate of its flow (i.e., speeds), haunts as it underpins all the evocative baroque of Foucault's interest in these institutional worlds apart. To cast this in Jameson's terms and give it a political valence, the political unconscious of Foucault's quasi-romantic interest in these mostly nineteenth-century spaces of the margins expresses itself in an implied wish not just to confront the imprisoning possibilities of the gaol and hospital, their ability to deny free movement, but also to face the possibilities for movement of subjects who escape through these customs points, relay stations, and rest stops into the broader open spaces of modernity. For these moving subjects, relations between sites can be established only by shuttling between them at partially regulated speeds.

At the embarkation point for his epistemic cartographies, Foucault betrays the influence of the quasi-mystical evocations of space by Bachelard; another of Foucault's undoubted influences, however, was Henri Lefebvre, the pioneer of the idea that understanding space is crucial to any materialist account of modernity. Lefebvre's finest work on space and politics, *The Production of Space*, appeared in 1974. When Foucault notes belatedly that the ship, that heterotopic space without a place which is a floating repository of dreams, has also been the engine of global economic expropriation, he gives a bow to the work of Lefebvre. Lefebvre in turn, together with the theorist of world systems, Ernest Mandel, is a crucial influence on the postmodern materialist criticism, also obsessed with the signifying power of spaces, of Fredric Jameson. By uncovering the contradictions contained in Jameson's central essay "Cognitive Mapping," which I will read together with a moment in his *Postmodernism, or, The Cultural Logic of Late Capitalism*, I will show that movement, flow, traffic, and speed turn out, even more than in Foucault's cartographic genealogies, to be an abiding leitmotif. In Jameson, speed and traffic exist as elements which, lurking behind phrases such as "sensory bombardment and subjective disorientation" allow him to make the argument, apparently contradictory if we only accept the terms he explicitly gives us, that even in such a bombarded, intellectually crippling, and "decentered communicational network in which we find ourselves caught as individual subjects,"[14] we can still establish the coordinates of our situation and map distances (to moving targets?) that he suggests are the materialist's critical task. Without taking into account our rate of movement — speed — the cartographic metaphor to describe our critical duties is, I suggest, problematic.

Jameson's spatial turn might be expected to be based on the pinpointing of static structures demanded by traditional notions of mapping and cartography, given his interest in architecture and sympathy for the postwar Italian school of architectural theory characterized by the work of Manfredo Tafuri, Aldo Rossi, and Massimo Cacciari.[15] Tafuri's *Architecture and Utopia* is a scathing vision of avant-garde modernist art, most of whose innovations he describes as mere flirtations with technology, consumer culture, or the new mass forms such as advertising. He attacks the avant-garde as a palliative, willing educator of both elites and the masses in the ever-more-ferocious regimes of capitalism, working as "a programmed control of the new forces released by technology."[16] For a truly critical artistic intervention in the modern built environment, he suggests, the only possibility is to present an antiexperimental building whose stillness and solidity stand as a rebuke to the studies of controlled chaos that appear to attack, but only collude with, the capitalist order. Appropriately, the most celebrated built structure of this group is Aldo Rossi's cemetery at Como.

Jameson's sometimes totalizing materialism is attracted to the Adornian clean sweep of Tafuri's scheme, but as Jameson has explained in "Is Space Political?" he wants also to open other possibilities for a wholeheartedly utopian impulse to be inscribed in buildings, in order to incite potentially liberating forms of desire.[17] Apt, then, that in his best-known reading of any text, his pages on John Portman's Bonaventure Hotel in Los Angeles, Jameson reveals a relatively unspectacular conference destination in the bunkerlike downtown of Los Angeles to be in fact a cyberpalace, mini-city, and even the postmodern proof of "a mutation in the nature of built space itself." The charismatic critic makes the dull and entrapping seem to bristle with distractions—and possibilities. This reading was scorned as wholly bourgeois; Jameson, his critical eye firmly on the sight lines of the middle-class conference delegate for whom the hotel was intended, failed to see that the building's gimcrack excitements masked the cold shoulder it gave to people of other classes—the maids who use the back entrance, the homeless, and even the carless, who are effectively kept out. This criticism, however valid, misses the more fundamental contradiction in Jameson's argument. It is this: if, as he claims, "postmodern hyperspace has finally succeeded in transcending the capacities of the individual human body to locate itself . . . to cognitively map its position in a mappable external world" (44), how then can he, as one victim of this carnival of postmodern hyperspace, claim to see what is going on? How can he situate himself in the very space he describes so that he will have the *critical distance* needed to make his totalizing claim about postmodern spatiality? When one is writing about space, the issue of critical distance, that point with a greater field of vision than that of others from which one can make a valid critique, ceases to be merely metaphor and demands to be thought of concretely. Jameson's argument denies the possibility of practical critical distance in the Bonaventure while he stands at a critical distance to read the Bonaventure himself.

However, when we search for Jameson's all-seeing viewpoint in the hotel, we find that there isn't any. Rather, his situatedness, as he describes it in the essay, is adventurously mobile, riding the sliding escalators, gliding up the lifts, entering and exiting by those hidden doors, emerging unexpectedly on different floors by different routes. His, it appears, is a critical multiperspective precisely generated by disjointed movement. The nearest the text comes to showing us the point from which the critic views the hotel as a whole, in fact, is the reproduced photograph of the building from

FIGURE 4. Photograph of the Hotel Bonaventure, Los Angeles. Courtesy of the Hotel Bonaventure, Los Angeles.

without: it seems to be a photograph taken, with complete appropriateness, through the windscreen of a car speeding along the Harbor Freeway (figure 4). Likewise, at the very moment of his analysis of the hotel's "disorientation," Jameson turns instinctively to automobile speed:

> It may now be suggested that this alarming disjunction point between the body and its built environment, *which is to the initial bewilderment of the older modernism as the velocities of spacecraft are to those of the automobile* — can itself stand as the symbol of that even sharper dilemma which is the incapacity of our minds, at least at present, to map the great global multinational and decentered communication network in which we find ourselves caught as individual subjects. (44; italics mine)

Bewilderment, here, is the effect you put down to ever-faster speed technologies. It can be overcome, the critic promises, by mapping on a totalizing scale. What the essay "Cognitive Mapping" shows, however, is that mapping itself may be an inadequate descriptor, or even an unequal metaphor, for the coming tasks of the materialist cultural critic. The slip of the tongue into the speedscape of cars and spacecraft masks an uneasy sense that what really matters in the new world order takes place in the flows of traffic, at specific speeds, between nodes, even if they are nodes decked out as superbly and frustratingly as the built and thus static environment of the Bonaventure. This hotel, in other words, works as a shadow play of the traffic flow on any of the nearby freeway interchanges. Jameson sees this but is bedazzled into becoming a post-Foucauldian reader of heterotopias, discerning in the hotel's furbelows the whiff of an aura—an aura mostly derived from the premonition (an inside-out nostalgia because it comes before, rather than after, the catastrophe) of the hotel's inevitable, perhaps already heralded, obsolescence. This is, remember, L.A., where built environments, from Irving Gill's W. L. Dodge House of 1916 to the Richfield art deco skyscraper of 1928, have always been instantly disposable as movie lot facades if the traffic flows in another direction, at another speed. Jameson celebrates a building in *the* modernist city that has always functioned on the principle of the dispensability of the fixed and architectural.[18] The Bonaventure can only be grasped from the freeway: it is speed perception, then, that needs to be analyzed. Jameson's metaphor for the critic of this site should have been not the cartographer but the traffic cop.

In "Cognitive Mapping" Jameson presents a history and offers a program. Brilliantly, he traces Ernest Mandel's three stages of capitalism in modernity onto corresponding stages of culture. Realism he aligns with the classic nineteenth-century era of market capitalism, when the world's space was desacralized and abstracted. The stage of imperialism is paralleled to modernism: when the experience of the individual was constricted to one corner of the globe while the truth which underlies that experience is located on another continent, modernism rose to "inscribe the absent global colonial system into the very syntax of colonial language itself."[19] In the third phase, late capitalism's bombardment of the senses corresponds on the cultural plane to postmodernism's "death of affect." Jameson sees the progress of capital as three successive reorganizations of capitalist space: the role of culture in each case is to annotate people's perceptions to these reorganizations. He then invokes the architect Kevin Lynch's vision of ideal urban living—the ability to map one's place in the chaotic city by becoming familiar with fixed landmarks within it—as a model for critical theory that can respond to these reorganizations of space.[20] When the late capitalist world is thoroughly disorienting, the critical theorist, like Lynch's open-eyed urban flâneur, must work to cognitively map social relations on a global scale.

Critiques of Jameson have focused on his tripartite narrative: they suggest that cultural shifts might not so concisely correspond to global political trends: Even high modernism, for example, is not only, even in the last instance, concerned with the capitalist reorganization of global spaces. Nevertheless it is Lynch's guidelines, taken on board by Jameson, that prove threadbare for the task of mapping postmodernity. His narrative of city navigation, dreamed up for Boston rather than L.A., has the whiff of Baudelairean *flanerie* about it, not the airlessness of the circuitry and concrete that engirds and networks the post-Pynchon metropolis. Lynch's is still a city of spires, needing *fixed* landmarks to which the city-navigator-*flâneuse* can raise her eyes to feel confident of her location. Jameson's call for the critic's totalizing vision is far removed from, and its scope at odds with, Lynch the humanist urbanist's desire that city dwellers feel at home. The differences elided by the analogy become evident as Jameson explains that "cognitive mapping" is premised also on Louis Althusser's concept of ideology, which presumes *a gap* between the experience and perception of the individual and the reality that surrounds her. This gap, in Althusser's schema, is filled by ideology. The gap, then (even when it is used as a metaphor; again, when writing about space one's spatial metaphors take on a ghostly, insistent quality), belongs to a vision of spatiality that also demands fixed points. Gaps to be bridged posit a space, a distance between individual and world—a distance which, once both are static and can be measured, then become the basis of his critique of what lies "beyond the gap." This proposes a vision of the subject as a figure who (within the terms of the argument) is untenably autonomous, who, like the points that give her comfort, can, even if she is a flâneuse, imagine herself at given moments as stationary and fixed and can thus take critical stock of the world. The actual conditions of postmodernism, however, are such that—as in the case of Jameson's photograph of the Bonaventure shot from the freeway—the subject is the figure in movement at a new velocity who jettisons the contemplative, cartographic pause. It is the trajectory of this movement, its rate of speed, that the critic needs to measure, or else his "mapping" will be little more than the counterpart of what Tafuri or Althusser critiques: a self-deluding collusion with the forces of disorientation carried out to make the subject enjoy her confusion.

To this point, I have discovered speed as the ghost haunting two key texts, one key to the career of Michel Foucault, the other to that of Fredric Jameson. Both Foucauldian cultural studies and the wave of materialist criticism they helped to inspire have, from their origins, not only been concerned in complex ways with explorations of the cultural significance of spaces but have as their political unconscious an interest in dynamic movement in space. The Bonaventure speaks in the mysterious voyages of its escalators; the boarding school is outshone by the roving ship. This begs two questions. First, why has there been a return to space among cultural and materialist critics? Second, why is the ultimate interest of these critics not in space itself but in movement? To answer, I turn to the work, first, of the geographer and theoretician of postmodernity's "spatial fix," David Harvey, and second, to the pioneering theorist of space in modernity, Henri Lefebvre. For a moment, however, consider how the anxiety about movement, and about the rate of movement, speed, hidden in the space fascination of Jameson and Foucault has also been stoked in work in architectural theory and urban studies.

When they write about built environments and their relation to communities and cultures, both Foucault and Jameson undercut their focus on the built with a covert attention to the permeability of these structures, the flows that might occur between them, and the movement they hinder and allow. They disentangle the ways in which the structures cut up and frustrate the movements of their users. Recall that their interest in space, in fact premised on their interest in traffic and its speeds, happened alongside an obsession in Western criticism with the estranging, disintegrating, counterdiscursive qualities of textuality and narrative—with poststructuralism. Space studies might be read as a counterweight to theory's grammatological tendencies. Radical developments in architectural theory, however, often profess themselves to be inspired by Derrida, the ideas of architects shocked into the new by reading deconstructive theory. Critics such as Mark Wigley on architecture and deconstruction, the feminist historian of architecture Beatrice Colomina, Anthony Vidler in his evocative psychologically inflected investigations of haunting and (anti-)structurality, and especially the architect and theorist of action-architecture Bernard Tschumi, have all co-opted poststructuralist textual theory as the lingua franca of discussions of architecture.[21] While this has produced, in the work of Vidler, for example, a rich awareness of architecture's uncanny propensity to embody in its most vainglorious structures the seeds of otherness, strangeness, and versions of the structure's ruin, it is in the work of Tschumi that poststructuralism has meant a full-scale manifesto regarding the necessity to place movement and, in his terms, the issue of violence, at the center of any debates about architecture. In his book *Architecture and Disjunction*, which interjected into architectural thinking and practice the palpable sense of kinetic power evident in the Futurist Manifesto almost a century earlier, Tschumi elaborates the proposition that "there is no architecture without action, no architecture without events. . . . By extension, there is no architecture without violence."[22] In Tschumi's ideal building, its users are moving, coursing, interacting individuals, so that the building is "engaged in constant intercourse with its users, whose bodies rush against the carefully established rules of architectural thought." He dreams of buildings that do not do violence on their users—with narrow corridors, forbidding facades—demanding, rather, structures which recognize that architecture was also about the movement of "bodies in space, that their language and the language of walls were ultimately complementary. . . . Architecture ceases to be a backdrop for actions, becoming the action itself" (148–49). Here one of the most daring innovations of modernist architecture, Le Corbusier's concrete ramp, as in the ramp which brazenly cuts through the Carpenter Center at Harvard, his only American commission, receives its full theoretical articulation two generations later as the dream of buildings that, if possible, move like their users, becoming themselves accelerators of traffic flows.

In the triumphant finale of *Architecture and Disjunction*, "De-, Dis-, Ex-," Tschumi confronts what he calls the challenge to appearances of permanence—buildings of stone or even of glass—being replaced now by immaterial representations, the electrode images of television. Invoking the work of Paul Virilio, Tschumi claims that "*speed* expands time by contracting space; it negates the notion of physical dimension" (316). This is a polemic against postmodern facadism (Disney's Los Angeles office with its "seven dwarves" pediment, Charles Moore's 1975 Piazza d'Italia in New Orleans), rather than an announcement of the future immateriality of buildings as such. The end of literature is possible; the end of built architecture is harder to imagine. Despite the force of Tschumi's polemic, fixity and stasis would appear to be indispensable conditions of architecture in practice. Nevertheless, just as in the case of work by the cultural and materialist theorists, here one witnesses one of the most distinguished architects of the day, from the discipline which would appear to have the most profound investment in structure, fixity, and the power of the immobile monument, also come out, *au contraire*, on the side of movement, action, and speed. This turn in a range of fields can only be understood in materialist terms; it needs to be historicized.

Both David Harvey, geographer and theorist of globalism, and the pioneer of materialist studies of spaces, Henri Lefebvre, note that Karl Marx had little to say about the spatial dimension of the flows of modern capital. In *The Production of Space*, Lefebvre theorized and charted what he terms the relentless "abstraction" of space by capitalism. By abstraction he means capitalism's drive to reduce all the world's richly particular spaces to a single homogeneous gridded landscape. For Lefebvre, capitalism, in pursuit of profit, remorselessly eradicates the local specific features that constitute place and make it livable and memorable. What makes a space a unique place, its features, its landmarks, and its spirit, tends to be eradicated in the push to make a more efficient network for producing profits. Manfredo Tafuri writes in the spirit of Lefebvre when he describes the city as an efficient machine which enables circulation—of people, goods, money, and information—to endlessly generate profits. This abstraction homogenizes space, but it does not necessarily make all spaces seem similar: rather, it compartmentalizes spaces, creating different enclosures for work, leisure, and consumption and different zones for the owners, the bourgeoisie, and the poor. Zoning serves capitalism. Lefebvre's monumental work elaborates on Marx's account of the destruction of nature by capitalism in the name of "progress." As Lefebvre describes it, "The tendency towards the destruction of nature does not flow solely from a brutal technology; it is also precipitated by the economic wish to impose the traits and criteria of interchangeability upon places. The result is that places are deprived of their specificity—or even abolished."[23]

This imposition, then, has a history in modernity, which can be charted. Lefebvre, surveying twentieth-century architecture, charts it from Le Corbusier's and Frank Lloyd Wright's relinquishing of the materiality of the heavy supporting wall in their buildings to the computers that were arriving even as he wrote. Harvey went on to map this same process of abstraction at the level of global space, and at the level also of the political real.

This abstraction, erasing interesting places to create the blandest space, effects human subjectivity too. When you occupy a space first grimly abstracted and then recolored by the compartmentalization necessary for capitalist efficiency, you are granted an uncanny, unsettling version of your relation to what you might presume is your "own place." This uncanniness is related to one's feelings before the simulation effects that Baudrillard would later theorize as characteristically postmodern. Lefebvre describes this unease as welling up when "desire and needs are uncoupled, then crudely cobbled back together." In his account, speed, as the ease of movement made possible by the abstracting of place into space, gets to be capitalism's good: people will work, and goods will move, faster and faster. At the same time, speed's pleasure may offer a new compensation for the disorienting loss of old-style place. Thus speed might well be supplemental to capitalism's designs: a necessity of capitalism which manages to transform itself into something more, a new pleasure.

Lefebvre presents human subjectivity under space-abstracting capitalism as a psychic sundering. In this story of how people are alienated from the very spaces they occupy, the "gift of speed" to individual subjects — for example, when they become drivers of automobiles — might appear as the arousal of a perverse desire that matches no real need. The desire to experience speed, note, is not generated by a visible need; it is a desire without a visible object per se in the world of produced consumer goods; it is a desire that can only try and try again to consummate itself in ever faster, ever more desperate, and ever more dangerous speeds — a desire, in Tschumi's terms, that submits itself to violence and a kind of torture. One might therefore see it as a new twist on older desires that, in its very strangeness, novelty, and excessive supplementarity, could be a force dangerous to the status quo of capitalist progress itself. (Critics such as Virilio would reply that that is why speed is so firmly policed, legislated, and controlled by the modern state.) On the other hand, as a desire clearly nurtured by capitalism — in every mass-cultural genre from car advertisements to car chase films — it may be *the* desire par excellence in Western culture that is fostered and tolerated in order to reconcile human subjects to their lot as actors in a "dynamic" capitalist economic milieu. Speed, intimately woven into a new paradigm of the modern subject's nexus of desires, becomes the new opiate and the new (after)taste of movement as power. As Lefebvre notes, much of even the most rational discussion about space has been about utopias. But if utopias are fantasies of ideal places, and places as such no longer exist (having been abstracted into more efficient spaces), then speed fantasies replace utopian dreaming as dangerous escapism or (even) as novel political discourse. Guy Debord managed to capture some of that ambivalence when he claimed, in his "Situationist Theses on Traffic," that "[The automobile is] the sovereign good of an alienated life and the essential product of the capitalist market."[24]

For Henri Lefebvre, space is "produced" as a social product under capitalism. Pitching his concept at the totalizing level of nature itself, he notes that Marx adds "the earth" only at the very end of *Capital* to "Capital" and "Labor" as the sources of wealth in the money economy. Space, in the triumvirate of "capital," "labor," and "the earth," is therefore instantly made real as the earth—a limited resource. In modernity, space, it becomes clear, is something "whose nature is nothing more than raw materials suffering gradual destruction by the techniques of production" (334). The history of space in modernity, for the critical theorist, will be a history of the dawning realization that this resource, nature itself, is not unlimited. Modernity witnesses a radical new awareness about space: a sense of global confinement and a sense of the exhaustibility of space itself.

Space, during the long history of Western colonization, had seemed unlimited: the most open resource of all. In the age of colonization up to the final days of imperial expansion in the nineteenth century, there remained space which could be thought of as unknown, blank, and conquerable. LeFebvre implicitly connects the new anxieties about space evident everywhere in modernist art, novels, poems, and films to an unconscious dawning awareness of the dilemmas that the fact that world space is limited will cause for capitalism. When he asks, at the opening of *The Production of Space* (16–19), why it is that, after five centuries of the credibility of Euclidean perspective in the West's visual representation of space since Masaccio, it could collapse in the early twentieth century in the psychoanalytically inspired spatial distortions of the surrealists or the spatial disruptions of Georges Bataille or André Breton's *L'amour fou*, he begins a project of exploring anxieties about spaces in modernism which insists that an understanding of perceptions of space is key to thinking the relations between modernism and modern capitalism. He formulates a dialectics of space to grasp the full charge of the modern. Each twist of the dialectic brought closer the sense that the space into which capitalism could expand was finite, that at some point (to be reached in the early twentieth century) it would all be colonized. Modernist spaces, such as the noir-shaded city nightscape, are uncanny not simply because they invoke memories of a lost sense of a more richly inflected "place" where one might have felt at home but because they cannot suppress the sense that the "other" space, whose exploitation pays for the comforts offered in the Western metropolis, will soon run out. At this juncture, the geographer David Harvey's notion of capitalism's need for a "spatial fix," the need of capitalism to constantly expand its territory, makes clear why this fear, of being boxed in, is for capitalist culture such an urgent one. Once "other spaces" for capitalist expansion run out, it can only grow by exploiting more intensely the space it knows.

Harvey puts Lefebvre's dialectic to the test of practice. He charts capitalism's conquest of space in detail and discovers it to be a process riven by contradictions and crises. For him, space matters because capitalism, given its structure, needs always to expand. Its compulsion to growth leads to its first contradiction: making money is based on the application of living and mobile labor power, but also on the use of technological change, which supplants living labor. Surpluses cannot be absorbed by unemployed labor; thus capitalism needs to find new spaces for the circulation of capital. Capitalism needs its "spatial fix": it always tries to expand into new territories so that crises at home are diffused. Spatial organization, a more detailed version of Lefebvre's "abstraction," accomplishes this. For Harvey, the ever-expanding behemoth of capital works like a giant pyramid scheme, whose ever-larger base is accommodated in the control of more and more, and increasingly abstracted, global territory.

Harvey's account of capital's geopolitical expansion functions as a materialist history of imperialism, of the postcolonial "three worlds" phase after World War II, and of the current globalism. His work builds on the tradition of earlier materialist theorists of colonialism such as Rosa Luxemburg, who even in 1913 in *The Accumulation of Capital* argued that Western nations pursued empires primarily to discover new markets for their excess consumer products. For Luxemburg, the aim of colonialism was, in the last instance, to turn each colony into a territory of consumers. As in the cases of Foucault and Jameson as Lefebvrians, Harvey wishes to come to terms with the abstraction of global space known as imperialism. Jameson's account in "Cognitive Mapping" of how the "secret" of the artistic and literary experimentations of Western modernism may be located in the hidden, far-from-the-metropole colonial reality of imperial space abstraction, cleanly answers Lefebvre's question of why Euclidean space was finally shattered sometime around 1917. For Lefebvre too, Harvey agrees, the answer is indeed "empire," if through a more dynamic, jarring process. Jameson posits a gap in knowledge, a suture, of which modernist art is a symptom, even as the art salves it. Harvey instead posits a radically convulsive, dynamic process in which capitalism lurches from crisis to crisis, addicted to profit and ever chasing new territories in which its contradictions at home can be overcome. And it is at this point in his argument, appropriately, that Harvey introduces the concept of speed into his discussion.

Speed, for Harvey, enters his argument under theoretical cover, by economic-formula stealth. He elaborates on the "spatial" component of Marx's original phrase regarding the exploitation of labor by capital, its aim "to annihilate space with time," to consider how "that contradiction is expressed through historical-geographical transformations."[25] His answer to Marx's conundrum is to elaborate a dialectic of static space versus dynamic movement. When it develops technology to speed up production, capital commits itself to a fixed infrastructure and, in doing so, to a fixed place. On the other hand, in developing markets, in finding cheap labor opportunities elsewhere, in the work of abstracting the new territory necessary for achieving the spatial fix that will resolve its crisis in the existing markets, capital must commit itself to improved, increased movement of cash, goods, and people. This contradiction has generated changes that can be traced historically by checking the speed of movement of goods, people, and money:

> The history of capitalism has therefore been marked by dramatic reductions in the cost of time of movement together with improvements in continuity or flow. Space relations are thereby continuously subject to transformation. The territory within which infrastructural coherence prevails is loosely defined as that space within which capital can circulate within the limits of profit without socially necessary turnover time being exceeded by the cost of time of movement.[26]

Here Harvey posits two variables of movement, two speeds: the first, in which the cost and time of movement are below "socially necessary" and profitable turnover time, possible in the space where "infrastructural coherence prevails"; and another, where the cost and time of movement are for the time being above it, too great for profit. This economic equation defines the economic forces which determine the imperial and postcolonial expansion of global capitalism. It hinges, note, on the speed of movement of goods, people, and money. Harvey's account of the dynamics of the "flexible accumulation" of imperial and postimperial economic expansion provides an explicit rationale for why space has become a preoccupation of Western theorists in a range of fields. Implicitly, it explains why the issues of movement and speed trip up the study of space at every turn.

That available space for abstraction is finite, as Lefebvre pointed out, was bound to deny the possibility of continuous spatial expansion. The time of the "spatial fix" that Harvey describes is running out. Western theorists are interested in space because the spatial fix is necessary for the continued growth, and hence maintenance, of capitalism: they are fascinated now in particular with movements and flows, because, as Jameson also avers, a new and different stage has been reached in the way in which the spatial fix abstracts new territory. In short, the whole globe has now been colonized for capital, and the search for new territories in which to resolve contradictions is almost over. High Western imperialism of the Victorian era had provided capitalism with the reassurance that there were more and more territories to colonize, more places to abstract and reorganize for the penetration of capital. At a certain point early in the twentieth century, however, when none of the spaces on the world imperial map, as Joseph Conrad's Marlow in *Heart of Darkness* described it, were any longer blank but were all red or yellow or blue (for the Congress of Berlin of 1884–85 had doled out the last unconquered areas between the Western powers), imperialist doubters brought home to Westerners the idea that writers such as Lefebvre would not articulate until the postwar years: that global space was not a source of boundless expansion, frontier energy, and cultures that could be read as exotically other, as well as a source of wealth. Rather, global space was a resource, and a finite one at that.

A pivotal moment in the British establishment's acknowledgment of this problem was an essay by Halford J. Mackinder, "The Geographical Pivot of History" (1904), in which McKinder, first reader of geography at Oxford University, used the term "closed space" to describe the wholly mapped world.[27] This realization has had effects comparable to those that the end of the frontier myth had on the North American continent, but on a global scale. New notions of a more complex spatial order, or ways to overcome the centrality of spatial expansion to capitalism altogether, had to be developed at every level. The result: spatial disruptions described by Harvey, and all the angst about spaces as frightening and frustrating in the high cultural productions of the early decades of the twentieth century. Among others, the arch-modernist James Joyce, himself the product of a city, Dublin, whose anomalous abstraction through close-in colonialism he anatomized in his books, could have his hero Stephen Dedalus ruminate apocalyptically that "I hear the ruin of all space . . . Shattered glass and toppling masonry, and time one vivid final flame."[28] For him, as for other modernist writers from W. B. Yeats ("the center cannot hold") to Virginia Woolf, whose most characteristic heroine is a nervy flâneuse for whom a backfiring automobile is as loud as a pistol shot (see chapter 3), the cadences of the poet William Blake's jeremiads a century earlier, in poems horrified and transfixed by the first stages of modern British capitalism and the "machine age," now ring more true than ever.

Movement, velocity, and in particular, in Tschumi's terms, movement as violence: these interests were always incipient in modernist representations. They could enter the field of vision of critical writing only after a further crucial change, when the mechanical age gave way to the electronic. Now that speed is measured against the instantaneous transmittal power of the computer, we can at least dream that movement imagined as locomotive power faces obsolescence. In terms of Harvey's formulation of those global spatial flows, once the "cost and time of movement" are reduced for information (and thus money) to virtually nothing, then "socially necessary turnover time" is freed in ways that can now begin to be imagined. Technology has mastered the virtual and transmits its images instantaneously: so we sense that movement and its rate, its speed, soon no longer matter. At that point, the era of speed, the rate of movement — will be over. Writing its history, therefore, becomes urgent. It matters less now than a century ago that this conquering of space by time proceeds in different spaces at different speeds: after all, the possibility that the colonies would become territories of consumers was (in part) fantastic too. What matters, for capitalist confidence, was the project of maintaining the sensibility of dynamic growth into ever new areas, which sustained a corresponding sense of dynamism at home. Thus speed enters the critical debate, and soon the mass popular consciousness, as a species of deep ideology, a pleasure by which one could be cheered, a personal, possibly harmless, power to be seized, and a memory, bolstered paradoxically by nostalgia, of an era when capitalism could still move and expand not merely in its confined "home" territory but ever outward for the enrichment, it insisted, of the world. The personal thrill of the new-century motor speeds and the politics of late imperial capitalism turn out to be unexpectedly and uncannily related.

By acknowledging speed as a prime force implicated not only in technological and cultural innovation but, more pervasively, in economic and global change in the twentieth century, we can trace two levels of a history of speed at once. First, undertheorized relations between the domains of technology and cultural production can be rethought, their symbiosis made evident. This relation is not merely a matter of a bridge between the "two cultures" of science and the arts of which C. P. Snow spoke in 1959. Nor is it even the glamorous but often superficial borrowing from one sphere to the other: clunky technology (the car engine) gets streamlined by being wrapped in design, while "culture" confines its dreams of the technological netherworld to wishfully utopian or didactically dystopian lowbrow genres, the science fiction thriller or the race driver memoir (although all these genres are great sources for evidence in the history of the modernist cultures of speed). Rather, by making speed a political issue, we bring to the fore the deep imbrication of technology in culture and vice versa, the necessity of technology to radically alter the very bases of perception so that its advances can seem inevitable. We can make visible a culture's readiness to educate different audiences in how such changes might be imagined, dreamed, dreaded. Thinking through speed lets us see that technology exists in modern culture as the deepest, and hence least evident, form of ideology, producing through the work of culture not just populations that are pro-technology but, more, ones whose expectations and perceptual equipment demand the prosthetic pleasures that specific technologies provide. This is ideology through machinery, a pleasure of modern culture, and it is centered on speed.

Second, taking speed seriously lets us see how technology has assuaged, enabled, and diverted attention from a global space abstracted by the relentless expansion of capital. If we read speed symptomatically and ally it, as Foucault has taught us to do regarding spaces, with the global spaces in which it fascinates and in which it has a history, then we can politicize speed. Its arrival into Western consciousness can be read as a symptom of a new stage in the history of imperialism and the ideology that supported it, marking the moment in capitalism's appropriation of all available global space. Speed had its great moment in modernity between the dread moment at the height of empire when the West discerned that the spatial fix, capitalism's potential to expand into previously unknown territories as a means to overcome crises at home, was not unlimited, and the more recent moment, in our time, when technology's achievement of instantaneous communication over vast distances seemed to make the variable of speed not matter anymore. It was the period when the sensation of speed for millions of individuals matched the actual speeds required for the progress of capital on which their overall well-being depended. Only now, when speed, at least as measured in terms that can be experienced unaided by human beings, seems about to be superseded, can we discern its symptomatic power and construct a history of it. This book, then, will be a history of the epistemology of speed in the specific historical period between the beginning of the end of imperialism and the beginning of the era when speed seems superseded by computer instantaneousness. This corresponds to the period in the history of culture termed "modernist." Last, however, consider the outstanding cultural theorist of the speed phenomenon of the twentieth century, Paul Virilio, whose work overshadows everything implied about speed and movement by Jameson, Foucault, Lefebvre, Harvey, and the theorists of architecture. Virilio has focused on military strategy as the engine for the development of new speed technologies and for the recruitment of citizens to learn the speed of their use. His work on speed in warfare sharpens the issue I have already sketched of speed's role in a geopolitical consciousness.

Virilio's history of speed—attentive to the Cold War's conflict between the first and second worlds[29]—might seem to eschew the geopolitics of imperialism and postcolonialism elucidated by Lefebvre and Harvey. Yet Virilio has almost certainly been influenced by Lefebvre, despite their political differences. Lefebvre's vision of the abstraction of space for capitalism's maximization of profits becomes, in Virilio's vision, an account of how the city, and then the state, worked on the one hand at policing traffic, managing the mass movement of vagrant workers outside its walls or borders and charging tariffs for goods at the gates, and on the other at coercing or persuading those same masses into becoming marching, moving armies that would, under the generals, rush toward the cannons to save themselves and grasp more territory for the state. Those in power, Virilio insists, struggle to control the engine of the masses' speeds. For him, bourgeois power is primarily military: it is after Napoleon (who said that the strength of an army is "as in mechanics, its mass multiplied by its speed"),[30] rather than after Adam Smith or after early engineers like Stephenson, that philosophers unconsciously begin to use dynamic metaphors.

Virilio presents himself as a theoretician of military history. His two books with his most specific readings of cultural productions both have a military slant: his early *Bunker Archeology* (1975) describes the German bunkers that face Britain along the French coast during World War II, and *War and Cinema* (1984) traces how the technology of the movie camera was driven by the needs of military photography, surveillance, and sighting. In *Speed and Politics*, his military historian's perspective serves up a materialist reading, one more thoroughly class based, more concerned for the downtrodden, even in its cynicism, than the analytic materialism of Lefebvre. The walled medieval city, Virilio notes, is the successor to a settlement that grew up around a crossroads and traffic intersection. Its successors are the city-state and later the nation-state. Each is, then, a "poliocretics of traffic control . . . confusing social order with the control of traffic" (41), organized by the dominant class to control the rate of movement—that is, the speed—of the others. This allows Virilio to think of revolution as a mechanism which jolts and interferes with the even speed and smooth movement of traffic. He begins *Speed and Politics* by noting how revolutions have always been about the right of the masses to the streets, whether in marches, or in the blocked streets of the barricades, about which he quotes Weber on Rosa Luxemburg and Karl Liebknecht: "They called to the streets and the streets killed them" (3). Revolution, whether bourgeois or proletarian, Virilio defines as symbolic and actual interventions in the state's regulated speeds of circulation of people and goods, interventions which supplant regimes that act as traffic police with new orders promising freedoms—freedom, first, of movement.

Virilio's account of speed in modernity concludes with the idea that the nuclear era, when the military arm is capable of almost instantaneous mass destruction, has produced a "state of emergency" in which "the strategic value of the non-place of speed has supplanted that of [fortified] space."[31] Here speed is the preeminent index of power, and it lies wholly in the hands of the militarized state. Nevertheless Virilio holds open the possibility of the use of speed as a politically liberating and revolutionary force, in a way that neither Lefebvre nor Harvey ever has the audacity to envision. It is as if each of them, writing out of a long tradition of materialist critiques of imperialism, from Lenin's *Imperialism* to the dependency theorists of the postwar years,[32] who suffered from the lack of a theory of geopolitical space in Marx's own writings and consequently produced mostly theories of static domination of colonized by colonizer, found it difficult to escape the point of view of the imperial center even as they critiqued it. On the political valence of space and speed, Virilio, renegade military historian, escapes this tradition; attending to speed as modus of military strategy, he focuses on movement as power play and shows the speed dynamic operating between the economic, military, and civic arms of the polis. His cynical commentaries on Britain as supreme colonial power, when it channeled its violence and its speed inventions (army, ships, trains) outward, map neatly, nevertheless, onto Harvey's account of capitalism's spatial fix.

Virilio then goes further. He claims that this dispersal of forces of violence, speed, and technology into an unseen, distant abroad was replaced, as the empire waned and its version of the spatial fix seemed less productive, with a turning of the same forces inward, so that their activities came to be practiced, if in other forms, on the population at home. This process he calls "endocolonization," and it has enormous potential, first, for understanding how the imperial colonizing efforts actually and concretely impacted the lives of the populations at home, and, second, for coming to terms with the vastly increased mechanisms of interpellation and suggestion to which the citizens of both Western nations and former colonies have been subjected since the end of colonization.

It has become a critical truism that Western modernity and its most developed expressive forms, the various modernisms, have been haunted by the "worlds elsewhere" of empire. From Picasso's African mask faces to the uneasy Indian world of E. M. Forster, this particular ghost has been recognized as an enabling discomfort at the Western modernist feast. In empire was located the uneasy political unconscious that fanned the obscurities of even the most Western-obsessed music, art, and texts.[33] It is this idea that Jameson twists into a full-bodied historicism in his "Cognitive Mapping" schema, when he sees modernist obscurities as the symptoms which betray a lack of materialist consciousness. While the modernist text might describe the home country, its discordances betray an unconscious awareness that the economic exploitations which underpin the comforts of the home country are taking place elsewhere — in an African rubber plantation or a Shanghai sweatshop. This account shows an admirable determination to discern the politics of even the most avowedly apolitical of texts; however, it gets mainly to praise the texts for possessing (albeit unconsciously) the very kinds of sensitivities which they may well appear not to have. Rather, the materialist critic should first seek to discern in the high-art text the forces that operate in the home culture it represents. Then the critic does not have to posit a gap — between Western self-serving insouciance and colonial realities — which the high-art text manages to cross.

The various modernisms, flaunting their discordances and obliquities, may be betraying unconscious political awareness of the guilty secrets of the West regarding its colonies; they are also reacting to the onset of the idea that empire was coming to an end, as there were no more lands to conquer. No more territorial expansion was possible, and at some point, spatial fixes too would run out. Western national economies were beginning to turn inward, and endocolonization was launched at home. At that point, Western high art could indeed identify its subjects with colonial peoples, as the Westerners were now being subjected to the regimes that had been pioneered as initiatives of colonial expansion. This reimportation of the methods of colonial administration to the home country—what Virilio terms "endocolonization"—marked an early moment of the universal system we now term "globalism."

How are endocolonization and speed related? Colonialism has always been partly a matter of strategically deploying speed technologies; as Virilio points out, the imperial powers could always defeat the native populations because they excelled them in speed—of travel (ships), and of projectiles (guns). Once this regime of speedy movement reached its limit, then its force had to be reabsorbed at home. The colonial regimes differed from those of the home nations not merely because they were undemocratic, alien, and failed to offer the same rights as did the metropolitan governments to their subjects but because they were regimes based almost wholly, as Frantz Fanon points out, on raw force—and this force was expressed through superior speed.[34] When the characteristics of this system of rule began to be practiced at home, therefore, with the more explicit aspects of the exercise of brute force erased from them, endocolonization meant the arrival of the regime of speed to Western nations in a new, more intense form. As Virilio makes clear, the postimperial regime was well positioned for this work, as the nation itself, in its emergence from the city-state, had primarily been concerned with the management of traffic flows of goods, services, information, and, above all, people by the empowered bourgeoisie. The new order, however, meant that in the late-imperial nation, via the quite sudden appearance of speed as an experience available to the masses, every citizen could now be offered the experience of speed as his or her own destiny. The mass production of cars, to take the key example, which began in precisely this period (after 1896), must be considered in part as a political development. Critics have had no trouble seeing the mass production of the Volkswagen and the building of the German Autobahn system after 1933 as starkly political;[35] we may also read politically similar moves in every western European country, and in the United States in the interwar decades and before. The first census of U.S. roads was taken in 1904;[36] the earliest British mass-marketed "family car," the Austin 7, was first produced in 1921;[37] Hitler was filmed breaking ground for the first segment of the Autobahn on September 23, 1933.[38] This new, much more intense and technologized stage in the mass experience of speed was matched by newly intense and modern traffic management: André Michelin, for example, created the Car Travelers' Information Bureau in Paris in 1908, undertook in 1910 to map France to the scale of one inch to three miles, numbered all roads in 1913, and then marked these numbered roads with standard square milestones of pumice stone covered in vitreous enamel. In 1900, with the three thousand cars then in circulation in France, he had produced the original Michelin guide, *France*.[39] The new individual speed culture, endocolonization, and the new level of bureaucracy in the nation-state were put in place at once. It was in Paris taxis that many recruits were hurriedly transported to the front in the early days of World War I.

At the same time, this period when the experience of speed at home would itself—as in more car production—stand in for the spatial fix that colonialism had offered abroad was, as it were, doomed from the start by the even greater speed of information transfer offered by the telephone. It is curious that the thought of abandoning the colonies arose at the very moment when new technologies meant new ease in administering them. As information, and hence (fictitious) money, could be transmitted almost simultaneously, locomotive and projectile speed was left to catch up. Once instantaneous transmittal became the norm, the era of speeds experienced as pleasure was over, and their history could be written: this is the point that has now begun to be reached. The interest in space in the West results from the experience of endocolonization; in speed, from the ending of the era when locomotive speed was offered to masses of people as a simulacrum of force and a source of imaginary personal empowerment. (Today, in the era of instantaneous telecommunications, people are being individually offered the Internet in very similar terms.) A history of speed since around 1895 offers a chapter in the life of nations in which the experience of velocity was thoroughly politicized and became a symptom of access or the lack of it to political and economic power. Read this symptomology: consider how some of the cultural expressions of this speed culture reacted to the new kinetic and sociopolitical order.

"Cooperating with Mechanics": Speed Criticism

In the latest fin de siècle, an advertisement in the *Economist* offered snippets of the wealth-generating advice available in a financial newsletter. On real estate, it suggested that the reader invest in a seaside villa in Albania. Albania: now the only section of the Mediterranean coastline where waterfront land could be had for next to nothing. The Mediterranean shorefront is a fixed limited resource in high demand, much of it already built upon; values in the long term, even in Albania, are bound to rise. On such arid beaches and impoverished coves, the newsletter's readers may even now be signing checks and dreaming of fantastic returns on their investment.

Such are the twilight dreams of colonialism, the first dreams of a new globalism. Henri Lefebvre's version of the space of the globe relentlessly abstracted by capitalism is nearly realized as available space becomes real estate — space as tradable commodity. Dreams of empire, the state's version of the land grab, developed under the archaic logic of the ancient empires, in which control of a greater territory meant increased prestige and power. In the cultural history of global space, the key fact around 1900 had been the abstracting of space into property known as imperialism. As we trace the links between this pervasive politics of space and the individual consciousness of space of each citizen, to grasp this is to begin to understand why frustration at slowness, scratched like an itch by Conrad's prose, became important in most high modernism. It comes close to explaining why flânerie, walking on foot through the city, became a modernist obsession at the very moment when new speeds were being achieved. It also complicates, but preserves, Jameson's intuition of the centrality of colonial-metropolitan relations for explaining high-modernist obscurities. For example, Eliot's langours in "Prufrock" become an index of the contrast between the efficiencies of the arriviste empire (that of America, where Eliot was born and raised) and the frustrations of the worn-out one (that of Britain). Likewise, Joyce's Irish stop-and-go flânerie in *Ulysses* indexes the clash between metropole and colonial city as the rhythm of a setting (Dublin) where home and heterotopia were entities whose status was deeply unsure.

Space, in philosophies of perception, may or may not be a sensory illusion; the concept of space, at any rate, thoroughly organizes human consciousness and thinking, as proved by our use of metaphors of space, distance, perspective, and dynamism in everyday speech. For example, as Mark Wigley points out, Jacques Derrida's first published essay, "Force and Signification" (1963), attacked the structural and spatial metaphors in the thought of Jean Rousset; Martin Heidegger's famous essay "Building, Dwelling, Thinking" first makes explicit the continuous use of architectural terms, metaphors, and tropes that form the grammar of thinking in the German philosopher's subsequent work.[40] No one, from the philosophers to the speaker of a banal everyday phrase such as "my personal space," is using such spatial metaphors outside a social and cultural context; all of us are subject to versions of space which have a history of which we are part. If that history in the twentieth century has been a history of imperialism, then the spatial consciousness which allows us to think space in our time, and from which our stock of spatial metaphors which influence all our thinking and even dreaming come, might be termed (to use a key term of the French theorists Gilles Deleuze and Félix Guattari) territorialization. Territorialization implies that we imagine space primarily in terms of its appropriation and ownership, for the increase of our own power and profit. In the twentieth-century discourse of space as territorialization, a crucial moment occurred early in the century when the realization dawned that the whole space of the globe had been accounted for, that there were no more Kurtzian "white spaces on the map" and no more frontiers. Could the rise in speed culture in the West at this moment be something more than a compensation for what was lost? Could it augur a new way of imagining space that we are only now beginning to theorize?

Certainly, as Marcel Duchamp remarked about *Nude Descending the Staircase*, "the whole idea of movement, of speed, was in the air . . ."[41] And Ilya Ehrenburg aptly captures the experience of speed in his strange novel *The Life of the Automobile* (1929): "In the dark theater, amid the smooching couples and the comfortable rattle of the projector, Bernard unexpectedly started trembling. A car raced across the screen. The entire audience was racing in that car. Bernard suddenly felt that he too was racing somewhere."[42] The offering of a speed experience to masses of people, primarily through the mass production of the automobile, radically altered people's perception of scale, perception, distance, and space. It also altered the spatial metaphors and tropes they introduced into their thinking and dreaming on all aspects of their existence. (The British urbanist and transplant Rayner Banham could wonder, for example, at the way Californians spoke of distances in terms of the time it took them to travel by car.)[43] As people experienced the new speed technologies, we need to ask, how did the new perspectives, metaphors, and senses of space generated by this new speed culture chime with, and enhance, the determination to further abstract real space, now that the blank, exotic spaces had all been colonized? This new stage of the abstraction of space at home, following Virilio, may be termed endocolonialism: the application in the home country, in novel forms, of ways developed in the colonies to intensively govern space and movement, which came into effect as imperialism waned. This increased organization of space is the social and political counterpart to the thrill of technologized speed being experienced by the masses of new automobile owners at the same time. Speed's appearance in both high and low culture at this moment in the early twentieth century may be read as evidence of people testing new regimes of spatial organization as they enjoy the pleasures and thrills of speed culture for themselves.

How do we read for speed? Most critical attention to representations of speed has looked at high culture artifacts of the various Western modernisms. The Western modernist elite were machine obsessed: think of Léger's machines and mechanic bodies, Wyndham Lewis's enthusiasms for speed culture in the journal *Blast* and his discussion of spatiality in *Time and Western Man*, Man Ray's photographs of Meret Oppenheim's naked body next to the dark symmetry of the wheels of a printing press, Duchamp's upturned bicycle wheel revolving endlessly in the air. Consider the speed-obsessed work of Italian Futurism, in sculpture, painting, poetry, novels, and a slew of manifestoes. Artists and writers themselves were the first to acknowledge that modernist experimentation has been influenced by, and has worked to come to terms with, a new stage in the machine age; the criticism which aims to account for the dance of art and technology nevertheless had an intrepid air. Stephen Kern's fascinating *The Culture of Time and Space, 1880–1918*, for example, traces myriad correspondences: a typical chapter, on speed itself, moves from early national speed limits to the Otis elevator, which caused a stir at the Exposition Universelle of 1900 in Paris, the first electric chair (New York, 1888, a "revolting spectacle," according to contemporary accounts), Taylorism in the workplace, "moving pictures," Marinetti's Futurist Manifesto, Umberto Boccioni's sculpture *Unique Forms of Continuity in Space* (1913), George Beard's book *American Nervousness* (1881), and Octave Uzanne's *La locomotion à travers le temps, les moeurs et l'espace*, a book full of nostalgia about the fin de siècle days of clopping horses, published in 1900.[44] Exhibiting evidence as profusely and as brilliantly as any showstopper in one of the great expositions from Chicago to Paris which were a feature of the period he describes, Kern orchestrates a dance of cause and effect; he elaborates on speed as a phenomenon, "what it felt like when the idea of speed was in the air." In another brilliant work of cultural synthesis, *Shifting Gears*, Cecelia Tichi shows how the new era of the car, electricity, and the telephone revolutionized the very form of American poetry of the 1930s.[45]

The difficulty for many studies of the relation of technology and culture is that they must participate in categories such as "technology" and "modernist poetry" to stage the critical act of overcoming them. The high culture component, despite the critics' intentions, gets to seem reactive, a catch-up job for a field which notices that technology, the competition, has been inventive enough to put a new sensation "in the air." For the critic who would consider how modernists such as Joyce, Picasso, Woolf, Eliot, Gris, or Balla revised the sense of space, and movement in it, in their culture this is a problematic critical method, as it embodies a notion of critical distance and thus of a fixed point for the author-artist and her subject, at odds with the dynamic of movement which the artist, "responding" to the new technology, manages to display. Critiques of modernist art or writing that aim to demonstrate how a defamiliarizing text subverts the established order on which it is modeled likewise persist in attributing to the artwork an assumption of this critical difference as perspectival distance. Undoubtedly many works were not merely reacting to, but were consciously reactionary in relation to, the new (dis)order where "speed was in the air." Utopianism in art in the age of speed could take the form of a celebration of slowness. However, to see this as the norm, to see art as the holdout for an out-of-date slowness, and indeed to praise the work of art for this "critical distance," is to render it impossible to see how technologically driven speed culture not only infiltrated but perhaps was itself altered by the high art that has been sanctioned by museums, schools, and other arbiters of taste as the great art of this century.

It is here that my argument with Jameson's critical paradigm in "Cognitive Mapping" is situated. In that essay, Jameson helpfully brings the modernists' concern with a radically altered sense of geopolitical space to the top of the modernist critical agenda. Yet he accounts for modernism's thoroughgoing strangeness by reading it as a symptom of suppressed anxiety regarding ignorance: the text's strange turns, the picture's multi-faceted perspectives, are to be read as symptoms of the work's own near apprehension of the fact that while life is being enjoyed in the West, the enjoyment is made possible by the exploitation of people elsewhere, in the colonies. I don't wish to deny the existence of this uncanniness as the basis of defamiliarization in all kinds of modernist artifacts. However, I suggest that it too cannot quite escape the logic of critical *distance* from its real subject as the measure of artistic value, even if Jameson, with a striking materialist aesthete's sleight of argument, makes the modernist artwork's distance from colonial realities a matter of a gap of inadequate consciousness. By allowing *distance* to be the key to his argument, and by claiming that the imaginative overcoming of this distance, even at an unconscious level, is precisely what leads to the value of the work's strangeness as an unconscious index of imperial unease, Jameson participates in a critical tradition where distance — measurable distance relative to fixed and static positions — is still the imperative of a sound critical judgment.

"Distance" in criticism is a spatial metaphor, based on the notion that an adequate distance will allow the spectator to have the correct perspective or enable her to enlarge her field of vision to see the issues in a larger context. This set of metaphors is derived, inevitably, from what I have described earlier as the "territorializing" mentality, even as it attempts to cut against the grain of the mentality of territorial takeover that drove imperial conquest. As such, Jameson's critical method in "Cognitive Mapping" should be perfect for understanding the mentalities discernible in late-colonial works. If, however, the territorializing mentality that undergirded the modern colonizing and imperial project was upended in the early twentieth century with the realization that the conquerable global space was finite, then his methodology applies only to works from before that date. Aptly, then, Jameson's major work, *The Political Unconscious*, which applies to historicization and to time the same distancing effect that is delineated in spatial terms in "Cognitive Mapping," considers literary works ending with Joseph Conrad's *Nostromo*, which was first serialized in *T.P.'s Weekly* in 1904. Later twentieth-century works he leaves untouched. In the essay and the book, he may be mapping the demise of critical distance in art as a trope which matches perfectly the territorial sense of spatial relations that undergirded imperialism, and which the new impressionism he notes in *Nostromo* helped to undermine.

What would a criticism — or an artistic and literary practice — which attempted to forgo critical distance look like? The new-century modernist movement that most explicitly chased speed in its aesthetic practice and also strove to obliterate distance was, of course, Futurism. Marinetti's barrage of manifestoes, Boccioni's sculptures, Balla's movement paintings of birds in flight, a dog straining at a leash, and cars traveling at speed, Severini's pointillist-inspired, movement-alert scenes, Enrico Prampolini's sets for international exhibitions, Benedetta's tactile tables, and Marinetti's novels all celebrated speed as signs of modernist engagement with the real. Speed would sweep away static historical contemplativeness, and what the group saw as the dead weight of Italy's overvenerated artistic heritage. Speed, for Marinetti, was the new beauty. "We cooperate," he declared, "with mechanics in destroying the old property of distance . . . for which we substitute the tragic lyricism of ubiquity and omnipresent speed."[46] The dream of destroying the notion of artistic distance that had been based on a classical perspectival scheme was indeed imbued with a "tragic lyricism," because, in Marinetti's original manifesto in *Le Figaro*, it could only, notoriously, be imagined as a car crash, albeit a glorified one, in which the uninjured Futurist mechanic-artist enjoys the communion of metal and mud in the "infernal ditch" into which he drives the fast car. This is the first and crucial car crash in high art; it may remind us, however, that the aesthetic desire for a communion with the real has an even more extensive history than the aesthetic-critical tradition of contemplative distance. What is needed for a thorough critical analysis of cultural forms that match the endocolonization through speed of Western experience in the twentieth century is a criticism which forgoes, on the one hand, the cartographizing demarcation of exact critical distance between spectator and object and, on the other, also avoids a quasi-visionary and inevitably apocalyptic criticism that can speak only of the "chaos" or "breakdown" of dynamic systems.

Such criticism would itself be a speed technology: annotating the speeds of moving trajectories as they survey each other in passing, making always contingent judgments which continually alter based on the changing points of view. It would be a speed technology that matches the traffic policing which is to the era of endocolonization what the task of the cartographer was to the era of high imperialism. Now, when—as the announcers of postmodernity have claimed in the wake of Baudrillard—this latter era has ended because speed culture senses its own obliteration by the instantaneousness of computer transmittal, then the need for such a criticism becomes visible. It would be a criticism to match Einstein's insight in physics, first developed (appropriately for our schema here) in 1905 and elaborated in the following two decades, that "there is an infinite number of spaces, which are in motion with respect to each other, and, in measurement, the relative velocity of the object and viewer was the crucial factor, not the distance between them."[47]

It is a criticism which forgoes dreams of a totalizing vision based on achieving the ultimate correct perspective; it is, rather, a contingent criticism in search of contingent cultural forms. It would refuse to see the text as merely reactive to technological "advances" or, on the other hand, to see it as somehow beneficently unconscious of the world order it does not manage to represent. It is avowedly political, unlike most of the technology-to-culture criticism which refuses politics altogether; it demands the limberness to focus on both the global issues of the appropriation and exploitation of geopolitical space and the specific political issues raised by the culture of speed itself, such as its blatant sexism (in that speed has almost wholly been presented as a male desire), its complete imbrication in consumer culture, and its enjoyment by the wealthy, excluding the poor. The challenge: to discover a criticism that has the dynamism, elusiveness, and powers of escape, the ability to overtake, the rush of energy, and the overall torque of its subject. What is needed is criticism to match the aesthetics of speed.

The first principle for this new critical form is this: it must be *au fait* with modernist pop as well as high culture. This truism of cultural criticism reaches the point of necessity with the culture of speed. The metaphors of the older regime of spatial organization—distance, perspective, stasis—fit all too readily into the metaphoric scaffolding of philosophy or cultural criticism; the metaphors of the new regime of speed, as they now exist, come from the new speed technologies, from the attempts to police speeds, or from the media technologies that have been instantly turned into ubiquitous pop-cultural forms: the phonograph, radio, and film. Consider, for example, these scattered terms from the first category of metaphors of the new regime of speed, derived from technology itself:

waves
circuits
short circuits
shocks
turbulence
aerodynamics
torque

From the second, the measuring and policing of speed:

speed limits
rpm
mph
horsepower
Mach 1 (and Mach 2, 3, 4, 5)
acceleration
braking
speeding
road rage

From the third, the new communications technologies based on speed

frames per second
slow motion
moving images
voice-overs
car chase
frames per second

These terms and many others thrown up by twentieth-century speed culture have implicated themselves in people's consciousness: we employ them in all arenas to make sense of experience. They show us, through their pop-culture origins, that speed has had first and foremost a mass appeal. They suggest that high culture, especially in the jagged-edged experiments of making-strange, has had to huff and puff in an after-the-facts game of catching up. The experimental, turgid arrows of the Italian Futurist Balla in his automobile painting, for example, *Speed of an Automobile and Light and Noise*, painted just before he abandoned concrete representations altogether to show speed wholly through abstract forms (he had in the previous year portrayed leashed dogs, violinists, and swifts in flight), may strike the viewer now as an all-too-levelheaded attempt to seal, within the archaic medium of an oil painting, the roar and onrush of an automobile. The same machine in movement, on the other hand, could have its velocity represented with ease in the simplest of early caper films, like the one that made Ilya Ehrenburg's hero leap from his cinema seat in excitement in *The Life of the Automobile*.

Film, a form of viewing enabled by new technologies of movement and light, reeling by at a rate of twenty-four frames per second, introduced audiences to all the other speed pleasures. Film is the vision machine of the age of speed. Actual "moving pictures," with the camera moving as it saw, came into being as an idea when M. A. Promio, a cameraman with the Lumière brothers, thought of taking continuous film from a moving boat in the Grand Canal of Venice. Around the same time, early film audiences had fled from their seats at the sight of a train, filmed arriving at La Ciotat station, rushing toward them on the screen (no Futurist art shocked so literally or effectively).[48] Within ten years, one of the biggest thrills of popular film was the car chase. For this speed technology, the portrayal of machines moving at speed was integral. The various new media technologies featured representations of, and plots based on, the variance in one another's speeds (think, for example, of *Dial M for Murder*): they operated as propaganda for speed's excitements in their very form, even as they underlined it in their story lines. Popular art forms proved most receptive to speed's excitements. Consider the newly popular faster tempos of jazz. Mass lowbrow novels, products catering to the tastes of railway commuters, which were sold in train station kiosks and were meant to be read while being carried at speed, were most often "thrillers," travelogues, police procedurals — romanticized accounts of the mass traffic control of the police state. Or they were sensation fiction, pulp romance that processed feeling as a rush of bodily sensation. All this made high cultural forms seem marginal relics of a more slow, staid world and hastened the distancing of high from pop culture that had opened significantly with the rise of mass literacy since the 1870s. T. S. Eliot, writing about Marie Lloyd, could sneer at "the encroachment of the cheap and rapid-breeding cinema."[49] Speed culture has given rise not only to novel technologies, from the roller coaster to the car phone, but also to new mass-cultural forms, from detective fiction to the car racer video game, all geared to entice mass audiences into speed's joys, conveniences, and thrills. Any account of speed culture must dwell on its unending capacity for mass persuasion, and on how pop culture and speed pleasure live off one another.

The history of speed culture must also carefully consider the blatant, and peculiar, sexism which has attended the persuasiveness of speed. The car has almost always had its attractiveness to its imagined male consumer suggested through championing of the most stolid assumptions of bourgeois patriarchy. Since the days of the daredevil entrepreneurs of the Gordon Bennett and Vanderbilt Cups, car racing and speed competitions have mostly been male preserves. However, since the bicycling craze in the 1880s, women occupied the open road as equals to men, and for every detective hero like Lord Peter Wimsey or Maigret there is a Miss Marple to solve crimes by monitoring traffic, and women Olympic speed record holders have — despite repeated early attempts to deny them access — displayed the speed power of women's bodies in arenas first open only to racing men. In the mass culture of speed, "faster" has often meant "more masculine"; nonetheless there has been no shortage of hints of the glamour of sexual ambiguity surrounding the human attainments of high speeds and the policing of them: if James Bond, in the Cold War era, could attain the mass fantasy status of a "smooth" masculinity because he could muster the newest auto-technologies to achieve the maximum strategic speeds, then the fantasies of the policing of such outlaw speeds, at least, starting with the ambiguous bachelorhood of Sherlock Holmes, were often imbued with shades of discreet gender bending. (A later Cold War–era servant of speed would be the "air-hostess.") Still, the twentieth century's trope of the car crash death of a woman celebrity — most poignantly that of Isadora Duncan, the dancer famous for free and expressive body movements, who, when her flying scarf was caught in the wheel of the car in which she was traveling, was killed in Nice in 1925 — is always cast as exemplary of the body's vulnerability before the machine's aggressively powerful speed. Speed culture has accentuated, and twisted, the sexism and the gender anxieties of modern culture: its intensities and thrills have made for moments when the forces in the great twentieth-century gender conflicts have been starkly outlined.

Finally, a history of speed culture must come to terms with what, following Virilio, I have termed endocolonization, and its role in the modern state's investment in, and the policing of, the new mass speed culture. The nation-state, a descendant of the walled city, practices a sovereignty not primarily based on a community but de facto validated by a defended territory with patrolled borders. This territorial state is, then, a bunker culture, always implicated, despite its diplomatic rhetoric, in the mentality of the state of siege. The new culture of speed would seem to run counter to this: it fosters mobility, the crossing of borders, the erasure of stopping points, checkpoints, and entrances and exits which slow the driver down, the breaking of speed limits and a full-bore freedom of movement. Yet the opposition between speed and the state is never clear-cut: the state operates as traffic manager, managing the faster movement of its commuter citizens for more efficient work practices, opportunities for consumption, and so on. Capitalist growth demands faster movement, and the state responds by establishing itself as a centrifugal point of efficient speed management where it gets its own citizens on the move and tries to exclude the rest. The state controls its roads, its telephone lines, its radio frequencies and airways—all the channels of movement. It exists to improve them and to police them ever more intensely. The state's infrastructure has been thought to be primarily about sustaining ideology and nurturing a sense of community in its schools, offices, and monuments—when it is first and foremost about patrolling people in movement. Monitoring how this movement is itself monitored, fostered, and controlled by the state must be a key task of any speed history: a policing of the traffic police, of the state as highway patrol.

1 **2** **3** **4** **5**

⟶

Thriller: The Incitement to Speed

The spirit of the time shall teach me speed.
—Shakespeare, spoken by the bastard in *King John*

The term "thriller" came into vogue in the 1890s.[1] In one racy, titillating new coinage, it encapsulated the immediacy, excitement, and intimate interface between the body's nerves and the machine's propulsion that would characterize the new culture of speed. It brought into the open the new directness of experience that people felt they wanted—and wanted now. It also—in the thriller genre's use of shock, sensation, and gore—brought into the discourse of literary fiction radical new protocols for the expression and the handling of fear. The thriller demanded that readers let down their guard, lapse into being terrified, to enjoy the richest thrills from the shocks being offered. Compare it to the roller coaster, that early, awkward, creaking, but completely thrilling premonition of speed culture, which was invented at almost the same time: the first was opened for business by La-Marcus Thompson in Atlantic City as the Oriental Scenic Railway in 1886.[2] The roller coaster, you might say, put gravity at speed's service. It offered a simulacrum of what it would be like to drive recklessly at full acceleration: it incited people to speed. The thriller, as pulp novel with its shocks, jolts, and terrors, its trail of clues and streetwise private eye, trained people, as it thrilled them, in the new kinds of alertness and mind-eye coordination that speed culture demanded. Incitement on the one hand, education through terror on the other: this approach from both ends characterized the cultural impetus that rendered seemingly inevitable the world of cars and traffic, speed limits and speed records, instant communication and instant gratification, that constitutes the twentieth-century culture of speed.

Engineers may have invented the machines that made the new speeds possible, but it was in the cultural sphere that these machines and the experiences they offered were cast as intensities of desire. High culture was slow to catch on to these new velocities (Futurism is the exception that proves the rule here): although both *The Love Song of J. Alfred Prufrock* and *The Waste Land* are threnodies to the thump-shuffle of pedestrian traffic in London, T. S. Eliot wrote no poems about the joys of fast driving. Rather, the task of introducing speed culture *in advance*, before it even existed, was taken up by popular culture genres. The detective story, with its origins in the French *policier* and its evolution into the American thriller, performed the role of rendering fear exciting in the context of the street. The gumshoe thriller hero is the first literary character to go everywhere by car, and his Holmesian predecessors in hansom-cab-clogged London are first and foremost traffic navigators. For them, the notion of "street smarts" might have been invented. In a fiction machine wound tightly to strain every nerve and manipulate every clue to heighten suspense, readers were taught the street smarts and the task list of rapid-response moves that speeders needed in traffic. Suspense is the literary mechanism that in the very act of reading induces the desire for speed. In public mass entertainment, the cultural forms that best incited people via pleasure toward speed culture were the most popular, subliterate of all. Welcome to the roller coaster, to which add the world of escape artists, strongmen, acrobats, and the new sports star breakers of speed and endurance records.

The mass culture of modern speed turns out to have been fostered in the fairground. Take as an example the extraordinary popularity of Houdini, the magician turned escape artist who specialized in self-release from locked trunks and chains, in precisely this period. The fairgrounds for the masses — as in Coney Island or Blackpool, or urban fairgrounds such as the Prater in Vienna — were a novelty of the new mass leisure industries of these years; their carnivalesque attractions presented the potential joys of the new speed culture — escape, new sensations of freedom, and newly perceptible sensations of *vitesse*, literally of being newly alive — as the finest of the joys of a life that grasped the opportunities of the new leisure. Both the thrillers and fairground attractions manipulated the terrors and the excitements surfacing at the first moments of twentieth-century speed culture. Only in some wayward flashpoints of high culture, and soon in the new movement-images of film and the movies, was the nexus of fearful thrill and carnival excitement elaborated with equal quality. The implications of unleashing these newly intense thrills and spills were at first obscure. However, the real meaning of detective fiction, of fairground speed tricks like the roller coaster, and even of the lonesome flânerie of modernist fiction becomes evident in the first movie car chase.

Watch this chase: in it, the raw thrill of speed is churned up—and screwed tighter by the social fear of being caught by the police, so that state repression matches techno-modernity. The emergence of twentieth-century speed culture was made possible by the development and management of an insidious kind of fear. This fear was propagated gleefully by the emerging genres of pop culture. Pop genres have always betrayed an unscrupulous transnationalism: enjoyed, condemned, or impolitely ignored at home, they can reemerge in unlikely locales abroad, easily taking on other lives, influencing other histories. Thus it has been with detective fiction, perhaps the preeminent pop form developed to exacerbate and assuage the mass terrors of modernity: the form's fluid and, in terms of conventional, nation-bounded histories of genres, unlikely transnational lurches from mid-nineteenth-century France to new-century Britain and hence to the West Coast of the United States in the 1930s prove the permeability of national barriers where it really counted. By the time that Walter Benjamin, at his desk at the Bibliothèque Nationale in Paris, was coming to understand the crucial role of Eugene Sue's detective fiction for the education of the city masses in suitable forms of flânerie in nineteenth-century Paris,[3] the meticulous high-camp detective story of Conan Doyle's Sherlock Holmes and the late-empire horrors of R. L. Stevenson's *Dr. Jekyll and Mr. Hyde* had become classics, and urban terrors were being revamped as gumshoe thrillers and the beginnings of film noir in and around Los Angeles, California. Here, then, is a cultural offering from the greatest nineteenth-century experiment in the reorganization of modern urbanism, Baron Georges-Eugène Haussmann's Paris, to the greatest twentieth-century experiment in a radically new and exploded urban form, Los Angeles, tempered by a period of development in the world capital of modern imperialism, London. This transnational cultural transmission of proto-thriller fiction from metropolis to metropolis implies that this emergent pop culture form grasped the answer to a key problem of the newly vast city: in brief, that traffic needs management. The relatively choreographed and personalized carriage and foot traffic of the Parisian boulevards merited plodding police work compared to the ingenuity required to even envision the symphonic complexity of motor traffic in L.A. The earliest photographs of urban streetscapes, for example, those by William Fox Talbot in London and Dublin, show half-empty streets where there were not even rules about traffic needing to keep to the right or left;[4] as traffic grew more dense and public transport developed, the urban detective story offered to the individual a sense of her place in the increasingly ordered but apparently chaotic traffic-scape.

Traffic is the grammar of mass movement. It is governed by the conglomeration of rules, explicit and implicit, enacted to ensure the smooth flow of information, goods, and human beings. The elements in the flow must achieve a certain uniform speed, the rate of speed must be maintained, vehicle collisions must be prevented. In retrospect, one can see that every device to move traffic and to calm it had been practiced for centuries; customs barriers and toll gates, from medieval city gates to C. Nicholas Ledoux's elegant pavilions strung along the customs wall around Enlightenment-era Paris, were principally state-controlled mechanisms for the regulation of traffic. It was only with the massive expansion of the metropolis in the nineteenth century, however — by 1880, four European cities, London, Paris, Berlin, and Vienna, had a population of more than one million, and all of them had vast suburbs for the working, lower-middle, and upper classes[5] — and the arrival of new modes of transport, the underground railway, the bicycle, the electric tram, and soon the motor-tram and car, that traffic became a political issue as well as a logistical problem. Within decades it had become a science and a profession with the advent of traffic engineers. Noted as a problem, seen as a teeming, unruly mass, this newly visible traffic gave rise to intense anxieties.

The crowd, as in Matthew Arnold's mid-Victorian fear of the Chartist rioters, had been a bogey and familiar bourgeois horror: the crowd was assumed to be the proletarian mob, ripe for revolt. By the first years of the twentieth century, this class-bound distaste had developed into a more fundamental kind of despair at the spectacle and implications of mass-moving people. The seeds of the strangeness in individual psychology that Edgar Allan Poe had marked in his story "The Man of the Crowd" were being elaborated on by the sociologist Georg Simmel, who wrote about both the "heightened awareness, a predominance of intelligence," of people in urban crowds and, more darkly, of "a structure of the highest impersonality . . . the *blasé* attitude [which] results from the rapidly changing and closer compressed contrasting stimulation of the nerves."[6] This blasé quality would soon be recast by a spate of modernist writers as a grim anomie, and the lonely flâneurs of Joyce's *Ulysses* (both Leopold Bloom and Stephen

Dedalus), Eliot's *The Love Song of J. Alfred Prufrock* (Prufrock himself) and Robert Musil's *The Man without Qualities*, as well as the heroine of Virginia Woolf's *Mrs. Dalloway* and Kafka's Gregor Samsa, would all discover the grotesque depths of alienation possible in the lonely urban crowd. This dismay at the crowd,[7] however, begins to seem like a classic case of practical bourgeois political fear transformed at the aesthetic level into personal angst, especially when one places it over against, on the one hand, the ominous philosophies of the crowd being dreamed up by figures such as Gustave Le Bon and Georges Sorel in the same period and, on the other, against a countercurrent that relished the excitement of mass, anonymous, and fleeting crowd contacts and the opportunities they represent. This latter tendency runs from Baudelaire, with his paeans to "love at last sight" in *Les fleurs du mal*, to Benjamin, and includes all kinds of low genres, from holiday ballads and later holiday postcards in Britain to boulevardier songs in Paris. Between crowd loathing and crowd relishing hovers the reading matter of the new commuter, which uncannily arouses mass fears and assuages them at once: the detective story, the crime novel, the thriller.

Even if high literature often seems repulsed by traffic while popular literature revels in it, it would be a mistake to imagine either that these categories can be fixed or that the different genres inevitably served different ideologies. Nevertheless one can credibly claim that the embrace of traffic and its opportunities was somehow inimical to the sense of fixed territoriality on which the state, with its massed cultural capital, had built its power. It is tempting to contrast the state, which worked to control, "calm," and take note of traffic, and a nebulous countermovement of the masses to literally move and, by moving, escape state control. The state (in its national form, a largely nineteenth-century ideological apparatus) has, however, historically been engaged in the fostering as well as the control of traffic: encouraging traffic may even be the state's principal function. When we think we discern, in the cultural sphere, the ideological interpellation of citizen audiences into attitudes toward traffic that appear to run counter to the state's interests, these incitements often turn out to have a paradoxically opposite effect. A maudlin immigrant song, for example—every nineteenth-century European nation had a number of examples—may call on its audiences to deny themselves the horrors and opportunities of one of the massive new international kinds of traffic that began in earnest in this period: taking the immigrant ship. Listened to in another place and time, however, such a song may be drawing its listeners into just such traffic by providing them with a moving—if tearful—affective narrative with which to justify their desire to become part of a transnational labor market. In the same way, the horrors of high-modernist anomie in the face of the crowd shown by Musil or the German painter Otto Dix may be read either as explicit lessons in the dangers of immersing oneself in the moving masses, or as a covert call to experience a new intensity of anguished sensation, and sensational anguish, in the monotonous callousness of the traffic-beaten street. Countering such melancholy, new high and popular forms which emerged from the experience of being part of traffic celebrate possibilities and assuage anxieties that arise moment by moment in the new rhythm of urban movement—how to judge the stranger who jostles you, how to nod and move on your way with the minimum knowledge and politeness, how to spot and make snap judgments about the surface signs that emerge from the flow, how to hold your own in this kinetic environment to whose rate of speed you are only beginning to become accustomed.

Note how many people, even when immersed in the new traffic, keep in touch with pop culture: reading on trains, reading and watching films on airplanes, listening to car radios, all are being educated by these popular forms into the speed culture in which they participate. Nowhere is this more evident than in the detective story. There are three striking features of a Sherlock Holmes story (and by extension of every urban detective fiction, a staple of the railway or airport novels, since): the blithe manner in which the hero-detective considers urban violence (speaking of the mugging that precipitates one plot, Holmes says that it is "one of those whimsical little incidents which will happen when you have four million human beings jostling each other within the space of a few square miles");[8] the assurance they offer throughout that one *can* read the surface signs as clues successfully and, thinking it out, know what caused the disturbance, robbery, strangeness, or murder; and, finally, the way in which fears are whipped up only invariably to be assuaged. This popular world of urban traffic and its culture offers an epistemology of surface appearances, snap judgments, quick studies, and (as Simmel understood) heightened or sharpened perceptions—all leading to fewer collisions, incidents, horrors, and accidents and the resumption of traffic's smooth flow. The detective's mannered urbanities offer a playbook of the traffic lessons taught by the new popular forms. These forms made possible mass acceptance of traffic and its culture.

The first successful urban mass genre, the detective story, faced the new phenomenon of mass traffic in the early years of this century by raising anxieties to assuage them, by denigrating the notion of home as fixed structure or refuge, and by indulging in escape fantasies which marked movement and participation in mass traffic as a gesture of freedom. These pop narratives avoided direct celebration of the new speed culture: this was carried out, as it were, locally, in the magazines for cyclists and early car enthusiasts, in advertising for tourist travel, in the technological boosterism surrounding the world's fairs, in the celebration of speed heroics by the winners of early motor races such as the annual Gordon Bennett Cup, and after 1909 in the more highbrow polemics of the Futurists and their popularizers. Before these scattered signals coalesced, however, the resounding note was one of anxiety that could be assuaged by quick-witted action. What occurred was a configuration of the mass perception of spatial organization to the point where, to quote the architect Bernard Tschumi in another context, space itself came to be seen as inseparable from action.[9]

With the new mass traffic, the prestige of fixed static spaces and structures as (apparently) immutable totems of power and authority waned. As a result, the monumental aims of buildings became uncannily evident, and their very solidity produced anxiety. The contradiction between, on the one hand, a building as a signifier of immutable power and, on the other, its function as a node of circulation grew apparent. Take the train station, temple of the greatest Victorian innovation in speed technology. By the end of the nineteenth century, the station had become a starred and anxiety-provoking space, and in the strong, overdressed architecture of the last great metropolitan railway stations (Milan, Los Angeles), as well as in the terrors named and soothed in the humblest travel guide or cheap novel in these buildings' bookstalls, we can trace the forms that this anxiety took. At the same time there were fewer spaces to retreat to: the idea of space as refuge, and in particular of the home as sanctuary and guarantor of personal prestige and identity, was coming under attack. The detective novel's plot makes the privacy of the home available to the inspection of the stranger-detective to render it safe for habitation. This was the era too of the haunted house (*Dracula* was published in 1897; its finest film adaptation, F. W. Murnau's *Nosferatu*, appeared in 1922). Here the notion that "even in the home one is not safe" was supplanted by the idea that the home was invariably haunted, a place in which to be tripped up by uncanny memories and a Pandora's box of personal history from which one could only free oneself by escaping. The new century saw the motif of escape become one of the driving forces of popular fantasies: remember, again, that stoker of fantasies of mass audiences at this moment Harry Houdini, who won fame for repeatedly escaping, against all odds, from locked trunks, straightjackets, multiply padlocked chains. Claustrophobia — the fear of entrapment in closed, locked spaces — can be read as a dominant pathology of this period; the escape artist is popular culture's riposte to the nostalgia for home and fireside that can be traced in some middlebrow Edwardian fiction.

The varied horrors of fixed, static, enclosing, or monumental spaces were accompanied by a new aversion to what came to be perceived as slowness. With speed came a new phase in the history of impatience. Only as speed became conventional could slowness become perceptible. Before the celebration of speed, a pervasive and profound aversion to slowness became a noticeable cultural tic. Flânerie, the phenomenon of the pedestrian wandering the city pavements, had been a rich motif of nineteenth-century urban culture; now the figure of the flâneur or flâneuse was abandoned, although he lingered on in high literary locales such as *Ulysses* and *Mrs. Dalloway*, a wistful, past-his-sell-by-date kind of character — and in effect unceremoniously plumped into public transport or his new car. (The unctuous Fr. Conmee, who climbs on the tram at Newcomen Bridge to avoid the rough streets of Fairview, leads the way in *Ulysses*. Even Sherlock Holmes is forever hailing hansom cabs, and Leopold Bloom dreams of a bicycle outing to visit his daughter fifty miles away, in Mullingar. Clarissa Dalloway's daughter rebelliously takes a tram up Fleet Street.) It was, however, around the image of the ship that the horror of slowness was most provocatively painted. Along with a frenetic and heavily publicized drive to produce faster and faster oceangoing ships in these years, which was brought to a sudden halt by the sinking of the *Titanic* in 1912, the seafaring narratives of this period betray an increasing impatience at the impossible slowness of ships. The great writer about ship life as monotony was Joseph Conrad: his elegies to the life of the sailor are also all treatises on killing time. *Heart of Darkness* has retained its striking hold over generations of readers neither because it is a great liberal text berating colonial cruelties, nor because it exactly mirrors the deep racism of its Western readership, nor because it is a deeply moving account of humanist despair (although it bears traces of each of these elements), but rather, more fundamentally, because it registers on every page an almost allergic reaction to slowness and the perceived lack of liberating movement and efficient speed. Slowness, in *Heart of Darkness*, is the true horror.

With Conrad's eerie tale, we can see how the new horror of slowness never exists outside political realities. If what is happening at this point is that the perception of space is being reorganized, so that built spaces seem less a static stage for the projection of power and prestige and more a permeable space where action and movement are possible, then older notions of a hierarchy of spaces and places, of the powerful and monumental center and the minor, unembellished periphery, become less tenable. The Enlightenment dualist organization of space that Foucault describes in "Of Other Spaces," with its real, lived, and "present" spaces and its other, heterotopic, quasi-sacred marked-off spaces (prisons, holiday resorts, desert islands, brothels, libraries, museums), begins to break down. In the late nineteenth century, the ultimate, as-yet-unknown heterotopia, the one that validated and lent its spectral aura to all the rest, was the unknown, as-yet-to-be-colonized territory of the unmapped parts of the globe, the white spaces on the map that, as Conrad notes, had so exercised the imagination of the young Marlow (see chapter 1). Once these had been occupied and the spaces unknown to Western cartographers had become an all-too-actual "heart of darkness," then the overall organization of earthly, global spaces into real spaces versus heterotopias had begun to be dismantled. This was a new step in what Henri Lefebvre characterizes as the modern abstraction of space, its reduction to the single common denominator of its usefulness. With the latest and most voracious stage of this abstraction, the possibility of the efficient movement to and across all spaces on the earth becomes the locus of new possibilities of pleasure, supplanting dreams of new heterotopias as yet uncharted and unseen.

So it is that at the very moment of the end of colonial expansion, slowness gets to be perceived as the new horror. Then, with endocolonization, this comes to apply not only to the colonial hinterland limned by Conrad but to the home space as well, as both are now equally known and abstracted. What has happened is that *place* — either as known, culturally loaded center of memory, affect, and identity or as heterotopic, fantasy-imbued, and even feared peripheral locus of otherness — has been rationalized and abstracted into *space*. In the use of this newly instrumentalized space, a space denuded of fantasies either of identity or of strangeness, it is movement and speed that count and must be made exciting. Slowness gets notated pejoratively as the temptation to linger in the haunted home or to wander in search of the heterotopic other space, the dream world that no longer exists; slowness is more and more often in these years rendered as something to be feared, to induce horror. Through a cultural regime that instilled a deep-seated aversion to slowness, rather than any desire for the proactive pleasures of speed itself, the culture of speed was installed in its participants in the early twentieth century.

The Rise of Non-Place

Double Indemnity (1936), James M. Cain's novel about insurance, murder, and means of transportation, begins as follows:

> I drove out to Glendale to put three new truck drivers on a brewery company bond, and then I remembered this renewal over in Hollywoodland. I decided to run over there. That's how I came to this House of Death that you've been reading about in the papers. It didn't look like a House of Death when I saw it. It was just a Spanish house, like all the rest of them in California, with white walls, red tile roof, and a patio out to one side. It was built cock-eyed.[10]

California gumshoe fiction makes evident what had been perceptible in British detective stories of thirty years earlier: these tales have no respect for, and a definite anxiety about, the residence, the house, the home. On the one hand we have a detective, and his alter ego, the criminal, who occupy the street and deftly negotiate its traffic; on the other, the solid, immovable house, home of the victim and scene of the crime, about which will always hang the stain of a crime that has been committed, or the anxiety about an entry that is always about to be forced. Cain's Spanish house, home of Mr. and Mrs. Nirlinger, their stepdaughter, and their maid, is both "House of Death" and nothing special, utterly conventional "like the rest of them," and, he implies, a kitschy fake, Spanish but in California. He gazes at it and it cannot quite gaze back, for it is "cock-eyed," twisted, askew. Moreover, in its very prosaic quality lie the seeds of its grotesquerie. This is how detective fiction and related genres such as the "true crime" reports invoked by Cain's narrator have always dealt with the houses that are nevertheless crucial to such stories: they are ordinary yet seem to contain some mark of the horror that has occurred or will occur within. These houses are *anomalous*: that is, not precisely or radically different, utterly comparable to every other ordinary dwelling, but still uncannily marked as disreputable. Other examples include the door to which the reader's attention is drawn in the opening paragraphs of Stevenson's *Dr. Jekyll and Mr. Hyde*, unremarkable in every way except that it is "neglected," which nevertheless "is connected in my mind," says Mr. Enfield, "with a very odd story."[11] Or consider the innumerable suburban villas of the Sherlock Holmes stories or the depressingly ordinary yet minutely described seedy inner-suburban London terrace houses in the fiction of Ruth Rendell.[12] The focus on the house in detective fiction is so insistent that one might wish to see it in psychoanalytic terms; this fiction's interest in secret rooms, sealed spaces, and dark corners relates it to earlier folk forms such as the fairy tale. Why, then, does the detective story's interest in the house's strangeness go hand in hand with an insistence on its ordinariness?

The answer lies in the house's diminishing affective role as home in the period. Readers, ensconced in their homes, read detective fiction and relish the attitude to houses in it, because they see that it mirrors their own fears that the privacy of their home, valued as refuge from an inundating modernity, can likewise at any moment be invaded and destroyed. Yet this does not account for the contempt with which, for example, Cain considers and dismisses the "House of Death." Detective fiction suggests to its readers, as it stokes their fears, that the house as home has already been evacuated of all significant meaning and affective content and that the chance of its association with a gruesome crime will offer the only, last-ditch opportunity of reinjecting it with a trace of the aura it has lost. For the reader in search of suggestions of homeliness, the detective story invariably offers only false pleasures: it induces an aftertaste of the old aura of the home, but an aftertaste only in the form opposite to that which the aura originally took. Whereas the home stood for security, the detective story portrays it as the locus of insecurity. It reminds the reader that the desire for this security is wistful thinking, better abandoned.

In the same years that waves of detective story writers in France, Britain, and the United States were making evident their contempt for the home place as aura-laden space in the Western metropolis, anthropologists from the same nations were busy following a set of disciplinary procedures that led them, in far-flung colonial villages, in the opposite direction. The first anthropologists were eager to see what Westerners had previously taken to be empty or raw space as a terrain composed, instead, of starred, intriguing, and interesting places — as villages with names, customs, kinship patterns, histories, and unique microcultures. The work of the anthropologist was to cite and confirm, in the authorizing language of Western scholarship, the uniqueness of places. These places occupied space which it had suited an earlier stage of colonial conquest to read as banal, undifferentiated, and empty. Popular genres were busy dismantling the affective aura of home in the metropolis; anthropologists were busy inventing multiple auras for places discovered in the colonies. Anthropological work can thus be read as a displaced nostalgia, on the part of the Western occupiers of the very spaces they are in fact radically abstracting through industrial and consumerist imperatives, for an archaic sense of place. It shows a triumphalist fascination on the part of the West with inhabitants of spaces who as yet refuse to surrender their affective attachment to their (invariably doomed) place. The colonies and former colonies have been nominated by the Western science of anthropology to hold the world's last places: that is, spaces which are given meaning by their affective ties to communities united by shared histories. However one reads the politics of this disciplinary turn, it has led to anthropology being the discipline, more than urban studies or architectural theory, most conscious of the lack of differentiation between places as a metropolitan problem. Whereas the detective story held up this issue to mass Western audiences as a mirror of its lingering anxiety, it is in anthropology that the end of place and homeliness has been at last read as a theoretical issue. A brief look at how the discipline deals with these concerns will illustrate what is at stake for the consciousness of Western subjects when they grow anxious about the untenability of the home as fixed, feeling-laden place.

A prime example: the work of the French anthropologist Marc Augé, *Non-Places: Introduction to a Theory of Supermodernity* (1995). Augé sees two kinds of lived spaces: the first are "places," sites susceptible to anthropological description, that is, rich with a communally held history, markers of a dense web of power relations, and signs of a set of beliefs embodied in monuments and markers. Then there are "non-places," the increasingly common stark zones stripped of such meanings, histories, associations, signs of community activity or history: freeways, airports, malls, car parks, chain hotels. Augé speaks of a place as "the one occupied by the indigenous inhabitants who live in it, cultivate it, defend it, mark its strong points and keep its frontiers under surveillance, but who also detect in it the traces of ancestors or spirits which populate and animate its private geography."[13] Non-places, in keeping with their name, are as yet for the anthropologist only to be defined against those richly lived-in places: "If a place can be defined as relational, historical and concerned with identity, then a space which cannot be defined as relational, historical, or concerned with identity will be a non-place" (77–78).

For Augé, places will be marked by stability, devoted to a long view that allows the site each occupies to develop a physiognomy of its own that is readable by the traditional anthropologist. He sees the strangeness of the anthropologist's disciplinary mode of operation: she gambles that the materiality of the signs in the designated site guarantees the permanence of the community they mark and, implying the gamble won, allows them, for her, to signify "place." Still, Augé continues to feel a nostalgia for these kinds of places; inevitably, his most memorable example of such a place is the French village from which he implies he comes himself. Now, in the new world of dominating non-places, this village is bypassed by a motorway, and merely indicated by a historical marker which you glimpse as you speed by: speed has no time for "place." Augé's best example of the preponderance of non-place in contemporary life comes when he imagines a business traveler at the cash dispenser, on the auto route, in the parking lot, in the departure lounge, on the plane, planning to stay in an anonymous business hotel in Bangkok. For speedy travel, "non-place" proves efficient. In a world where homes are often uncannily present only as "houses of horror," this description of the new proliferation of non-places is utterly credible. Augé's division of lived space into these categories needs to be interrogated, however, if the implications of the nostalgia for places are to be overcome.

First, Augé's history of the phenomenon he implies—the rise of non-places—is open to question. He sees such spaces as characteristic of "supermodernity," a recent stage of geopolitical history which corresponds to Baudrillard's or Jameson's postmodernity but with a key difference: whereas for Baudrillard the postmodern spectacle means an explosion of appearances as a simulacrum that is more pleasurable than the real, Augé's supermodernity, *au contraire*, has given rise to zones that appear to have been emptied of all signs of meaning. There is no *Blade Runner* glamour in the "non-place." The freeway, unlike the gaudy postmodern corporate headquarters, does not push a fake façade before our eyes. It is a modernist invention of clean utilitarian lines, not a postmodern pastiche. Augé's non-places have existed longer than he implies: the division of which he speaks (like modern anthropology) is keyed to the modernist rather than the post- or supermodern period. The first autobahn was inaugurated in 1933; the first airport lounge at least a decade earlier. The first years of the twentieth century mark a prehistory of such non-places. This was also the period of the ideological work which persuaded people used to the stable comforts of reassuring place that such havens, as types of communal and spatial organization, were stifling. Both high modernism, with its half-glamorous angst, and the new pulp genres, with their half-titillating high anxieties, taught people to find comfort in the apparent freedom of unencoded non-place. The glorification of the minimalism of modernist architecture by its practitioners from Adolf Loos to Walter Gropius, too, can be read as an aesthetics of non-place.

Second, because Augé avoids historicizing the discipline of anthropology, he is blind to the impetus which has produced his categorization. Anthropology's work of naming and describing places was almost always the humanist arm of the late-nineteenth-century colonialist project, work that continued as the empires began to be dismantled. Colonial locales were being denominated by Western anthropologists as places with a (now) recorded culture and communal life at the very moment when large swaths of Western space were being redirected from places to the sorts of anonymous non-places that have become such a prominent feature of urban and suburban life. Leaving aside the geocultural implications of this,[14] we may surmise that the Western anthropologist's desire to demarcate place in colonial settings was a response to the laying waste, in different ways, of many such places in both the imperial metropole and the colony. Note in the same years a fascination with the slum life of London and Paris, as in Jack London's *People of the Abyss* (1903), a fascination mined in early detective fiction such as Conan Doyle's opium den tales; and also in "country places." This was the golden age of local historians and folklorists, which absorbed high art from Hardy and Yeats to Cézanne and found a popular outlet in romance and nationalist fiction. These nostalgic turns in the first decades of the twentieth century, when anthropology was still enthusiastic about its ability to demarcate place where the cartographers had merely mapped territory, and when the new non-places were sufficiently new to be presented as wondrous, suggest that the disgust at life in rationalized spaces, inaugurated by the romantics a century earlier, was now a cultural given. It led to a backlash of antiquarian nostalgia, and the fascination with exotic places that drove most advanced tourism. At the same time, the Grand Concourse in the Bronx was considered as wondrous in its day as Haussmann's Avenue de l'Opéra had been deemed half a century earlier; "marvels of engineering" had not yet come to seem as soulless or banal.

Anthropology's search for place, then, in the sense Augé defines it, has been propelled by nostalgia. Place in this sense — particularly with its validation of permanence and stability — has in modernity always been an illusion, a golden mean promoted by the relatively new discipline to underpin the logic of its village ethnographies. It might be more useful to consider, as the author Italo Calvino put it, that "home is where one's parents are buried" — that is, in part, a setting that is invariably in the past, the creation of memory, susceptible to dreams. In Augé's work, the terms of Foucault's similarly dualistic division of lived space into real and heterotopic sites seems to be reversed. For Foucault, space was divided into real spaces and heterotopias, homes, streets, and factories versus institutions, cemeteries, holiday camps, brothels, honeymoon hotels, and jails scattered on the periphery of real space, but where our fears and desires can dwell. For Augé, real dwelling occurs in relatively enclosed and demarcated places, while all around rolls the novel vacuity of non-places. If places themselves, however, are archaic and illusory, then they become the heterotopic repositories of what Foucault saw as the residue of the sacred in modern culture.[15] Non-places become those in which we live the vital moments of our daily lives.

Note that Augé's non-places are all sites, nodes, or modes of transport, traffic, movement, speed. From his first definition, he makes this clear: "The installations needed for the accelerated circulation of passengers and goods (high-speed roads and railways, interchanges, airports) are just as much non-places as the means of transport themselves, or the great commercial centers, or the extended transit camps where the planet's refugees are parked" (34). This does not mean that ethnographies within the older tradition cannot be carried out regarding specific cultures or subcultures inhabiting such zones; one of Augé's own previous works is *Un vie dans le metro*. Nor does he speculate on why it is at intersections of traffic that this new blankness of non-place has developed. Yet it is around this issue that he articulates an implied history, for he associates the "spectacular acceleration of means of transport" (34) with a global world order of shifting populations, emigrants, international movements of capital (the reference to refugees in the last quote is characteristic), in short, to the transnational geopolitical milieu that succeeded the imperial phase of colonial expansion.

Augé's work implies that a new version of the relation of spaces and communities has been needed in Western anthropology since the moment when imperial colonization gave way to the globalist geopolitical order. He calls for a new anthropology to explicate these new spaces: a booster for his discipline, he declares that given changes in scale (by which he means that a global gaze is now necessary, and that a focus on one place is impossible), "we are poised to undertake the study of new civilizations and new cultures" (35). This is still the lingua franca of the liberal humanist branch of imperialism, but it launches a new stage of inquiry into lived spaces; Augé courageously begins the task. He comments on the fashionable new words associated with non-places — *interchange, route, communication, transit* — and considers the solitude that such spaces engender, the coincidence of the plainest functional space and the surprising proliferation of written notices about them (road signs, airport screens, departure and arrival boards), and the way in which such signs encourage the idea that different spaces can be consumed, as in tourism. He stresses the need to remember that "what is significant in the experience of non-place is its power of attraction, inversely proportional to territorial attraction, to the gravitational pull of place and tradition" (118). We will follow that injunction. We need also to historicize and locate in geopolitical realities the emergence of this new global constellation of non-places to which he refers.

And so, again, to home. The home is the most "emplaced" locale in Western bourgeois consciousness, and the space that in the Western nineteenth- and twentieth-century imaginative literary tradition has most closely corresponded to that occupied by the colonial village in anthropology. The ideological work of persuading people that non-place is indeed deeply to be desired, in inverse proportion to the degree to which the home place was to be feared, was carried out in the early twentieth century by the new reading matter for commuters and emergent popular culture.

"House of Death"

Detective fiction, prime reading matter for the transient occupiers of the new non-places, offered early lessons in successfully negotiating the new eerily unmarked spaces of mass movement common by the early twentieth century. It gave lessons in traffic management to commuters. It did this, suggesting the pleasures of non-space, by arousing fears of its opposite, the anthropologist's place, which most commonly, in late-Victorian bourgeois fiction, was signified by the house as family home itself. The amateur detective, self-proclaimed policeman, patrolled the streets for miscreants, a flâneur with a purpose and a plot. He scanned the traffic for deviations—missed trains, the impossibility of getting from point to point in a given time—and ordered them under the aegis of a logic that created a convincing counternarrative to the criminal's alibi. Moreover, he demanded the right to intrude on the privacy of home spaces; in "A Case of Identity," Holmes tells Watson how wonderful it would be "if we could lift the roofs off every house and peer down into the rooms of their inhabitants."[16] Ever alert for clues—that is, signals from surface appearances that the keen passerby must discern in an instant—the detective offers a way of useful knowing in non-places that has replaced the extended acquaintance common to the village place. Clue reading becomes a method for an amateur epistemology of any non-place and its occupants. Detective fiction portrayed the street as a turbulent, ever-changing conduit of activity and its monitoring, while the house, robbed of its affective power, was again and again portrayed as a sinister relic of corrupted forms and archaic desires. To show how fear of home met engineering flow in early-twentieth-century pulp fiction, consider a story which dwells on the claustrophobic terror of the house as prison, Conan Doyle's "The Engineer's Thumb."

Detective fiction, poker faced, lacks humor; it compensates by serving up large doses of camp. (Camp goes hand in hand with the suspense that the thriller genre works to create, for, like suspense, it demands a suspension of belief). In "The Engineer's Thumb," otherwise a somber tale, the camp element is supplied by the all-too-obtrusive phallic imagery of the misadventures of the gimmick thumb of the title. In the story, a handsome young engineer has his thumb whacked off ("It gave even my hardened nerves a shudder to look at it. . . . It had been hacked or torn right out from the roots") when he goes one night from London to inspect a large mechanical press in a country home inhabited by two men and a young woman.[17] She saves him, he takes the train back to London, he notifies Holmes. So far, it is a case of the castration anxieties of young men who confuse their careers with a life at home and how these fears are proved true. Yet there are complications. If the camp symbolism is self-consciously (but, as always in detective fiction, as in other camp genres, never overtly) comic in its obviousness, nevertheless its vividness produces a flash point—the exposure of the wound, the revelation of a lack—that alerts the reader to be ready for further flash points in the story. The correspondingly vivid, equally terrifying moment turns out to be a gruesome evocation of the terror of claustrophobia.

What happens is this: the young hero, brought at night to the mysterious house, is invited to inspect the hydraulic press, which the owners claim is a device to press fuller's earth into bricks. Led upstairs along narrow corridors, he inspects the press and solves its mechanical problem. The press turns out to be a room in the house, with timber walls, but with a roof and floor of metal: the metal ceiling can be lowered hydraulically and "comes down with many tons upon the metal floor." With this room, in a Conan Doyle story of the early 1890s, the house as "a machine for living in," which Le Corbusier would a quarter century later describe as the end-all of modernist architecture, is dreamed of in advance; moreover, it is revealed as a nightmare. There follows the inevitable: the engineer is inside the machine-room, inspecting it a little too curiously for his own good, when the owner steps out, closes the door, and turns the lock.

> "Hallo," I yelled, "Hallo, colonel! Let me out!" And then suddenly in the silence I heard a sound which sent my heart into my mouth. It was the clank of levers, and the swish of the leaking cylinder. He had set the engine to work. The lamp was still upon the floor where I had placed it when examining the trough. By its light I saw that the black ceiling was coming down upon me slowly, jerkily, but, as none knew better than myself, with a force which must within a minute grind me to a shapeless pulp. I threw myself screaming against the door, and dragged with my nails on the lock. . . . The ceiling was only a foot or two above my head, and with my hand upraised I could feel its hard rough surface. Then it flashed through my mind that the pain of my death would depend very much on the position in which I met it.

Only with Kafka's Gregor Samsa is the horror of incarceration in the bedroom of the family home so morbidly advanced, and only there, through Kafka's leap from the paranoid night-city logics of detective fiction into surreal symbolism, is the effect equal parts po-faced comedy and visceral anguish. The detective story, at such moments, achieves the heights of its avatar, Victorian mass sensation fiction, and becomes very literally a thriller. It wrings the last resources of realism into physically palpable agony and short-circuits an emotional appeal to tap into the reader's visceral desire for self-preservation. In the case of the torn thumb itself, the effect is mainly unconscious. Evoking the terror of claustrophobia, the text appeals directly to the reader's sensations. This reader is invited to cower along with the hero-narrator: not to weep over his tragedy but to experience, as he does, a knotted stomach. In the image of a physical body about to be crushed by an ever-smaller closed room, the complex notes of realism's moralistic threnody are flattened, so that the effect is intensified: we experience the actual physical sensations along with the hero. The suspicion of the home that had been building throughout nineteenth-century realist fiction, and became explicit in the numerous dreams for escape from that home that litter the fin de siècle bildungsroman (Samuel Butler's *The Way of All Flesh* may be the bitterest example), and had found its outlet in the haunted houses of the horror fiction in the same period (*Dracula, Dr. Jekyll and Mr. Hyde*) is concentrated in a thriller moment where the detective names the home as crime scene. This home is not vilified because it is too richly a place in the anthropologist's sense, some haunted repository of family memories; even if its passages and thresholds seem to him "hollowed out by the generations that had crossed them." The engineer sees very little of the house, and by the end of the story it has burned down, with few regrets expressed by the narrator, and only a tangle of machinery and a human thumb notable among the ruins. Whether haunted family home for generations or modern machine for living in, this house merely stages, first, the castration anxiety of the young male professional of the new motor order, the engineer, and second, the claustrophobic nightmare that any home, with its conspiratorial family, represents in the cosmology of this new order.

Moreover, the setting of these two thriller moments, the deftly spun web of the detective story plot which shows Sherlock Holmes connecting the clues and nabbing the criminals, analyzes the shock of the two images flashed before us of the victim's torn, endangered body. This detective story plot is a kind of machinery itself, and it enacts a set of substitutions: the vulnerable body is replaced by the alert mind; the meditative, professional engineer who sees little is replaced by the snap-judging amateur detective who notes all; the claustrophobic house is replaced by the free and open railway, road, and street. The story itself is a narrative machine, not for living in, but for moving along inside. It is a story about timetables, times spent in travel, speeds of transport. Focused on rates of traffic flow, it was ideal for reading in traffic, especially on the train itself. (The length of a Sherlock Holmes story is nicely calibrated to the time necessary for it to be read on a suburban train commuter's trip.) The engineer is ordered to arrive on the "train from Paddington which would bring [him] in there at about 11.15" (197), to change "not only [his] carriage but [his] station," so that he was on time to be met by his client in a closed carriage. Distance and speed, correctly calibrated, are the keys to solving the crime: "It was only seven miles, but I should think, from the rates that we seemed to go, and the time we took, that it must have been nearer twelve" (200). Afterward Holmes spots the ruse: the engineer had simply been driven in a circle; the house abutted the station. The point of the interminable timetable lore and the calculation of speeds by the vehicle's passenger is to allow Holmes to describe the devious confusion that criminal elements can sow in traffic. Holmes solves the mystery by understanding speed.

The criminal, to put the engineer off the scent, is a would-be modernist: self-consciously circling, he celebrates chaos, whips up confusion. The sleuth demonstrates that such cubist antics before their time can be neutralized if the discerning passenger uses a battery of traffic-checking procedures. (These are the very procedures that would later become the tasks of a new profession, the highly responsible one of traffic controller, who holds our lives in her alert eyes as she guides airport traffic from the control tower. The detective is a traffic controller without the visual clues, after the traffic facts.) Holmes collates the timetables and the times, adduces comparative speeds, monitors landings and departures, and in this way solves the mystery — that is, what exactly had been going on in the home. This mystery turns out to be what a materialist reader considers the most fundamental kind of circulation, that of money: the house is a hideout of forgers, the hydraulic press revved up to mint debased coins. The home is a fake, a cover for fraudulent circulation. Its occupants, keepers of the nightmarishly claustrophobic room-machine, had colluded to render road traffic seem chaotic in order to keep their house hidden, but Holmes triumphantly succeeds in rationalizing that traffic — and in doing so comes upon their house as a burned ruin. At the tail end of the realist narrative tradition, the house as home, which that tradition had begun by celebrating, is, in the new social economy of circulation and traffic, revealed as ruin and fraud.

This pattern repeats itself in countless detective stories. The detective is either a flâneur, stalking his prey on foot, or, in noir thrillers, a cool-handed driver, barging into traffic patterns with a deadpan verve. The thriller not only warns its readers of the archaic fraud that the home has become; it encourages them instead to consider traffic's excitements and usefulness. The thriller trains them in the logics of a kind of traffic hermeneutics, a typology of ways to exist in traffic in a manner that serves their own ends. If, as Augé points out, the trafficked non-place is a featureless concrete-scape punctuated with written signs (for example, the freeway, or even the junction of two streets in what Joel Garreau has christened the contemporary "edge city"),[18] then every Sherlock Holmes story constantly tells us to stay alert amid the dullness, read the signs, and do so with sublime care. The thumbless engineer, for example, had noticed that the horse which had pulled the carriage to the station in Eyford to collect him was fresh — he tells Holmes so in reply to the detective's query — but he had failed to *read* this sign and thereby to realize that the horse could not already have traveled the seven or more miles that supposedly separated the station and the house. Such readable signs scattered on the traffic concourses are clues which, the detective story assures us, when arranged in the right sequence, will be reconstitutable as a viable, if unlikely, realist tale.

If realism, since the 1830s, had been the literary form that had soothed anxieties about the joys of the hearth, house, and bourgeois home, one successor of the form, the detective story or thriller, found itself at odds with its origins. As the genre that, recasting realist logic as hyperacute observation, would represent the new order of circulation and traffic in satisfying ways, it discredited the static home. Sensing now that the home's solidity was a bourgeois dream, it nevertheless toyed with that dream, and organized its plots so that they were premised on the bourgeois impulse to reduce potentially uncontrollable movement to static surety. Thus the realist plot outcomes that close detective stories and "solve" the mystery are always tainted by a sense that they are arch: this is the outcome of the whiff of camp in all these texts. The camp element is the symptom of the text's attempt to reconcile its realist roots' allegiance to defending the solidity of the home, with its new allegiance to the new, exciting disorder of circulation and traffic. Detective fiction is a straining form of realism that finds itself determined to master the new order. Its scattered clues and liberally floated red herrings partake richly of the arch quality: they are the thriller's points of contact with the new traffic order. And, in their method of textual revelation, where the author acts as fairground magician and tells the reader in effect, "There, you see it, but you don't see it," they constantly cajole the reader to look harder, to see better (the village where the engineer should have looked harder is called Eyford), to be more alert, to "use those grey cells," as Poirot would soon chime endlessly. They offer the outline of a method for reading the grammar of traffic to those still wistful with memories of home.

This cognitive aesthetics of clue reading is the literary acknowledgment of the pioneering sociologist Georg Simmel's assertion that the urban dweller was more likely to have a "heightened awareness and a predominance of intelligence," which, however, is undercut by "an inconsiderate hardness and . . . general blunting of sensibility."[19] The detective story educates the mass of drivers, passengers, and pedestrians in this new kind of alert cognition. It does so not merely by instilling fear of the scene-of-the-crime house as a delectation of shivering pleasure but also by generating the half-fearful, half-enjoyable frisson of kinesis to be derived from moving smoothly in traffic. Or rather, it simulates this frisson through its strategy of moving the reader through the story, the arousal of suspense. Suspense has always been integral to the history-mimicking temporal schemata of realist narratives: we form expectations about subsequent events based on our judgment of what has gone before. Detective fiction dismantles the temporal primacy of this structure of suspense and reassembles it in resolutely spatial terms: the crime has happened, and a scouring of the spaces surrounding the crime, or more accurately, of the use of the traffic patterns in these spaces, will solve its mystery. By flattening suspense into an issue of understanding spaces and the speeds within them, what is achieved is an extraordinary distillation of the experience of suspense itself. Why does the turn from time as duration to space as crime scene distill suspense? Once again, space annihilates time even as (in the scattered clues) it renders it real.

The detective story plot promises that no longer will events follow each other in lugubrious order; they have already occurred, and the sole focus on where the perpetrator *is*, "out there," and on who he is, turns suspense into a totalized experience — the assumption that the reader, for the duration of the story, is to accept the notion that this suspense is all that matters, and accept it to the extent, one might say, of becoming (imaginatively) addicted to it. (The thriller, likewise, is the genre that has succeeded in rendering reading addictive.) This experience of distilled, gnawing, more or less physical suspense, built up from a narrative which details the canny reconnoitering of a space, represents the thriller's brilliant abstraction of the more dissipated and fragmented forms of suspense built around sequences of time familiar from realist fiction. It presents the reader with a visceral sensation, an extended thrill, which is *the* pleasure of detective fiction. This thrill, this distillation of suspense in the thriller genre, is manufactured through fast, keen looks while moving through a given space "against time"; thus it corresponds quite accurately to the sensation of fearful pleasure to be derived from being a passenger or, more particularly, a driver in traffic oneself. The thriller simulates for the reading commuter the very pleasure that might be derived from the traffic of which she is a part. This is the true pleasure of reading thrillers on trains.

One final point on new-century images of hearth and home as fearful dwelling. This was not merely the provenance of thriller and detective writing, even if the trope's sharpest expressions came from this popular quarter. Images of the fearful dwelling can be seen too in the strange twists in the architecture of that relatively new mass genre of building, the suburban bourgeois villa. At the very moment when this kind of building for the "personal client" was becoming an acceptable benchmark or first notable work by ambitious young architects, these villas were turning in upon themselves in unprecedented ways. Villa architecture had throughout the nineteenth century provided structures where the most kitsch historical allusions and excesses of decorative additions had been encouraged, whether in the "painted ladies" of North America, the mini-châteaux of the Parisian suburbs, or the crenelated chimney pots and drawbridge of the clerk's castle, the villa satirized by Dickens in *Great Expectations*. By the century's end, such badges of sentimentality were being dispensed with in favor of what might seem like the stirrings of modernist minimalism but turn out to be yearnings for suggestions of the villa as bunker. Here the work of the prolific and gifted British architect Charles F. A. Voysey is typical. His country houses might appear to be more accurate, academic imitations than heretofore of large rural farmhouses, but their mostly small and low windows and broad expanses of bare wall, heavily overhanging roofs, lack of discernible major entrances, and interiors awash with long, low corridors and beams often suggest, rather, a determined bunker architecture. It is as if Voysey felt that the client would need suggestions of the fortress, or even of the prison, all dressed as Arcadian manse, to make him feel patriarchal and at home. Consider the final "country house" commission of Voysey's contemporary Edwin Lutyens, never completed and barely lived in, Castle Drago in Devon for the tea merchant Julius Drew,[20] where the broad, smooth stone walls, slit windows, and monolithic massing show an abandonment of rustic trimmings in favor of a home-as-bunker that seems inspired by Vauban's seventeenth-century fortress engineering. Only Lutyens's cardboard mock-ups exist of the unbuilt parts.

Such fortress homes, moreover, were not only the fantasies of eccentric and reactionary late-imperial Edwardians. The villas of the famously antidecorative Viennese architect Adolf Loos, for example, such as his star's

residence for Tristan Tzara on the Avenue Junot in Paris, or the famous
unbuilt house he designed as a publicity stunt for the jazz dancer Josephine
Baker, were replete with imprisoning sight lines within (as if the famous
dwellers inside would be seen and oversee, and hence play at control and
being controlled),[21] and blankly near-windowless and fortresslike without.
By the time the modernist Le Corbusier had reversed all of this, with his
stunning (but unlivable) drawing room open to the sky in the Apartment
Beistegui (1929–31) or the glass-walled airiness of his Villa Savoye (1929)
(of which Le Corbusier himself said, "A home is not a prison"),[22] the zeal
of the pioneer modernists' manifestoes and polemics might have obscured
the fact that the prison-villa had, in some strange cultural transformation,
itself become unlivable anyway, the subject of half-wistful surrealist satire
in *Les Mystères de Château du Dé*, a film made by Man Ray with settings by
the modernist architect Mallet-Stevens.

By the late twenties, as J. M. Cain's dismissal of the "House of Death"
in *Double Indemnity* makes clear, the era of the bunker house as perceived
threat was over, and the era of traffic and circulation as the prime space of
action had arrived. When Le Corbusier made a film about his early villas,
L'architecture d'aujourd'hui (1929), he opened evocatively with a shot of
the architect himself *in his own car* driving up to the entrance of the Villa
Garches (figure 5).[23] The glass wall in the typical Le Corbusier house signified the downfall of the house as a bunker; even more telling in his work
is the concrete ramp which climbs inside a number of his buildings and
smoothly cuts through others. A simulacrum in miniature of the concrete
freeway, this ramp eloquently bespeaks the takeover of the dwelling by the
traffic route.

The Agony of Slowness: Bunker Culture

Angst about home, a fear of dwelling, was in this period the counterthrust
to learning the lesson of the potential pleasures of traffic and speed. It stood,
however, for a broader cultural turn: from the pleasures of place as Augé
defined it and the reassurances, nostalgias, evocations, and allegiances that
place as totemic guarantor of identity could provide, to the more flimsy, un-
grounded, but thrilling pleasures of movement and speed. Given nationalism's hegemony in twentieth-century ideologies of community, this might
seem a strange claim to make, especially about the period leading up to the
mass sacrificial effort to defend one's nation that was the First World War.

FIGURE 5. Le Corbusier drives up to his recently completed Villa Garches. Still from *L'architecture d'aujourd'hui*, 1929, directed by Pierre Chenal with Le Corbusier. Courtesy of the artist's estate.

A deeply embedded affection for the homely in its various forms—whether house, village, country, nation, tribal territory, or even football team—persisted, even becoming magnified. The ideologies of homeliness, however, whether implying allegiance to family or nation, are constantly mutating and evolving. The change, around 1900, altered an old relation between "home" and "away."

I agree with Jameson's suggestion in "Cognitive Mapping" that a structural relation exists between the cultural forms broadly definable as realism and modernism on the one hand and the sociopolitical forms of nationalism and imperialism on the other. I disagree, however, with his claim that modernism's alienating strangeness, its ability to baffle, results from a subconscious cultural awareness in the early twentieth century that the life being lived in the West was removed from the space of the production of wealth that made that life possible—that is, the work of exploitation of native peoples and resources in the colonies. This is to place an altogether too sincere (and modernist) faith in the geopolitical social acuity of modernist shock tactics and experimentation. Nevertheless, since notions of home and away are interlinked, and since the idea of home shed much of its aura in fin de siècle Western writing, so that increasingly raw and strange forms of realism, such as the thriller, had to be fabricated to represent it and to inject it with at least a whiff of the authority to which it had been accustomed, one can be sure that a profound change occurred in the imaginary of the other place also. In late Victorian fiction, this other place might have been the slum, the brothel, or even the imagined underground or aerial worlds of post–Jules Verne science fiction; most often, however, it was the colonies. In the thriller, the home was feared; other genres reexamined those worlds of terror and desire that Foucault termed heterotopias. As the notion of home lost its power, the other place, and in particular the colony also, I suggest, lost its fascination for the Western imaginary—its power to arouse terror, excitement, fantasies, and fear. We shall consider the reasons for this change in a moment. First, to my proposition: despite scattered exceptions, the colonies ceased to be imaginatively decisive *for Western representations* of the West itself after about 1900. This is the point at which colonial spaces and colonial "native" actuality became explicit in Western texts and artworks about the West itself, from Picasso's images of African masks to E. M. Forster's *A Passage to India*. But this availability for overt Western representation, and integration of colonial elements into texts primarily concerned with representing Western social or psychic realities, meant precisely that the absolute otherness of the colonies for Western imaginations was over—and hence its unspoken and until then unspeakable effect on Western representations of itself, of its home, and of mass ideologies of homeliness such as nationalism was nullified also. Versions of home, then (on which the badge of selfhood, as ideologies such as nationalism had claimed, were imprinted), had to be radically reconstituted. It was in the era of nationalist realism that the unspoken imaginary of the savage colonial heterotopia was implicated (but unconsciously, as a symptom) in every text that demarcated the national version of homeliness; this is what readings of the troubled homeliness of *Jane Eyre* have proved. By 1900 the colonies had become too fully known to the West, so that their imaginative power faded, was neutralized.

Replace Jameson's argument, then, with what follows from that of Augé: the formerly other, exciting, and fearful empire territories became, in the new century, the first real non-places for the Western imaginary: merely sites, in Western terms, without enough features to fear. The work of anthropology, busy describing places in the European empires, which emerged as a respectable discipline at this moment, might seem to disprove this; but it is precisely anthropology's disciplinary premise that it can discover place in a waste of non-place. By not being systematic and totalizing but rather appearing to follow the old missionary-colonist logic of working from the village upward, anthropology enhanced, rather than contested, the new Western logic of a global wasteland of non-place beyond the tenuous homeliness of the European homelands. This vast change in the Western imaginary of global relations occurred at the moment when the whole of the globe had finally been mapped and claimed. While truly an other place exercising imaginations fundamentally committed to home, colonial territory had had an imaginative hold. Because it was still unmapped, knowledge of it seemed potentially limitless. Once the colonial world's borders had been determined, the imagination of the colonies in the West fundamentally changed.

For Western culture, this change was traumatic. Once Western imaginations realized that their unmanageable fantasies and fears could not be relocated to the imaginative heterotopic space of the colonies "on which the sun never set," these fears returned to haunt the space of homeland and home in, for example, the surge in invasion narratives and gothic writing in the 1890s.[24] The genres that had nurtured the fantasies of colonialist heterotopias were doomed; imperial adventure fiction, such strange dreams as H. Rider Haggard's *She*, which had played a significant role in developing young mass popular audiences, in a stroke came to seem passé. Once the "affiliative versus heterotopia" model of conceptualizing known place by countering it with the mass of the unknown broke down and the other territory was shorn of its capacity to be demonized, the home place's emotional hold as a place of refuge turned out to be nebulous also. There was a shift from a sense of space as places, whether loved or loathed, toward the beginnings of a sense of everywhere as non-place. Twentieth-century culture signaled a new acceptance of the idea that the rationalization of space, the breakdown and leveling of its peculiarities in favor of its more efficient use for exploitation and ease of circulation, had entered an important new geopolitical phase. Already, for example, the modern notion of tourism, as travel devoted to the nostalgic search for sites that retain a residue of their sense of place, had become wildly popular, and the "travel book" as we know it today was born. More important, no new version of otherness was found to demonize colonial space (although versions of the old one, particularly around tropes of "savagery," certainly persisted), so that a representational crisis in relation to the colonies arose, and this crisis not only presented an opportunity to colonial peoples to represent themselves but had profound implications for the representation of the West to itself of its own home places.

The contradiction in the old territorial imperative, which underpinned the very notion of colonial expansion, was at this moment exposed. As the territorial potential for the expansion of the empires reached its limits, the process of empire making — movement, voyages, travel, speed — came into its own and was recast in new ways as a new locus of power. The ship, the ancient, myth-encrusted floating dreamscape that had always been in the West the epitome of the voyages (itself a mythic term by now) that had upheld and developed imperial power, at this moment lost the power of romance. In the strangely gripping *Heart of Darkness*, Joseph Conrad, who turned out to be the writer of moving elegies for this romance of the ship, offers a grim testament to this new inability of Western imaginations to render Africa as a heterotopia in the final instance, and the trauma that results. This trauma at being unable to render Africa as exotic heterotopia then transforms itself into a narrative about frustration — about all the frustrations of being slow.

Heart of Darkness is a detective novel. Marlow, cold, shrewd, honest, is the classic detective investigator, even if his movement along the world's highways is conducted in ships and boats rather than in hansom cabs or on foot. Anticipating the private eye, he is in his own way hard-boiled, in a tale that is steeped in a glowering noir quality. Here is a story that wants to be an imperial adventure novel, celebrating the successful traversal of heterotopic unknown territories by undaunted colonist men, which finds it cannot help but be instead a detective fiction in an unlikely locale. This first African detective novel treats the colonial space much as the Sherlock Holmes story treats the British home: it shows it as traumatic, even similarly claustrophobic. Its massed terrors serve both to accentuate what it shows as Africa's traumatic quality and to inject into this space a whiff of the aura, which, the story itself implies, it thinks the place no longer projects. In other words, Conrad's story has no respect for Africa, which is not to say simply that it is racist — as the famous intervention by Chinua Achebe has amply proved — but rather that it is not ultimately interested in the specificity of any African place, no more than Conan Doyle is interested in the specific aura of the London home.[25] Instead it is in the journey, and in the speed of the journey, that our interest is implicated and our excitement and desire for thrills elicited. *Heart of Darkness*, then, is an apt title here, as it would be for any noir thriller: it implies the fear to be faced at looking, perhaps for the first time, at non-place. It forgoes the pleasures and cultural assurances of a world whose places could be divided into, on the one hand, a home deeply loved and, on the other, an alien place hated and feared.

Heart of Darkness is the imperial fiction which shows that the split between home and colony that had characterized the territorial mentality of imperialism is clearly no longer valid, now that there are really no new places to be discovered in the world.[26] The Victorian empires had represented themselves, whatever their political reality, through the simple imagery of territorial aggrandizement borrowed from the wars of Alexander the Great and the Roman Empire: the modern empire, in this mold, was simply a matter of one territorial unit taking over numerous others. In this schema, the nation's claim to territory, to land — that is, to space — was what made an empire large, and hence notable. This simplistic but predominant vision of empire tended to diminish all the nonterritorial kinds of political power — of exploitation, trade, cheap labor use, and strategic use in defense — that the empire brought, but it fitted perfectly with the sociocultural vision of spatial organization that divided spaces into home versus heterotopia. Conrad's novel, however, suggests that this vision of empire, being an imaginary construct, needed as an enabling half fiction the possibility that the empire could expand its territory indefinitely to sustain its power. At the story's outset, in a passage which seems to invariably draw readers, he underlines Marlow's discovery of how the globe's total colonization led to this crisis in the Western imagination of an older construct of world space:

> Now when I was a young chap I had a passion for maps. . . . At that time there were many blank spaces on the earth, and when I saw one that looked particularly inviting on a map (but they all looked that), I would put my finger on it and say, when I grow up I will go there. The North Pole was one of those places, I remember. Well, I haven't been there yet, and shall not try now. The glamour's off. Other places were scattered about the Equator. . . . I have been to some of them, and, . . . well, we wont talk about that. But there was one yet — the biggest, the most blank, so to speak, that I had a hankering after. True, by this time, it was not a blank space any more. It had got filled since my boyhood

with rivers and lakes and names. It had ceased to be a blank space of delightful mystery—a white patch for a boy to dream gloriously over. It had become a place of darkness.[27]

"The glamour's off": in this thoroughly modish observation, Marlow registers the demise of a previously evocative form of thinking about home and away. This phrase decrees the demise of the John Buchan–or Karl May–style imperial adventure novel. With the colonization of all spaces comes the unsustainability of the tropes of exploration and adventure, although both were so imaginatively powerful that they went on in the succeeding decades to have eerie, twilight afterlives in a rash of travel writing by figures such as Freya Stark and T. E. Lawrence, whose increasing eccentricities helped them retell, and resell, the now defunct fiction of exploration. Both travelers and explorers were being supplanted by a new generation of "adventurers," whose achievements were not now concerned with discovering the sources of African rivers but had mostly to do with encounters with machines—for example, the British aviators Alcock and Brown, and Charles Lindbergh—the new adventurers of speed.[28]

Such traces of the increasingly foolish-seeming explorer, however, merely underline the prescience of Conrad's novella. In its early pages, when a brooding chiaroscuro is swathed about both London and Brussels in the text,[29] the point is not simply to render another fin de siècle account of urban alienation but rather, it turns out, to present these Western cities in the same light as that in which the Congo jungle will soon be shown. When London is described as one of the places that also had once upon a time been colonized, the novel again announces its determination to cast all spaces, both home and colony, in the *same* terms. *Heart of Darkness*, with its suggestion of a new genre of imperial noir, then presents us with a radical version of what Henri Lefebvre termed a rationalized world space. The novel is at pains to point out that it perceived this capitalist reduction of all space to use value not in the industrialized, trade-intensive (London), or bureaucratic (Brussels) West but rather in the formerly heterotopic territory of Africa itself.

Further, a large part of the book's descriptions of Africa is taken up—as in the account of the Central Station—with, in fact, eerie representations of an industrialized Africa, one where industry, the blasting through the hills to build a railway, is presented as perverted but is shown as a version of tin-pot Western utilitarianism nonetheless. The "other" Africa, the one that presumably exists beyond the wall of the jungle, is presented to the reader not, even remotely, as the potential space of exotic and pleasurable strangeness. It emerges as a blankness whose possible value as a nature reserve of the primitive is relayed to us in tones whose blandness, and whose bleakness, can make them seem reverential but which betray no real interest. A typical account of the as-yet-unknown Africa speaks of how "the silence of the land went home to one's very heart—its mystery, its greatness, the amazing reality of its concealed life" (37). These sonorous abstractions ("amazing reality") bespeak no fascination for any possible particularities of this as an "other" world—so that when Kurtz, the only figure here who still adheres to the old spatial divisions of home versus colony, therefore finds the jungle a fascinating heterotopia, his dualism and his resulting "going native" can only be judged by the novel as dementia. Kurtz is much like the foolhardy adventurer Scott, who in 1912 would freeze to death after reaching the South Pole; the native woman of the novel occupies much the same role that the Sherpa guides played in Western representations when the British climber Sir Edmund Hillary became the "first man" to climb Mt. Everest. Seeing Africa, even at a remove, through the eyes of Marlow, as blankly abstract, and refusing to see particulars in the anthropological mode, make possible the novel's critique of the older style of territorial imperialism. Where the novel becomes radical, however, is in pointing out the newer style of colonialism, epitomized by the Central Station and its manager, which cares nothing for and indeed despises the archaic sham of the older form and is instead dedicated to trade, ease of transport, communication routes, and exploitation. It is an even nastier form of exploitation in that it does not care about the actuality of Africa even enough to despise it but rather would reduce the whole world to routes useful to the pursuit of trade. This is Conrad's sobering picture of the beginnings of global transnationalism. It is a featureless world, where the only real feelings swirl around the smoothness or otherwise—usually the latter—of the traffic that constitutes trade.

The trauma of the novel's exposure of the colony as a non-place abstracted by Western capital is concentrated in one uncanny image—that of the ship on land. In *Heart of Darkness* this role is taken by the biscuit-tin steamer in Marlow's charge, sliding through jungle grasses, always about to run aground. Whenever this image of the breakdown of what had been the natural division of traffic for centuries occurred, it had portended a crisis. As such, it has often been associated with colonialism (a late-twentieth-century version is Werner Herzog's film *Fitzcarraldo*, in which a ship is carried across a Peruvian isthmus).[30] Subtly, Conrad's steamer, putt-putting its way up the Congo, chugging between the tall riverbank jungle, is a version of the ship-on-land, an unsettling symbol of the transportation uncanny. Foucault, in his paean to the ship as itself a heterotopia, declared that "in civilization without boats, dreams dry up, espionage takes the place of adventure, and the police take the place of pirates."[31] This turns out to be an excellent summary of the plot of *Heart of Darkness*. At the moment when the ship itself, like the Africa to which it sails, stops being the heterotopic vehicle of exploration and adventure, an unruly image of heroic voyage since the time of the *Odyssey*, it is turned into land transportation to signal the full effect of its degradation. Around this uncanny image, the uneasily modern pleasures of the narrative of *Heart of Darkness* assert themselves. These turn out to be the masochistic pleasures of the repeated experience of frustration.

The massed pyrotechnics of "native savagery" around Kurtz's station at the climax of *Heart of Darkness* are a Colonial Exposition–style diversion derived from the evening shows put on with "native villagers" at the expositions of this period, such as the Greater Britain Exhibition's enormously popular Kaffir Krall of 1899.[32] The doomed, exotic, heads-on-stakes world of Kurtz's trading post is countered by the real world of the Central Station, and the most vivid and continuous pleasures of the text are provided not by the caricatured sideshow of native dances and rites but by the day-to-day frustrations of malfunctioning technologies of transport. This is signaled as soon as Marlow lands at the coastal station: even before he has a chance to witness the shameful enslavement of Africans in scenes reminiscent of, and influenced by, Roger Casement's reports on Congo atrocities in his British Government Report of 1903,[33] Marlow spots "an undersized railway truck, lying there on its back with its wheels in the air. One was off" (22). Soon he is drawn to "more stacks of decaying machinery, a stack of rusty nails" (22). Marlow's own task, to pilot the boat upstream, is sabotaged some months later when, on finally reaching the Central Station, he finds that after a stupid accident the boat had been sunk in the river. Once he retrieves it, he discovers that, far from being shipshape, his command is "like a Huntley and Palmers biscuit tin kicked along a gutter," and that he must wait some months for rivets to arrive to repair it. This is a world not of terrifying tribes in heterotopic spaces but of inferior technology bedeviled by gross (Western) inefficiency.

We readers are asked to collude in disapproving of such an apparently dull subject as the underuse of technologies of transport, even African transport, because Marlow's sense of what is honorable, and his high-minded attack on the very colonial exploitation in which he is a salaried participant, get subsumed to his practical sailor's discourse of efficiency and frustration at the lack of all due speed. Moral outrage gets expressed as traffic rage. Efficient speed becomes synonymous with moral authority. Those who are careless about boat accidents and finding rivets to fix them are corrupt; those who strive to make repairs and to keep on schedule, like Marlow himself, the ship's mechanic, and even the native engine stokers he employs on the journey upriver, are admirable. This slippage from the abstract virtue of the idea to the practical efficiency of mechanical engineering is the novel's crucial ideological shift of gears. Read this way, the darkness of the title seems to elucidate frustration in the face of colonial inefficiency, a frustration brought on by adherence to modernist progressive optimism of the Fordist or Bauhaus type—a faith that technology, exercised at efficient speed, will foster a virtuous, if featureless, world—rather than any nebulous alienated modernist pessimism. Conrad, through the character Marlow, transforms an old-style imperial explorer, the last colonist as pirate leaving home in search of heterotopias to plunder, into the new worker-as-mechanic oiling the cogs of the non-place world order of efficient traffic and enriched trade. The heroic sailor is reengineered as dependable manipulator of transport and machines.

This literary reengineering is effected by a genre shift from explorer travelogue to the strategies, if not the locale, of a detective novel. At the Central Station in particular, Marlow becomes a canny private eye: time and again we see him lying quietly on the boat deck, behind a levee, or in his darkened room as he overhears muttered conversations that allow him to piece together clues about what is rapidly emerging as the mystery of the arch-trader in ivory at the Inner Station, the marvelous Kurtz. Soon every sign—that upturned railway locomotive, the starched collars of the accountant, the wry painting of Justice in the brick-maker's hut, the drums sounding in the night air—acquires an uncanny, aura-murky status as clues to an overall mystery, and Marlow as efficient, would-be-honorable amateur detective sets out to solve them. (A striking reading of the complex array of nuances emanating from just one of the more uncanny clues, the "extraordinary find" in a deserted riverside hut of a book, *An Inquiry into Some Points of Seamanship*, is given by the postcolonial critic Homi Bhabha in his essay "Signs Taken for Wonders.")[34] Since Africa as a place in the anthropological sense will never be the focus of readerly fascination in *Heart of Darkness*, the pleasure of the text must be implicated in the investigation conducted as a trail followed, a detective story chase. What Conan Doyle did for the home in detective stories such as "The Engineer's Thumb" — that is, made us disdain it, and then reminded us that it once had a powerful aura by injecting it with a perverse residue of such affect in the shape of fear — *Heart of Darkness* as detective story does for the heterotopic space of "away"; that is, it refuses any interest in the specific differences of the African locale, but we are made to vaguely fear it in a reminder of its former power to fascinate. By rendering Africa as a site of detective investigation, the text again implies the continent's comparability to London or Brussels. In this new global non-place, abstracted for capitalist use, the proper citizen is again the regulator of traffic, aiming for maximum speed. In the new order of non-places, the taxonomy of alert behaviors and ways of knowing that have been borrowed from the policeman to be imaginatively reworked as the ideal behavior of the individual subject becomes not merely, as in a Sherlock Holmes story, a blueprint for an epistemology. More, this policelike alertness becomes, in Conrad's text, the basis of a new ethics: the sailor turned engineer and good driver redeems himself by accelerating and rendering efficient the movement of the traffic that makes the colony work, while by piecing together the clues along the route, he triumphantly comes to know the truth of Kurtz's possible transgression for the society and himself.

Nevertheless, the invention of this new-model hero, the ethical technician, bends the newly assured strategies of the detective genre as well. For one thing, detective stories usually proceed from a point where a general sense of uncanniness is discerned rippling across the social fabric, to the point where the blame is placed on a single figure who is thereby unearthed as a criminal. (In "The Engineer's Thumb," blame devolves to two or three figures: a conspiracy.) This blaming of a single subject makes the detective story inherently antipolitical, prone, rather, to explanations which amount to conspiracy theories: social problems are reworked as aberrations of an individual. *Heart of Darkness* likewise focuses on a single individual, Kurtz, but blame is attached much more ambiguously. The implicitly ethical disclosures of the narrator imply a continuous indictment of "the system" — especially the unnamed apparatus of colonial exploitation which stretches from a northern European city to the Congo basin. However, because this ethics is articulated by the figure of an avid, alert, and capable technician-engineer, and because in his terms ethical judgments get to be articulated as discussions about efficiency of speed and movement, the ethical critique which suffuses the book gets articulated as a continuous low buzz of frustration with real colonial machines and the world in which they so slowly move. The complaint is that imperialism is in practice inefficient, jarring, impatience generating, unsmooth.

The old imperialism, in other words, is too slow. At the point where the text might be expected to rev up as a sensation novel, therefore, where, like a good detective story, it short-circuits appeals to our emotions to appeal directly and viscerally to our sensations and converts its ethical trajectory into the generation of sensations that we as readers can imagine we experience and so empathize with the implications of the text—at that point, the novel itself frustrates us and refuses to be a thriller. Instead, climactic moments such as Kurtz's famous death scene are shored up with a barrage of abstractions ("I saw on that ivory face the expression of somber pride, of ruthless power, of craven terror—of an intense and hopeless despair" [99]) that purport to appeal grandiosely to our emotions via our intellect and thus cannot but appear portentous too. The thrill is missing: "The glamour's off." The refusal to thrill us directly is palpable throughout; palpable, because what we as readers experience is a steadily administered dose of the frustration experienced by Marlow himself. The glumness of this frustration spreads like traffic haze over the various and diverse locales named in the text: the very listeners to the overall narrative (in the famous framing device) are, literally, stalled on a yawl in the Thames: "The only thing for it was to come to and wait for the turn of the tide," concludes the novel's opening sentence. Marlow's frustration at slowness is the novel's palpable evidence of its ethical point, and it seeps like radioactivity through the entirety of the text. *Heart of Darkness* is an anatomy of the modern horror of slowness.

The novel scratches the itch of slowness at every opportunity. The tale's listeners, already on the opening pages, in wait, are deeply bored, a sensation exacerbated, as any denizen of queues and lines knows, by their implicit group acknowledgment that their frustration should go unnoticed. When, on the second page, the novel tells how "and at last, in its curved and imperceptible fall, the sun sank low, and from glowing white changed to a dull red without rays," and so on, the reader is well aware that here is impressionist writing at its time-passing best, both yawn inducing and frustrating in a novella which, being short, we expect to be "fast-paced." This frustrating languor spreads, and Marlow's frustration at it becomes explicit: so much so that any character operating at speed, in contrast, seems threatening, as when the notoriously emblematic Brussels doorkeepers "knitted black wool feverishly" (15). Innumerable accounts of the implied and overt enormous levels of frustration at the colonizing companies' slowness follow. The steamer to Africa keeps stopping pointlessly at every port: "We pounded along, stopped, loaded soldiers, went on . . . nobody seemed particularly to care" (19); the shameful chain gang at the first station moves with deathlike lethargy: "They were dying slowly — it was very clear" (24); soon "I had to wait at the station for ten days — an eternity." Then the walk to the next station is interminable — fifteen days, two hundred miles — to be succeeded by the months-long wait for the infamous rivets. The trip upriver itself is, fittingly, the most grimly slow of all; it culminates in a magnificent scene of ethereal, otherworldly, fogbound stillness. Stationary in the fog, at dawn in the river eight miles from Kurtz's station, the party is attacked. This perpetual sense of slowness is a version of suspense so diffused through the fibers of the text and rendered so constantly tangible in the experience of reading that it becomes the spirit of the book.

To the extent that this constantly invoked frustration with the pace of activity — of travel, of movement, of technical work on the boat, of the steamer journey on the river — fosters standard-issue narrative suspense (about "what will happen next"), this is dissipated once Kurtz's station is reached and he is found and brought away. Yet although the novel's quest narrative concerns Kurtz and the gist of the detective story elements in the novel concern the quest to find him and to know him, nevertheless, as he is not branded the criminal within the standard framework of the thriller, this pervasive impatience in the face of slowness represents more than keeping the reader hooked. Clearly it is a dramatic condemnation of, and display of impatience with, the speed of yawls, cruisers, and steamers by a sailor. The ship is the symbol of the old colonialist mind-set; in this newly revealed featureless space of the modern colony, the ship is too creaky, too thoroughly colluding with the rank inefficiency of the colonial endeavor, too maddeningly slow. More, this slowness — and impatience with it — is sharply directed at the old idea of empire. The Congo, presumed site of the story, occupied an anomalous role between the archaic "territorial" idea of empire as aggrandized territory and the stirrings of a less sentiment-ridden geopolitical order. It conformed to the heterotopic idea of empire, but with a modern twist: in a caricature of the old vision of the ruler conquering an empire, the Congo was *owned* by King Leopold II of Belgium as a private fiefdom. Choosing the Congo as setting, Conrad, in focusing on this anomalous case, avoided directly critiquing the British Empire, of which he had, after eight years in the British merchant navy, become a citizen. He exposed for his readers the futility of heterotopic fantasies that perversely mirrored the aura of home. He also had them experience secondhand the way in which the trauma of moving from that older, more dreamy version of a bifurcated world order to a new one where all spaces, home and away, were equally abstracted for exploitation would only be overcome by those who demanded efficient speed and excellent transportation. The masters of the abstracted global world would show a properly ethical (and "manly") impatience at the inefficient slowness of those trapped between visions of empire, old and new.

Conrad's curiously frustration-driven, curiously resonant text responds to a change in geopolitics with an ethics derived from thinking about technology. He convincingly ties the political issue of new ways of imagining empire and the division of the globe under late imperialism to the material issue of the arrival of a speed culture. In caring more about fast turnaround time and better boats than about the particular strangeness of Africa, Conrad's work may well be the first, embryonic account of what became the globalist world order. He shows that if the home is an illusion (as the novel's closing, defiant kick, the chilling account of Marlow's visit to Kurtz's intended, back in a Brussels drawing room, proves), the colony as exotic heterotopia is also a sham. What is left, he insists, is a technology-driven ethics for this new world of instrumentalized, featureless, and exploitable non-places. This is based on principles of efficient engineering and transport—a scientist's ethics of beneficent speed. Whereas the pure detective story pleases by generating and assuaging fear, the deployment of detective story strategies in *Heart of Darkness* works its effects by generating frustration at slowness. This brilliant, subtle strategy of negative inference posits speed and a smooth journey as a global badge of effectiveness, "good work," achieved desire, and even (as Kurtz's case shows) a necessity for the maintenance of life. Speed culture in the West, the novel implies, would surmount the slowness of an imperial geospatial idea that is petering out in entropic inefficiency.

This lesson learned in the colonies could be realized in the West, the novel implies, because in the end Marlow does return home. In the city that at the book's outset had reminded him of whitened sepulchers, he visits Kurtz's intended and feels trapped waiting in a very white room—once again we witness an engineer experiencing claustrophobia. In this return to the West, the novel plants the suspicion that the venality conducive to the slowness characteristic of the imperial hinterland is embedded even more relentlessly in the closed air of the home-infested West, where slowness is replicated and caricatured in a horrible sense of stasis and stillness. Jameson, in his periodization of literary genres and the corresponding political stages of imperialism, would have it that people like the "intended," who didn't know or refused to heed the truth of the colonies, soon became modernists, and intuited colonial exploitation in the jarring and grating of their defamiliarizing prose. Marlow, however, the sailor turned detective, and by the end as cool as Sam Spade himself, returning to a city even more dank and static, purports to already know the reality of colonial exploitation and suggests that the colonial reality already exists in a more vehement form back in the home nation than it does in the colony. He suggests that the stasis signifying this reality is evidenced by the inefficient, excruciating slowness of the colonizing endeavor and that the only ethical basis for action in the circumstances is a vivid impatience with, and detestation for, such stasis. When he tells his lie about colonial reality and the Intended accepts it ("The last word he pronounced was your name" [110]), he says, "It seemed to me that the house would collapse before I could escape, and that the heavens would fall upon my head" (111). (At least he escapes with both his thumbs.) With this image of the collapsing Western home, the novella's focus shifts at the end from the grimness of the featureless colony to the grimness of the enclosing quality of the Western home and state: they are shown to be two sides of the same coin. Conrad's text decries the hypocrisy of home, felt, while again he waits, as a sordid, claustrophobic stillness. His ending becomes a critique not only of a newly utilitarian version of colonial exploitation but also of the territorial and bunkerlike quality of the Western state that had sponsored colonialism in the first place.

If the Sherlock Holmes stories show us how to fear the house as home, and Conrad's novel shows us in the end how to fear the state, and its colonies, as similar kinds of bunkers, then just as we saw a suspicion of the dwelling space reflected in a crisis of domestic architecture in the period, likewise we can detect the uneasiness with the state's bunker qualities in the hyperbole of the era's monumental national buildings. The nation-state, as Paul Virilio points out, has during its history struggled with the same contradictions that would soon dictate the contrary ways in which it envisioned its colonies: on the one hand, the state was, one might say, a color covering a specific, clearly bordered territory on a map, that is, a relatively vast imagined community that derived its identity in the final instance from the specific territory—the portion of global space—that a group occupied and defended, while on the other hand, the state operated as overseer and director of movements of people, goods, and money, both among its own people and between them and others. When new transport technologies meant that global and local movement increased, so that traffic became a science and its management a dominant national function—national passports, for example, were made compulsory in Britain only with Regulation 14.c of the Defense of the Realm Act (DORA) of November 30, 1915, as a wartime emergency regulation—the state's traffic-policing function increasingly contradicted its dominant self-imagination as static territory.[35] The uncertainty this generated is evident in the almost comically histrionic scale of some of the vast transport projects and transport-related buildings undertaken at the start of the twentieth century by state or by national companies. The last of the great urban European railway stations are the most grandiose. The railway terminus building of the Ferrovie dello Stato in Milan, the largest city of one of the last nation-states to emerge in western Europe, for example, shows in its extraordinarily hyperbolic façade the state's overbearing assertion of its power over national transport; a bravura last cheer, perhaps, for the great era of rail travel. The contradiction that had characterized all such structures is more evident than ever: in the front, a massively monumental building; at the rear, a series of light metal sheds covering the tracks—where the real work of moving vast numbers of people was quickly carried out. In Milan, the facade with its massed arches is so solid that it might be taken for the plinth of some gargantuan, never-undertaken statue. Within, the *pièce de résistance* is a fantastically high, impractical flight of stairs. A hymn to national grandeur, it resembles the vast marble monument to Vittorio Emanuele II, the first king of Italy, in Rome. That structure, designed in 1895, is wholly and only a monument: it backs on to the Forum, proclaiming the history of the Roman Empire as precedent for the new state. The Milan station backs on to the train tracks: aiming to imply the state's power over its transport networks, it suggests, rather, that, with its awe-inspiring power to monumentalize, the state is locked into a commitment to stasis, the static, fixed space of its national territory. Its power to impress applies only to the fixed facade of the terminus, foolishly beside the point for a structure dedicated to traffic and the movement of people. When Degas painted his impression of the Gare Saint Lazare in Paris, he chose to represent not the gravitas of the building's facade but rather that point — full of the expectation of speed — where the iron-framed shed opens to the tracks that lead outward and beyond. If we read the vast station's pretensions after seeing Degas's picture, the state's intervention is a pitiable kind of facadism. A railway terminus is effective to the extent that it can be efficiently traversed; decked out as a monument, it betrays a state unconsciously aware that its power, based on the prestige of its static territoriality, runs counter to the new fluidity of movement and traffic. The stage is set, in architectural symbols, for the era of speed to be at odds with the state.

In 1929, the same year as *The Maltese Falcon* celebrated the night traffic on the streets of San Francisco and helped inaugurate a genre in praise of chaotic Pacific Rim traffic that would reach its apogee years later in Ridley Scott's film *Blade Runner* (1982), the French surrealist Georges Bataille articulated a critique of all architecture, all static immobile structures, as territorializing edifices that counter the people's own traffic, their potentially revolutionary movement:

> Architecture . . . is the expression of . . . the physiognomies of official personages (prelates, magistrates, admirals) [with] . . . the authority to command and prohibit. . . . Thus great monuments are erected like dykes, opposing the logic and majesty of authority against all disturbing elements: it is in the form of cathedral or palace that Church or State speaks to the multitudes and imposes silence upon them. It is in fact obvious that monuments inspire social prudence and often even real fear. The taking of the Bastille is symbolic of this state of things: it is hard to explain this crowd movement other than by the people against the monuments that are their real masters.[36]

Here statist bunker culture is attacked with utter directness. Bataille's two other entries in the *Documents* series are on abattoirs and museums — the first he sees as centers of modern sacrifice which nobody visits, the second as reminders of death set up by the powerful to which the bourgeoisie sheepishly troop. Written two years after the proportion of U.S. families owning automobiles had reached 55 percent,[37] at the moment when the construction of the German Autobahn was about to be publicized internationally as a major plank of the Nazi empowerment of Germans,[38] in the year of the Wall Street crash in which the international circulation of money in the modern wireless era suffered its first major upset, and almost twenty-one years after Marinetti's Futurist Manifesto extolling speed as a new aesthetic virility, Bataille's bravura surrealist piece makes explicit both the fears of house and home expounded in the now familiar thriller and detective novel and brings to their logical conclusions the frustrations embroidering texts like those of Conrad, where the stolidity of exotic territoriality, the other side of the coin of monumentality at home, exasperates the engineer who sees goodness in efficient speed.

With surrealist panache, Bataille makes clear how high modernism—of which surrealism can be taken as a culmination—simply shocked by openly naming the implications of the fears and frustrations which the more popular forms had merely implied. (Proto-modernist high fiction such as Conrad's had deployed lowbrow forms to imply them too.) Yet Bataille goes further. First he impugns all architecture—by which he means any humanly built structure, any human modification of space, and, by implication, any human imaginative manipulation of spaces—both as home and as heterotopia. He connects the state to grand architectural and monumental structures and, by implication, accuses the state itself, with its justification for its existence in the last instance the fact of its static demarcated territory, as perhaps the most vicious and oppressive of such structures of all. Finally, in his image of the attack on the Bastille, he sees movement by the people—that is, the people's access to speed in the public thoroughfares not blocked by monuments—as potentially revolutionary and as the beginning of their emancipation. (Ironically, the Place de la Bastille, where the prison stood, has become a great traffic circle.) With the example of the French Revolution, he implies that this movement, this seizing of speed, is itself integral to the democratizing impulse of modernity. Thus he literalizes the metaphor of velocity implicit in the first key word of modernity, *progress.* His analysis is nevertheless—like that submerged in the detective stories and in Conrad's last, highbrow example of the colonial adventure yarn—still confined to critique. Beyond the destruction of awe-inspiring, fearsome monuments, what is the crowd to do with its seizure of speed? How will it enjoy speed's pleasures?

In the aftermath of the French Revolution, the people's speed was reharnessed by the state to wage a war fueled by an ideology of conquest. "La Marseillaise," as has been pointed out, became, like every national anthem, a tune to mark the rhythm of the marching soldier's speed, a martial road song.[39] It was only in the twentieth century, once the ideology of territorial expansion that sustained empire building in the classical sense became untenable, that the era of mass speed could at last be unleashed for the benefit and pleasure of the masses themselves (although national regimes always stood ready to reharness it for territorial wars). How new forms of subliterary mass culture grasped speed as a possibility for popular entertainment, how high modernist writing made the new unfamiliarity of non-place comfortable and even desirable, and how, above all, the newly invented entertainment media cast the new medium of speed as an individual pleasure will be the topics of the final section of this chapter. In it, we trace an arc from the fairground roller coaster to the demolition of the melancholic flâneur in literature, on to the first movie car chase.

Experiencing Speed: First Phase

A reimagining of the significance of particular kinds of spaces, both local and geopolitical, is discernible in both mass and high culture around the beginning of the twentieth century, achieved by the arousal of intense emotions about spaces, ranging from frustration to fear. In the late nineteenth century, the detective story endowed the city with a curious noir quality; it demonized the house and home, highlighting instead the pleasures of a lonely flâneur existence. It appropriated the staid aura of the home, recycling it as danger and replacing it with a sense of the glamorous danger of the thoroughfare. In the same years, the brash and jingoistic hymns to adventure of the popular colonial novel grew hollow. The genre literally lost its nerve, to be recast in higher literary form as a dryer and bleaker elegy to imperial adventure by Conrad. Adventure fiction discovered its own insubstantiality in the face of the knowledge that geopolitical space was finite. Exotic fantasies of otherness were replaced by stories about trajectories of exploitation and routes of transport. Sherlock Holmes stories replace the newly nightmarish aura of the home with the more obscure glamour of the policing of the street; Conrad's novella replaces the heterotopic delights of exotic other spaces with a cool, ever-murmuring, barely restrained frustration that the thoroughfares of the empire are mismanaged, unsmooth, don't let business run on time. Staging his as a narrative of a failure, Conrad goes further than Conan Doyle (and all detective fiction), whose golden rule is that the story must always be narrated as a success. Conrad instead incites us, by sharing Marlow's frustration, to presume that smoother, speedier, more efficient movement ("progress," but literally, by barge or train) might somehow equate with a more honorable use of the colonial space. That space is now undifferentiated, except to the degree that its profit potential is assessed. Whereas Holmes, traveling in the open streets, shows us how to be careful and alert, Conrad's novella implies an engineer's ethics where efficient movement—good driving—itself renders us honorable. In tandem, each announces the old aura-filled perception of space to be obsolete: Conan Doyle's stories demonize the home; Conrad's novel implies the unsustainability of the fantasy of the heterotopia. With Conan Doyle and Conrad, each side of the dualist equation is demolished. Why was it at this historical moment that the older dualist conception of space as home versus heterotopia became obsolete?

The Western discovery of the finitude of the knowable world, the realization that all the white spaces on the map had been filled in, merely precipitated the sense that the home-versus-heterotopia vision of space was obsolete: it should not be mistaken for its cause. For this we need to search further, to the spatial imperatives of modernity itself. As David Harvey explains in detail, space in modernity has been viewed primarily in utilitarian terms: that is, its specific and particular features have been increasingly abstracted to make space a matter of better surfaces for the more easeful creation of wealth. In this world of increasingly abstracted space, Foucault points out in "Of Other Spaces," residual islands of "sacred space"—spaces that were once significant and full of aura and now linger on or are preserved as monuments—still intrude. I suggest that for much of modernity these islands still exerted the awesome power of their presence on people's entire view of spatial organization, so that increasingly a spatial order that was more and more abstracted and turned into what Augé terms non-place was still being seen, anachronistically, in the now mythic terms of the older, hierarchical, center-periphery, home-heterotopia version of the spatial imaginary. At some point the divergences between the archaic imaginary constructions and the reality of the more rational new spatial organization were bound to become apparent. The limits of colonial expansion, once reached, provided such a moment. This was so because imperialism's rationale of territorial extension—that a nation could take over heterotopic spaces and make them its own possessions—operated in parallel with the older sense of spatial organization, but it supported a reality that had more to do with trade and exploitation, in short, with traffic, than with territories drawn on any map. Once this became clear and the geopolitical spatial order was seen as relatively abstracted, then the belief in home as its center was likewise laid bare. (The notion of the nation, the home territory that sustained the empire abroad, was then liable to be seen as archaic also.)

To grasp this is to begin to understand why frustration at slowness, scratched like an itch by Conrad's prose, became important in most high modernism. It comes close to explaining why flânerie, walking on foot through the city, became a modernist obsession at the very moment when new speeds were being achieved. It also complicates, but preserves, Jameson's intuition of the centrality of colonial-metropolitan relations for explaining high-modernist obscurities.[40] For example, Eliot's langours in "Prufrock" become an index of the contrast between the efficiencies of the arriviste empire (that of America, where Eliot was born and raised) and the frustrations of the worn-out one (that of Britain). Likewise, Joyce's Irish stop-and-go flânerie in *Ulysses* indexes the clash between metropole and colonial city as the rhythm of a setting (Dublin) where home and heterotopia were entities whose status was deeply unsure. If, however, the world was now to be considered as an abstracted non-place, with every place equally featureless and robbed of its particular auratic points and centers, then how was this space to be navigated, crisscrossed, used, even enjoyed? Conan Doyle and Conrad, distilling distaste for the old, had only hinted at the pleasures of the new. Non-place for them is still dark, misty, murky, fraught with dangers, surprises, and evil purposes — and so it was for even the most optimistic high modernists who succeeded them. It was an enormous task for culture, both high and low, to construct discourses in which this new version of an apparently featureless spatiality could be described, celebrated, and made culturally ready for use. This turned out to be the work of the lowest genres of culture and of the most rarefied forms of the high, and as new technologies were harnessed to create new cultural forms, such as the phonograph and film, these new forms proved utterly adept at developing representational strategies where the new non-place could emerge as the most exciting of all. This excitement centered on the ease of movement in abstracted space: that is, it centered on speed.

What occurred, and what is brilliantly captured in Augé's division of all spaces into place and non-place — that is, into spaces that can be represented and spaces that cannot within current protocols be represented at all — is that there was a massive crisis in the representation of spaces, so that for a moment space ceased to be credibly representable. This led in part to what critics have noted as the obsession with time in the various modernisms, from Joyce's stunning compression of *Ulysses* into a single day to Proust's baroque of nostalgia and remembrance. It meant too, however, that there was a new attention to the means by which space was in fact experienced. This experience was seen to exist in the kinds of *movement* possible through newly abstracted, utilitarian space. This movement was cast as necessarily efficient, profit making, and maximally exploitative of all the resources of any space encountered. Movement, however, could also be pleasurable in itself; this maximum extraction of use value could be cast as pleasurable. Hence speed. Maximum efficiency meant maximum speed — but this drive for speed, at speed, had to be cast as the greatest pleasure. The work ethic and the pleasure ethic could be deemed not merely to coexist but to become one. Capitalism, as the French critic Jean Tissot has written, did not invent speed, but the experience of speeding could rightly become the physical and experiential co-equivalent of the pleasure of capitalist competition. Further, such human speeding, as befits the era of mechanics and engineering, was not merely to be an attribute of the human body, even if it had its basis there; it is certainly no accident that the era of modern international competitive sports, with running the thousand-meter dash at their highlight, began at precisely this moment. The Olympic games were about human speed, and they celebrated, above any one place, the whole world. They were, however, a spectacle for all except the competitors: they showed, rather than granted the experience of, the wonders of unaided human speed. What was needed was that people be given the experience of it en masse — and this was accomplished with the aid of machinery. As the first Olympics were being run, the first mass-produceable car was going into production. The opening of the experience of unheard-of speeds for individuals had now begun.

The precedents were the fast oceangoing liners and the trains, which were traveling at a respectable speed by the beginning of the twentieth century. In *Harmsworth's Magazine* in 1901, J. W. Wintle, in an article titled "Life in the New Century: The Most Striking of New Inventions," noted that "quite a sensation has been caused in nautical circles, by the performance of H.M.S. *Viper*, which travels at the rate of forty-three miles per hour. This extraordinary speed has been obtained by fitting her with steam turbines."[41] The crucial development was to move the masses from being passengers in boats and trains to being drivers. People could be transported quickly, but to actually experience that movement as physical pleasure was another matter. Here the simple fairground attraction of the roller coaster works as an example of the way in which mechanics would, with the simplest device, render speed not as an image of others' momentum but as a taste of a new experience that would be one's own. It did not allow driving, but it offered speed as physical thrill. One of the earliest roller coasters was built by LaMarcus Thompson as the Oriental Scenic Railway in Atlantic City in 1886;[42] in 1901 Edward Prescott built the famous Loop-the-Loop at Coney Island.[43] Here, at the beginning of what Jean Baudrillard would later term the age of simulation, we have an icon of modern mass enjoyment that is thoroughly committed to raw physical experience, celebrated among holiday crowds and in public. (The first modern amusement park opened in Coney Island in 1895.) In the very years of the flowering of mass consumer culture as we now know it, when the mass image and the spectacle were asserting their nebulous but vastly seductive powers in areas from state pageantry to the mass advertising of soaps and powders,[44] controlled and commercial access to actual experience centered on speed. Speed was offered as a sensation, a contrast to the simulations—such as advertising—of contemporary capital.

Yet speed and capital were always intimately combined. This speed experience, however visceral, was also only a game in a fairground—it too was controlled, regulated, lively and invigorating but not really dangerous, granted without risk, or very little. (The advertisements for the Loop-the-Loop claimed "No danger whatever.")[45] It was conducted in public: bodily pleasure of the speed sort could and should, the roller coaster implied, be public, and this separated it from the private bodily experiences being explored in psychoanalysis and avant-garde literature in the same period. (Freud was dividing private sentience into two spatial fields, the conscious and the unconscious, at the same moment when such dualist divisions were breaking down in the perception of real space.) In the fairground show, destination for the urban working masses on Sunday outings to Coney Island, speed became the sensation which could be experienced publicly by everyone. It marked the point at which the new enveloping order of spectacle and mass consumption gave way to a taste of experientiality that could be enjoyed and still met with the approval, even the encouragement, of the authorities and the powerful.

Key to the fairground's roller-coaster thrill is that it was a physical *experience*, at the very moment when experientiality itself was beginning to give way to spectacle as the medium that ruled individual lives. This particular managed experience should be read in detail, as the roller coaster provides the strategies that would, in automobile culture, organize the pleasures of the next, more widespread, version of the sensation of speed. First, notice the simplicity of the mechanical device that propelled the customer toward her pleasure: with its scaffold structure and creaking rollers, it was primitive in a way that drew attention to the unsophisticated haphazardness of its technology. This might seem the opposite of much technological self-representations since, where ergonomics and aerodynamics often hide under a streamlined skin, versions of machine design that arrived in the 1930s or before. Early automobile design, however, likewise prided itself in its rough-and-ready quality.[46] Exposed rods and joints in early autos suggested improvisation and encouraged automobile customers to look to the future when surface appeal would improve. The roller coaster's thrown-together look also implied that function — and the experiential enjoyment that came from following function — came from form. In its naked functionality, the roller coaster, as design, anticipated the modernist architects' rhetoric of honesty and transparency: with its exposed girders, it anticipated Richard Rogers's and Renzo Piano's Centre Georges Pompidou, whose outside escalators provide a ghostly memorial, a trace, of the roller-coaster experience. This rickety machine, scaring and thrilling the masses, taught them, and celebrated the idea, that a vivid experience demands the engineer's minute attention to functionality. It arrived, paradoxically, at the same moment when design, packaging, and advertising were all getting into their stride, and the age of the appeal of surface glamorous appearances was also being born.

Next, note that this machine that sold speed solely as pleasure did so by using the simplest of forces — that of gravity. Speed, the lesson went, was a force of nature — enunciated, evidently, by the technical know-how of structural engineering. This was an engineering-aided version, with a vengeance, of back-to-nature. It was to be experienced best of all in that sinking feeling you endure in the fell swoop when the car goes over the precipice and *falls* — when all sense of control must be surrendered and nature as pure force of gravity takes over. Consider that downhill skiing was initiated as a mass, if elite, sport in this period too, when various speculators, among them an entrepreneurial author, saw the potential popularity of speeding downhill on skis and began to import them from Sweden to Switzerland. (One skiing entrepreneur was A. Conan Doyle, he of "The Engineer's Thumb.") The downhill thrill — whether on skis or in a roller-coaster car — is all about how the ration of personal control and personal surrender to the force of speed conjured by nature must at all times be calibrated. You give in to nature's force, and then experience speed as pleasure with an undertow of fear. You begin with a certain control, and that control (as in revving an engine, propelling oneself faster) brings one level of pleasure, along with a sense of purpose; but it is the moment of surrender to a force of nature larger than oneself, along with the fear of loss of control that comes with it, that deepens the pleasure. This heady interdependence of surrender and willpower, calibrated continuously and by means of split-second decisions, is what makes up the modern machine-enhanced but utterly natural and gravitational experience of speed.

This sense of surrender is enhanced by the relatively minimal safety precautions built into the machine. Constrained merely by a bar, you learn that the force of gravity, nature itself, will protect you from the machine's dangers. At the same time, not strapped in or restrained, one's personal responsibility — to be a good consumer of speed — is made evident. The lack of restraints and of cover accentuates the fear. This fear, accepting and overcoming it, the ride implies, is the absolute basis of, and a prerequisite for, the pleasure. The pleasure feeds on the fear — of an accident, of nature's power, of the technology's crash. Pleasure, the machine implies, comes when a willing rider overcomes the fear of these possibilities. This fear must be present, but it must be disregarded. The depth and complexity of the pleasure are thus intensified, and it appeals to a whole spectrum of sensations and emotions. This thrill is better than that of the detective story, as it is absolutely physical. It carries the rider along by appealing first to fear, then to her sense of her personal power. This power is underlined in the freedom the rider is given to disobey the simple rules: allowed freedom of movement, the rider, it is implied, is responsible for the speed — even if, in the case of the roller coaster, this is an illusion. In the coming culture of the automobile, just this onus on the individual to control her fear and to exert her personal responsibility within a firmly established rule system will be the ground rules for the people's accession to the pleasurable experience of fast cars, fast lives.

Next, notice the ratios of public participation to private pleasure embodied in the experience of a roller-coaster ride. The machine marks, you might say, the demise of the era of the passenger: it is the last vehicle in which being a passenger for its own sake is presented as a really enjoyable experience. (In the airplane, the passenger's pleasure was to be based mostly on recognizing one's class.) The roller coaster marks the moment in the history of passenger travel where photographs of late Victorian revelers enjoying their seats on a charabanc outing gave way to images of glum commuters, or of airplane travel that had to be photographed glamorously if it was to be seen as exciting. Like the coming car culture, however, the roller coaster offers speed as a mass experience, to be enjoyed in public. The enjoyment itself, nevertheless, is private, individual, and essentially selfish. This division, which neatly instills a modernist version of the gap between community and individual, puts the thrill experienced by the lone individual at the heart of the fulfillment of desire. It implies, however, that the consummation of one's pleasure can best be experienced in public view, so that it orchestrates a breakdown in the conventional split between public and private lives, refusing the notion that private pleasure must retreat to the home. This has been replayed again and again in the anomalous status, at once very private and absolutely public, of car travel. In the world of streets and of mechanical trajectories of speed like the roller coaster, privacy would be deemed the enemy of personal pleasure. At the same time, killing the chance for a politics of this new speed pleasure, no sense of community was necessary to enjoy it; on the contrary, the individual alone in the crowd of strangers was the ideal candidate for this thrill of technology and speed. The more technology thrilled, the more you felt the thrill alone.

All of this, moreover, took place at a funfair, often at the seaside. Modern speed technology was born in a popular carnival atmosphere of excess, enjoyment, leisure, and abandon. The innocence and the simplicity of the pleasure, the sense of license, of holiday, the sense of wagering, all combined to make the roller coaster a hilarious, as well as riotous (if very controlled), experience. Carnival pleasure, which in Mikhail Bakhtin's terms might have been harnessed as a force with the potential for limited communal opposition to the status quo, was managed, diverted, and channeled into a form of intense personal pleasure that could be deemed instinctive and certainly cut off any of the contemplative positions possibly useful for imagining significant social action. This was an invitation to physicality, to a fast physical thrill, at the service of the coming revolution in transport. The holidaying masses were shown how potentially disruptive carnival antics could be bettered by a technological fix that offered each individual in the crowd a better thrill, a physical experience at once so general and so intense that it exceeded anything a game with one's peers could provide: individual lonely pleasure proved to be best. When people step off the roller coaster, they are laughing, terrified, excited, exhilarated, thrilled: enticed in advance into the coming car culture. This pleasure corresponded, like a gambling win, to the essential characteristics of capitalist competition, where the greatest thrills appear depoliticized and the greatest achievements, it would seem, are experienced alone.

At the opening of this chapter, I suggested that mass culture genres and forms inducted people into the new culture of speed by altering the ways in which they registered the spaces that mattered to them. The thrillers of pop culture, like detective fiction, did this by arousing fear—fear of the spaces, especially the home, where the older spatial certainties had once found shelter. Others, like the well-modulated colonial yarns of Conrad or, later, the flâneur stories of the high modernists, represented the frustrations of slowness. The incitements to leisure of the new amusement park, such as the rough-and-ready technology of the roller coaster and Ferris wheel, offered excitement by giving their customers an early taste and primitive rundown of the coming pleasures of speeding itself. These forces of terror, frustration, and excitement, in the new era, were never distinct. What speed promised to do, and what the fairground attractions foretold, is that it would only be in this mix of what appeared to be contrary impulses, in a straining, taut, and unending effort to keep all three impulses in operation at once and to calibrate the ever-shifting relation between them, that one could achieve the optimum pleasure of the new speed culture. In calibrating the ratio of fear, frustration, and excitement, the thrill, already represented in mass sensation fiction and the shrill advertisements for the fairgrounds, could now be realized by every individual as personal experience. The vicarious thrills and spills, accidents and emergencies, successes of vigilance and frustrations of the slow, to be read about in the popular forms of sensation fiction could now be experienced as physical, immediate, and personal when, with car culture, the promise of speed seemed open to everyone.

Through technology the masses were about to be offered the means to increase the speeds they would experience and to take personal control of speed's rate and power. The new avalanche of pop culture worked hard in advance to ensure that speed's customers had established a desire for speed's pleasures. The old-order pleasures of dreaming about more or less imaginary fixed spaces were made to appear quaint, even dangerous, out of date, both in the colonies and by implication in the "real world" of home. (It was the arch-modernist Gertrude Stein who said of the California city of San Jose, "There's no there there": the true joke is that, given the world's new spatial order, she could, increasingly, have been speaking of anywhere.)

Flowing along the new featureless routes of ruthlessly abstracted spaces would be the new task, and with speed it was guaranteed to provide a new and hitherto unknown intensity of pleasure. Experiencing extraordinary new speeds on these routes and controlling one's experience of them would become a pleasure that only in the twentieth century would vast numbers of people come to know, and to know it, as Huxley claimed, as one of the only truly new pleasures of modernity. Car culture was about to begin, and the masses had been indoctrinated in the complex of sensations that need to be calibrated to enjoy speed. At the dawn of the society of the spectacle, people were being offered an extraordinarily intense *experience* of such pure private physicality. This was an innovation of which modernity's alliance between technology and the human could be proud. Technology, still sticking to its utilitarian strengths, was now poised to profoundly impact the subjective realm of personal pleasure. Modernism would be marked by a new symbiosis between the technological and what it felt like to be human. Speed would be the symptom of this symbiosis, and also its selling point. When speeding, the modernist citizen of the world would feel in her body the thrill of modernity's energy. The years of incitement to speeding were over, and with the new century, the opportunity to seize speed had come.

Gaining Speed: Car Culture, Adrenaline, and the Experience of Speed

Speed is the form of ecstasy the technical revolution has bestowed on man.
—Milan Kundera, *Slowness*

Our little car was almost ready. She was later to be called Auntie after Gertrude
Stein's aunt Pauline who always behaved admirably in emergencies and behaved
fairly well most times if she was properly flattered.
—Gertrude Stein, *The Autobiography of Alice B. Toklas*

The automobile has come to show even the slowest minds that the earth is truly
round, that the heart is just a poetic relic, that a human being contains two standard gauges: one indicates miles, the other minutes.
—Ilya Ehrenburg, *The Life of the Automobile*

It was not until 1927 that the roller coaster had competition from the newest
attraction: the Dodgem car.[1] The roller coaster had offered speed as a thrill
and had shown how this private thrill could be staged as a public spectacle,
but it was still modeled on the train. The passenger did not drive; the journey was plotted in advance; there was a departure point and a known terminus. The Dodgem car made the thrills and spills the driver's responsibility:
your journey, your crashes, your skill. This experience, the attraction taught
you, was a huge comedy.

Robert Frank's photograph of a couple on a Dodgem car ride (figure 6)
was taken in 1952, in the postwar moment when all the dreams promised
by the speed culture built up in the previous half century appeared to come
to pass. The photograph flashes before the viewer in full the complex of
thrills—ecstasies, even—that a Dodgem car ride, and car culture itself,

FIGURE 6. Robert Frank, *Couple, Paris, 1952*. Silver gelatin developed-out print. National Gallery of Art, Washington, Robert Frank Collection, gift (partial and promised) of Robert Frank. Courtesy of the artist.

put on offer. First note the isolation: although there must have been a dozen cars on the platform, the rest, given the changes in visibility when traveling at speed, and when speed effects are photographed, become a blur of fairy lights. This thrill, too, then, is to be relished alone. The car gets to replace the fearful home, for here is a couple, and the ecstatic straining of the man's face—at the momentum, at the torque, with the woman—vividly inscribe the interface of sexual desire and technology that, from its first outing, the automobile fostered and came to represent. Then read the woman's smile: reaching out to the photographer in a kind of communication, yet with eyes quite shut against the car's speed, she laughs—hilariously, shamelessly, excitedly—because for the car's driver, the power to steer, to drive where one wants, on a stage where every crash is merely a thump of rubber on rubber and a collision framed in laughter, is a power so intoxicating and so childishly simple that it provokes glee. In the Dodgem car, the driving thrill is granted in isolation, it is suggestive of sexual ecstasy, and it is cast above all as comedy. The steering wheel rounds smoothly, the car careens in an out-of-control curve, the participants shriek and laugh wildly. Car culture and its psychosomatisms were in full swing.

This is a chapter about the invention of the automobile and its cultural effects; it is also a chapter on the invention of adrenaline. Adrenaline was first isolated as a human hormone in 1900; its molecular structure was determined in 1904. I, however, want to use "adrenaline" as a code word for a new intuition of the novel emotional, psychic, and somatic possibilities raised by the conjunction of the technological prosthesis of the automobile and the human organism. A rush of adrenaline is what underpins the grin and the drawn faces of the couple in that Dodgem car; it names a profoundly new conception of human energy, displaying itself in a complex of new human intensities, that is imagined to surge in the human subject as she interacts with the speed-producing machine. This rush is a new, if subtle, moment in the history of human awareness of the senses. "Car culture," then, is the annotation of the pleasures and the terrors that this new rush provides and the languages in which they could be expressed. The self-advertising tricks of the automobile as new technology launched this discourse; soon diverse forms were exploring the nuances of emotion, sensory heightening, and psychic awareness engendered by the interaction between new machine and human subject. Car culture, even at its most lowbrow, struggled to articulate passions that were up to now not quite imagined before, at least not in these forms. Doing so, it traced the outlines of a new version of what the term "culture" itself demarcates.

Karl Marx, when thinking a half century earlier of how workers related to machines, had spoken of "temporary paroxysms."[2] This adrenaline, this surge of expectant energy that is felt when human subject and machine take each other on, is worth dwelling on because it is in excess of the protocols and rewards described by the narrative of consumption usually used to explain the arrival of the automobile and its phenomenally eager acceptance. The rate at which the car was taken up is spectacular: in 1907, about 62,000 cars were built worldwide; by 1913, the figure had climbed to 606,124.[3] The Ford Model T began production in 1908, at the point where the possibility for workers to own their own cars was only beginning. The story is most often told as a narrative of brilliant technological advances by individual inventors. The work of these innovators—Benz in Berlin with his first motor-engine of 1885, a 0.8 horsepower, one-cylinder engine used to power a tricycle; John Boyd Dunlop with the vital component of smooth driving, the pneumatic tire of 1888; and the Michelin brothers in Paris, who first fitted an automobile with such tires—all formed a chain of developments that put cars on the streets of the world.[4] A succession of advances by intrepid pioneers, cash-rich investors, and canny mechanics who became race car drivers and, if lucky, car manufacturers makes for a tale with at least some of the trappings of the narratives of physical endurance and derring-do that were replacing adventure fiction in this period. To understand why (rather than simply how) this new speed machine became such a vivid component in the imaginative lives of people in a few years, so much so that it invaded the domain of their sexual lives and their very sense of what constituted human energy itself, we need to probe motivations rather than chart intentions.

Car Culture: Experience Trumps Consumption

Histories of early automobile production generally describe the rise of car ownership as central to the rise of mass consumer culture in the West in this period. The turn of the century witnessed the greatest of the great exhibitions (the Exposition Universelle in Paris, visited by fifty-one million people, opened in 1900),[5] the full flowering of department stores (Louis Sullivan's Schlesinger Mayer, later Carson Pirie Scott, department store was built in Chicago between 1899 and 1904),[6] new leisure time for workers, and a new level of disposable income even for some members of the working class. In this commodity carnival, the car became the most coveted consumer disposable of all. In the history of mass consumption, desire for this ur-commodity was stoked by a legion of new accounts of businessman heroism, super-endurance, and tough tactics. Henry Ford in particular was cast as a near-mythic figure. These tales of discovery, clever improvisation, and deft entrepreneurship worked as advertising for this new, soon-to-be-mass-produced product in part because they were reconditioned versions of late Victorian adventure tales. Endurance races across France, America, and the Sahara and lavish car shows were early innovations in this highly managed branch of consumerism. From the start, the car industry was about innovations in mass publicity almost as much as innovations in technology. The antics of the Paris-Madrid race, the Circuit des Ardennes, and the Gordon Bennett Cup were celebrated in newspaper dramas, offering free publicity for car companies and feverishly cast as adventure. The reading of car culture as the golden calf of early-twentieth-century consumerism, however, does not necessarily explain why the car, with its speed possibilities, came to stand out so dramatically among the mass of consumable goods available.

The car is a singular kind of consumer commodity: it is not merely an inert object, as conventional accounts of commodity fetishism imply that the commodity must be. Certainly, the car's value as a spectacular commodity — one that, once merely seen, is instantly desired — was enhanced by good design, a high-gloss body, and fine accouterments from brass and glass to chrome; as a static commodity, it was granted more glamour than almost any other. However, the car is primarily a machine, in which, it appeared, the act of consumption itself could be exceeded when the car was used to experience the new thrill of independent speed. Speed culture, the access to the adrenaline-inducing rush that twists the faces of the couple in the Frank photograph, does not quite fit with the notion of hapless consumerism that the usual accounts of the protocols and harnessed desires of late Victorian and early modern consumption would lead one to expect. Rather, it challenges and contests the model of a largely passive consuming subject.

Accounts of early consumer culture, especially as they relate to literature, have been deeply indebted to Guy Debord's account of the "society of the spectacle,"[7] as well as to Jean Baudrillard's even-better-known discussion of simulation in modern culture. Histories of consumerism have delineated its seductive mirage effects, the empty promises of happiness and personal fulfillment it holds out through advertising or through the simple display of the mysterious, glamorous commodities themselves. Baudrillard's notoriously apocalyptic account carries this much further, so that, as he puts it in *Symbolic Exchange and Death*:

> The end of spectacle brings with it the collapse of reality into hyperrealism, the meticulous repudiation of the real, preferably through another reproductive medium such as advertising or photography. Through reproduction from one medium to another the real becomes volatile, it becomes the allegory of death . . . a fetishization of the lost object which is no longer the object of representation, but the ecstasy of the degeneration and its own ritual extermination: the hyperreal.[8]

This description of a receding hall of phantasmal hyper-spectacles sums up what most accounts of early consumerism imply. There have been attempts to counter this deeply pessimistic vision, as in Jennifer Wicke's account of the "work of consumption" that is done, she claims, by women as consumers.[9] Such accounts nevertheless leave the overall conception of consumer culture as a mirage intact. Most of this writing is, in turn, indebted to Marx's totalizing account of commodity fetishism in the opening chapters of *Capital* ("A commodity is a very strange thing, abounding in metaphysical subtleties").[10] However, precisely because these Victorian origins of both consumer culture and the critical apparatus to analyze it focus on the act of consumption as the analogy of the act of looking at a spectacle, they consider it a static behavior, a tragic event where the spectator-consumer is fooled in his obeisance to a static commodity as spectacle. By the early twentieth century, however, new forces were arising to render this model more complex. Symptomatic of such changes was the new car culture.

We have seen that a change in late Victorian Western culture's conception of space was one key cultural shift related to the rise of speed culture for the masses. Nationalism at home and imperialism (or, for the United States, westerly expansion) were dominant ideologies; the dualist spatial ideologeme of home and heterotopia underpinned the representation of space in the West's cultural productions. Perhaps the greatest cultural innovations of the high Victorian era, however, were the wiles, delights, and oppressions that made up popular consumerism. The model of this consumerism developed by the Victorians, based on fetishization and a passive attitude before the spectacle of the commodity, fitted perfectly with the dualist envisioning of space fundamental to the national-imperial cultural imaginary. Both "home versus heterotopia" conceptions of space and "fetish of the commodity" models of consumerism cast the object to be known as essentially static, and the act of knowing as, first, the accurate measurement of the distance between fixed observer and object and, second, its takeover — as colony, as object to be known completely, or as purchased commodity. As Marx put it, in this vein, "Commodities are things, and therefore lack the power to resist man. If they are unwilling, he can use force; in other words, he can take possession of them."[11] This is consumption described by analogy to imperialism. We have seen in the previous chapter how, in the fin de siècle, this dualist system of imagining space broke down, and traced this to the moment of realization that the world was now completely mapped. This breakdown was evidenced in the new anxiety about home in the detective and thriller fiction that burgeoned as new literary (and sub-literary) genres of the period; it gave way to frustration over slowness in modernist literature after Conrad. At this same moment, the masses were being given corresponding kinds of new mass-culture thrills — as in Houdini's escape spectacles, or the roller-coaster fairground ride. Did a similar breakdown take place in relation to the relatively new protocols of consumer desire and consumption? I suggest that it did so. Just as the realization of the possible end of the age of empire diverted cultural imaginings from what was to be found at the end of the voyage (home or heterotopia) to the actual modalities of experience (at speed) of the journey itself, so too the dawn of the new moment of truly mass consumption meant that the static pleasures of gullible fetishization would not suffice as the sine qua non of consumer pleasure. It was not, however, that fetishization as such was superseded; it survives still as the prime consumer behavior. Rather, it now came to coexist alongside a new improvising logic of personal pleasure that was the logical extension of the consumerist imperative. Of this new logic, the car's speed culture was the first and prime example.

The new technology of the automobile, once masses of people became drivers, made such improvisation for personal pleasure inevitable. Spectacle, the image of the fetish that governed the protocol of the original passive consumerism, is a late moment in the history of iconicity. It was with the invention of the camera that the hold of the upper classes on pictoralism — the ability to coin images — was loosened. Spectacle (as it came in the early twentieth century to replace wordiness in advertising) may then be read as the rear-guard action of those in power to reclaim their hold on the image as a way to awe the masses, a power that they had lost with the invention of mass photography. The new speed and independence of the automobile, however, granted a new power — and a new capacity for personal pleasure — and it went into the hands of masses of people almost at once. In this lay its striking potential as a tool to improvise new ways of relating to the world. This speed — this ability to move rapidly and at will with the new technology of the automobile — was among the first of a series of new personal empowerments made possible by major new technologies — mass electrification provided another — to be granted to the masses directly. The car's allure, and the basis for car culture, was twofold: on the one hand, it was the ultimate commodity of the new mass consumerism that was offered to its customers using the full panoply of commodity spectacle under which consumerism operated; on the other, it was wholly new, a commodity that superseded all of Marx's intuitions about how a commodity's mystical character resides in its congealment of the labor power used to produce it, because it engendered in its consumers effects far beyond the usual run of commodity pleasures and suggested to them a range of behaviors, pleasures, and freedoms which they had hardly intuited before. The car was a radically hybrid commodity: its use value, as it turned out, far from being superseded or obscured by its exchange value, rather, complemented it. While still implicating use in its glamour, it made "use" itself into a complex of experiences which the consumer had not known she had desired.

We can see this division mirrored in, for example, the two directions taken in early automobile production: the craftsmanlike building of svelte, luxuriously made cars for the rich, who sat in them merely as passengers, as if the car were a private train, and the soon-streamlined mass-production of rattly, clanking cars for ordinary people, who did drive them, and for whom the experience of driving was to be as bumpy, and as *felt*, as possible. The first tendency led to the Hispano-Souza and the Rolls Royce, the second, to the Citroën, the Morris, and the Ford Model T. It can be seen too in the different attitudes to cars evidenced in texts from highbrow, as opposed to lowbrow, culture: modernist authors, such as Virginia Woolf in *Mrs. Dalloway*, seem nervous of the car and its "pistol-shot" noises, while popular forms, from the funfair to the *Boy's Own* annuals to silent cinema, take to the car enthusiastically as speedy, lively, useful, and often hilarious. In the cinema, the car and the idea of speed were sold to the masses as nonstop excitement; the car's new pleasure, beyond use value, was enthusiastically explored on film. (It was as if, in the movie car chase, even photographed speed could energize the medium representing it.) The early history of car buying emerges as a double narrative: first, with the emphasis on style, luxury, snobbery, and spectacle, the car was advertised as the ultimate commodity; underlying this was a (counter)current, scripted only as it emerged, of the car as speed machine that offered the greatest thrills not in its appearance but in its use. It is this challenging, not-quite-scripted effect, an effect in excess of the pleasure of the commodity form itself, even as the automobile was doing duty as the commodity's supreme example, that can be code-named "adrenaline." We can chart the struggle of this effect to operate despite, or in tandem with, the car's status as static commodity.

Speed Experience versus Consumer Desire: First Steps

Charles Dickens, if he had been born fifty years later, might, with his energetic, dynamic prose, have been the supreme novelist of the motorcar: he was famous as a young writer for composing some of *The Pickwick Papers* while seated in a moving stagecoach, and, at the time of writing *Our Mutual Friend*, was deeply traumatized by his involvement in the Staplehurst railway accident, in which ten people were killed and many injured.[12] By the 1890s, however, the anxiety of much high literary production to distance itself from the rising tide of mass-market railway novels and a litter of commuter writing manifested itself not only in little overt concern for new technologies in such texts but more fundamentally in a textual pace that was itself slow, contemplative, and anything but geared to speed. It is in such works, by Thomas Hardy and Henry James, for example, that when speed is granted an entree, it is analyzed with all the caution and, mostly, disapproval that suggests a fear of what is to come mixed with an awe at its prospects. In high literature of the twentieth century, speed, when it was regarded at all by serious writing, was treated with an almost puritan suspicion.

Prim disapproval riven by fascination, for example, sets the tone of Hardy in an intriguing scene in *Tess of the d'Urbervilles* about the sexual thrills and physical terrors of a racing dogcart. *Tess* was first published in *The Graphic* between July and December 1891, four years before the earliest commercial production of the motorcar, at a time when the speed limits for motorized vehicles on public roads in Britain was, under the 1865 Red Flag Act, still four miles per hour. (Moreover, a person carrying a red flag was supposed to walk before the vehicle. This rule was dropped, and the limit increased to fourteen miles an hour, by the Locomotives and Highways Act of 1896.) In chapter 7 of "The Maiden," the novel's first section, Hardy describes how the teenage and gullible Tess tries not to be frightened by the cad Alec d'Urberville, who drives her downhill at full speed in his dogcart. It is a passage that already, in 1891, contains all the elements of desire, fear, power-playing, and the relation of speed and sexuality that are at work in Robert Frank's photo of the lovers in Dodgem car bliss sixty years later. What for Frank's lovers in the photo is excitement at the use of speed was cast by Hardy as terror tactic in a vile seduction. The speed fiend (Alec) is a corrupt villain; the refusal of the thrill of speed by the lowly heroine (Tess) symbolizes the self-preservation of her sexual innocence. In a chorus of disapproval that would follow the automobile from its earliest days, speed, in advance, stood for a caddish masculinity, its refusal for demure innocence.

Nevertheless Hardy gives us a superb account of the feeling of speed (surely at more than four miles per hour) that whips up its own erotics of the force of nature and the joy of lack of control:

> Down, down, they sped, the wheels humming like a top, the dog-cart rocking right and left, its axis acquiring a slightly oblique set in relation to the line of progress; the figure of the horse rising and falling in undulations before them. Sometimes a wheel was off the ground, it seemed, for many yards; sometimes a stone was sent spinning over the hedge, and flinty sparks from the horse's hooves outshone the daylight. The fore part of the straight road enlarged with their advance, the two banks dividing like a splitting stick; and one rushed past at each shoulder.[13]

The poetic onomatopoeia of the "s" sounds and the taut countering of abstractions ("axis," "oblique set," "advance") and similes ("like a top," "like a split stick") are not just Hardy's mimeticism-searching impressionism in action; they focus in a brilliant amalgam the basics of a speed discourse *avant la lettre*. Boosters of car driving from Filson Young, author of *The Complete Motorist* (1904), to Henry Ford in his memoirs, as well as reporters writing of the Gordon Bennett Cup, and masses of writers for automobile advertisements, would be recycling such strategies of telling speed's thrills until they seemed very tired indeed in the coming decades. More telling, however, is the narrative which surrounds this evocation. Alec, male driver, wishes to race downhill ("There's nothing like it for raising your spirits"), but Tess is frightened; at the next hill, he promises to slow down if she allows him to kiss her. She veers aside, he threatens to go faster, and she allows him "The kiss of mastery" (56). Her hat flies off, she climbs down to retrieve it and then refuses to remount; in this style, Tess walking, Alec driving slowly, they go the six miles to his mother's house. In this set piece, Hardy presents the use of speed by a male as a means to sexual conquest, the gaining of what he calls sexual mastery. Speed is a weapon of the nouveau riche male seducer; refusing it, Tess, still the pure woman, holds on to her innocence.

Hardy's evocation of speed betrays an interest in its energy and its force as an experience, but speeding is not merely cast as dangerous in itself; it is a torture inflicted by the man upon the woman, the corrupted upon the innocent. Speed here stands for callous male sexual predatoriness, and its pleasures remain for this text unavailable within a puritan moral order. It is shown as a weapon of the rich driver; the account serves as a warning to the poor passenger, to the laboring classes, to beware of it. Consider the ecstasy of the presumably working-class couple in Frank's photograph sixty years later, bent on enjoying the limited speed thrill of the Dodgem car: the warning implied in Hardy's moralistic vignette was to be ignored or reversed. His canny association of speed and sexuality nevertheless foreshadows what was to become a staple of antispeed discourse, as well as a huge advertisement enticing people to car culture, in the coming century. Hardy is one of the last authors to write about speed before the advent of car technology. He writes before the car became a commodity, and his focus is almost wholly on speed itself, not on the vehicle. Once cars began to be produced, however, the concerns articulated in Hardy's speed scene were exacerbated, caricatured, and debated. Speed and sexuality—as a new subdiscourse of speed and power—were to be thoroughly related. This sexuality at speed could be sold as part of the allure of the car commodity; it could also appear in new versions as part of the experience of speed which might exceed commodity fetishism.

The car's fetish qualities, inevitably, inhered in the car as object. In the first thirty years of car production, it was the curve—of a hood, a fender, a roofline—that became established as the mark of the car as luxury consumer good. The curved car body subsequently came to signify aerodynamics; first, as it was expensive to curve metal and wood, it meant *luxe*. From the first, the making of cars involved not only the construction of a machine but the arrangement of a narrow and (after engines became powerful enough to carry a closed car) enclosed space. The car's space in twentieth-century culture often managed to eclipse and counter the home as site of sexuality, privacy, family gathering, and scene of generational changes. In the same way, the closed car in a real sense became the site of innovation of the most modern steel-and-glass architecture. In the earliest years (1890–1900), while innovations in the engine were still paramount— the modern carburetor, for example, was invented in 1893 by Wilhelm Maybach, the assistant to Gottlieb Daimler[14]—the techno-architecture of the earliest vehicles was awkwardly retrospective: these machines borrowed their contours from the horse-drawn carriage, and their spindly metallic look from the recently popularized bicycle. (One can read these tendencies even in the rich man's car photographed by Lartigue in 1911 [figure 7].) These early efforts used a wooden frame, the legacy of coach building, which continued even with the early Model Ts; this was only superseded when it was found that mass-produced welded metal frames were faster to construct. This frame was complemented with a mass of metal spokes,

FIGURE 7. Jacques-Henri Lartigue, *The Marquis de Soriano in a Gregoire Automobile in the Bois de Boulogne*, 1911. Gelatin silver print, 12 × 16 in. Courtesy of Friends of J.-H. Lartigue, Paris.

handles, engine parts, rails, and steering stick. Through this early arrangement of steel, iron, and glass, early cars conveyed a sense of practicality in mechanic plainness—as in the first Daimler car, of 1886, for example. As production boomed, however—in France there were 300 cars in 1896, 4,800 in 1900, and 16,900 in 1904, the first year in which the United States surpassed France in the number of cars built[15]—two types of car production emerged, one aimed at a small, exclusive market, and the other marked by mass-market plans. It was on the new luxury marques, individually built with bodies molded in the coach-building tradition, that the curved metal of the outer skin became the key sign of careful, expensive worker-hours and the lavished attention of skilled artisans. At first, these curves were made by bending parts of the wood frame, a time-consuming process; next, they were made of beaten metal, which involved skilled craftsmen working slowly on an expensive product.

It was only in the thirties that this new glamour-imbued, luxe-laden curve became a feature of built architecture, particularly in seaside and leisure buildings in the style that came to be known as "streamline moderne." By then, car architecture had become an inspiration for a new curvature which builders in concrete could copy. This curvature of the metal shell of the car was associated with increased comfort within. Its finest moment in the earliest stage of luxury car building came with a style known as the Roi de Belge. Also christened the "tulip phaeton," this was associated with the innovation of mounting side doors in front of the rear wheels, in cars with engines powerful enough to carry passengers in a commodious back seat. When the king of Belgium, it was said,[16] complained to the coach builder that the rear seat was too small for his bulk, his mistress Mlle. de Merode proposed a solution: place two large stuffed armchairs side by side there. To accommodate them, the car was given wide, bulbous sides and a rear of double-reversed curves in the shape of a tulip. The bulbous upholstery within was matched by a curvaceous bulbousness without. This became the much-copied style in luxury marques on two continents. In the Roi de Belge, the man who, as proprietor of the Congo, presented Conrad with the raw material for expressing the frustrations of slowness in his treatise-novella, also contributed to the fetish quality of the new technology that rendered the experience of speed luxurious.

The curve, then, which might seem at first suggestive of speed's smoothness, originally represented well-padded luxury as a complement to smooth and soothing technology. It was a new design signifier—with roots in art deco—and was the avatar of, and was probably suggested partly by, some sense of speed's aerodynamism as well. The swoosh of the car through the air meant that one saw it as meteoric—as a point trailing a tail—and this sense of flow the designers incorporated in car bodies with their gently undulating or furiously flowing curves. Already in the Vanderbilt Cup era, cars meant for racing were being built with the low, streamlined look of modern race cars; the Stanley Steamer in which Fred Marriott reached 127 miles per hour in 1906 at Daytona Beach was low, wedge shaped, and little higher than its wheels.[17] The luxury marques paraded their owners' wealth with excess baggage space, which was accommodated beneath the curves; Gatsby's cream-colored Rolls Royce in Fitzgerald's *The Great Gatsby*, for example, was "bright as a nickel, swollen here and there in its monstrous length with triumphant hat-boxes and supper-boxes and tool-boxes, and terraced with a labyrinth of windshields that mirrored a dozen suns."[18]

Companies known for mass-producing earlier machine commodities as luxury accessories for bourgeois households become involved in car making, suggesting the sense of the car as luxury commodity prevalent at the time: the Steinway Piano Company, for example, had bought the rights to manufacture Daimler engines as early as 1890, although the company never built cars.[19] That the owners of these cars were invariably rich gave the machines — which flaunted their owners' wealth — cachet: William K. Vanderbilt, for example, was reported to have a hundred-car garage filled with the world's most expensive makes at his Long Island villa, and in 1905, long before five dollars a day was considered a princely wage by a Ford worker on the newly operational assembly line, the most glamorous marques each commanded about $7,500.[20] As these rich buyers came from the leisure class, cars were from the first associated with leisure, with "touring," and with the habits of fashionable "resort" living (the Côte d'Azur, Newport, Long Island, Deauville) richly documented in the novels of Fitzgerald, most of which describe any number of cars, usually as signifiers of their owners' capacity for luxury and conspicuous consumption. This cachet was enhanced and stoked by early automobile shows (one of the first held in the United States, in Madison Square Garden in 1903, attracted the Rockefellers, Vanderbilts, and Astors) and the new habit of parading in one's car on the esplanade or parkway as a new version of the Victorian drive; *Automobile Topics* in 1901 spoke of how "in Atlantic City the automobile parade on the Pacific Avenue Driveway is becoming a daily feature of society."[21] This version of haute car culture was taken up in the earliest representations of cars in film. In one of the very first films, spectators had leaped from their seats at the sight of a speeding train careening toward them; the first cars in film were instead presented demurely as a procession of enviable consumer commodities. *Automobile Parade*, an Edison film of 1900, simply features a series of about ten different car makes as they parade by the camera, which itself is static. With a unique design centered on aerodynamic and luxury-signifying curves, the custom car for the wealthy customer, increasingly longer, wider, and lower in the first decades of the twentieth century, presented itself as the newest, most up-to-date, and most luxurious and ostentatious commodity of all. Underlying this commodity ostentation, nevertheless, was a fascination with the car's new kind of power: independent speed.

The possibilities of speed were illustrated obliquely in the aerodynamics of the car's appearance: they were evoked directly in the discourses about drivers, races, endurance, and "spills" that also fascinated the largely non-motoring public in this period. The very clothing deemed necessary in the first open cars—the panoply of goggles, veils, heavy leather or rubber coats, scarves, and gloves (the dancer Isadora Duncan would be killed, gruesomely, when the trailing scarf she wore got caught in the spokes of the taxi in which she was being driven in the south of France in 1927)[22]—all evoked a culture of the outdoors, of facing the elements, and of intrepid adventure. (The car could be enlisted on the side of public health: early debates on automobile use even included newspaper speculation that the car would "clean up" the city, where horse droppings had been a public health issue.) The association of the car as speed machine to adventure was fostered from the first by automobile races, often held over long distances and across national borders. The first such race, organized by the Count de Dion, soon to emerge as a famous car manufacturer, was run from Paris to Bordeaux and back, a distance of 732 miles; the fastest car in the race, driven by another manufacturer, Emile Levassor, covered the course in forty-eight hours and forty-eight minutes, averaging fifteen miles per hour without a single breakdown. Fifteen gasoline-engine cars, six steam cars, and one electric car entered the race; only eight gasoline- and one steam-engine car managed to finish. As Levassor's car was a two-seater and the rules had stipulated that the first four-seater would be the victor, the winner was a Peugeot driven by Koechlin.[23] These dangerous city-to-city runs culminated in the Paris–Madrid race of 1903, when so many accidents occurred, including one in which one of the Renault brothers was killed, that the race was stopped in Bordeaux, where police impounded the cars and they were dragged to the railway station by horses.

Drivers in these races, accompanied by mechanics, roared along dirt roads—in the Paris-Madrid, the winner had covered 342 miles at 65.3 miles per hour—with only rudimentary brakes: burst tires, breakdowns, and crashes were common. The 1903 experience did not stop the most thrilling and global contest of all, the 1908 New York-Paris race from Times Square to the Champs-Élysées via Vladivostok and Manchuria, won by an American car, the Thomas Flyer. Only three cars finished that race. New speed records were always newsworthy. The 100-kilometer-per-hour barrier was overcome by the Belgian Camille Jenatzy, who reached 105.87 kilometers per hour on April 29, 1899, at the Circuit d'Archere, in an electric car named *La Jamais Contente*;[24] seven years later Marriott's *Rocket* broke the 200-

kilometer-per-hour barrier (127.7 mph).[25] By 1939 John Cobb had achieved an average speed of 368.9 miles per hour at the Bonneville Salt Flats in Utah in the superstreamlined *Railton*.

These contests on the open road were the automobile world's version of the fascination with sports contests in the new era of mass leisure and of sport as mass spectacle. They were also renovated versions of the tales of heroic adventure of the Victorian fin de siècle, presenting intrepid drivers on dangerous courses rather than explorers in the African jungles. The New York newspaper whose best-known sponsorship in the nineteenth century was sending H. M. Stanley to Africa in his hugely publicized search for the "lost" missionary David Livingstone, was, in the new century, the sponsor of the most famous international motor race, the Gordon Bennett Cup. The *New York Times* and *Le Matin* sponsored the New York–Paris race of 1908. Newspaper interest ensured that these races became transatlantic sensations, reported in papers and featured as filmed newsreel attractions in the thriving new medium of the cinema. A surviving short titled *Race for the Vanderbilt Cup* of 1904, for example, displays a panoply of race cars and their drivers from all the contesting nations photographed from a range of camera positions. From the first, cars meant the toughest and most danger-ous—and exciting—of adventure sports; in these races, where counts and mechanics sat side by side representing their nations, at least the possibility of novel class alliances was suggested. Directed to a mass audience, this implied that each of its members might have access to this dream of mad adventure at speed.

Reading of these early automobile racers' exploits, one is struck by a new set of almost invariably male class allegiances that were forged in bringing the first cars onto the public roads and into the public eye: a mixture of often nouveau riche businessmen, arriviste aristocrats with money (de Dion), earnest engineers and the heads of factories (Daimler), along with assorted bicycle mechanics, amateur inventors, and hangers-on, who, through shift-ing deals, lawsuits, concessions, patents, and claims, as well as the mass publicity generated by the cross-nation races, managed to transform the car from a novel invention into a mass-produced commodity. This milieu is summed up cynically by none other than James Joyce in his story "After the Race," written after Joyce had been a reporter for the Gordon Bennett Cup. This race had to be held in Ireland in 1903, as the speed limit in Eng-land of fourteen miles per hour was too constraining.[26] (The race was won by Camille Djinnis in a Mercedes 60.) Joyce's sketch of the socially inept young Irishman Doyle contrasts him cruelly with the continental members of the "motoring circles" Doyle had encountered during a year in Cambridge. These include drivers in the race who see their business futures in cars:

> Segouin was in a good humour because he had unexpectedly received some orders in advance (he was about to start a motor establishment in Paris) and Riviere was in good humor because he was about to be appointed manager of the establishment.[27]

To represent the world of this new class of technician businessmen and sportsmen, Joyce—contemptuously—employs the kind of imagery that had been employed by his compatriot George Moore in his naturalistic depictions of horse-racing and betting circles in novels such as *Esther Waters*. Joyce, however, reserves his greatest contempt for the proletarian spectators who line the final miles of the route: these viewers of speed, enthusing by the roadside along which "the Continent sped its wealth and industry . . . Now and again . . . raised the cheer of the gratefully oppressed" (42). Doyle, as the go-between who is out of place amid both watchers and the racers, humiliates himself when, later that evening, he loses his money to the racers at cards. Joyce's story was first published in December 1904;[28] it was finally published in book form in *Dubliners* in 1916, when its author was long resident in Trieste. Unlike the Futurists writing in Italy in and after 1909, Joyce shows no interest in the speed of the cars as such; rather, this is a tale of class resentments, in which the spectacle of the terrific new speeds acts merely to exacerbate the sense of anger the narrator feels watching the foolish enthusiasm of the oppressed poor. Nevertheless there is an implied if muted respect here for that group of racer businessmen as a new international class to whose brand of hard-bitten glamour neither the spectators nor the hapless Doyle can aspire.

The rumblings of class resentment at these spectacles, first of the rich parading in the ostentatious symbols of their money, and then of rich adventurers, along with their humbler mechanics, racing each other on public roads, were choreographed by the new mass-circulation newspapers as an interplay of Luddite caution and whetted desire. An outcry about the dangers of the road races, especially in custom-built racers such as the Mercedes 60, which won the Gordon Bennett Cup in 1903, led to the discrediting of the long endurance races and the rise of Grand Prix racing over more restricted courses (Le Mans in France, Daytona in the United States) after

1906. Soon these were being raced in lower horsepower and much smaller "voiturettes," paving the way for modern car races on specially built tracks. Brooklands racetrack in Britain, with its extraordinary gradients suggesting the necessity for the curve in new roads as well as in car design itself, opened in 1907; the first Indianapolis 500 was held in 1911. Rich speeders in modern cities caused outcries, especially when they caused accidents and hit pedestrians: Mrs. Bridget Driscoll, crossing the street, was the first recorded fatality, hit by a car at Crystal Palace in South London in August 1896.[29] *The Horseless Age*, the first U.S. auto periodical, reported in summer 1904 that cars driving through working-class neighborhoods were so harassed by stone throwing that the drivers demanded police protection. Such incidents famously led President Woodrow Wilson to declare that the invention of the automobile was the greatest incitement of the poor to socialism, so great would be their envy of the cars of the rich.

The spectacle of speed — and the prospect of actually experiencing it — was, however, also held out to mass audiences. W. K. Vanderbilt himself enjoyed racing his red automobile through the streets of New York, with the police (for he broke the speed limit) in futile pursuit: such exploits by rich drivers were the origins of one of the most characteristic twentieth-century narratives, the car chase. A sensational automobile run in the United States in 1899, from Cleveland to New York in a journey that took forty-eight hours, was watched by almost a million spectators: it has been credited with introducing the automobile as a commodity purchasable by the public to U.S. consumers.[30] The Vanderbilt Cup, filmed in its inaugural run in 1904, attracted half a million spectators in 1906; it became such a popular feature of the years before World War I that it was the basis for a Broadway musical *The Vanderbilt Cup Race*, in which the champion driver Barney Oldfield drove a Peerless Green Dragon onstage.[31] While such spectacles of mechanical endurance were presumed to enthrall the masses — as in the crossing of the American continent by a Vermont physician, D. H. Nelson Jackson, and his chauffeur, Sewall K. Croker, in sixty-three days in 1903 — the cinema continued to stoke its audiences' interest in the experience of riding in automobiles. In the "Tim Hurst Tours," for example, the audience sat in a theater that resembled the interior of a touring car and watched films that had been photographed from a real car window along the great streets of the world's cities.[32] Class resentments about the ostentatious display of wealth by the rich in their access to speed were drowned by popular discourses and streams of images harnessing people's fascination not just with flashy commodities but more with their power to cover distances at terrific and enduring speeds. Woodrow Wilson could claim that the spectacle of idle rich "automobilists" spread socialism; the popular media, in retort, fed the popular fascination with speed. More, they lured with the dream that driving would soon be within everyone's reach.

While these opulent, superelegant cars for the rich paraded their aura of the most desirable of new commodities, as well as their role as engines for new experiences of endurance and speed, makers were also imagining more lowly — and enjoyable — cars for the people. Already in 1895 the French automobile manufacturer de Dion-Bouton had attached a 2.75 horsepower, forty-pound engine to a tricycle: fifteen thousand of these were sold in the following five years, even at a price (3,900 francs) that was about double the average annual wage in the United States at that time. These engines were used by companies such as Renault in France, Humber in England, Opel in Germany, and Packard in the United States;[33] the "bicycle boom" soon turned into the motor boom, and bicycle manufacturers such as Harry T. Lawson in Britain rushed into car production. But it was in the U.S. Midwest that forms of mass production enjoyed vast successes: Ransom Olds with the curved-dash Oldsmobile of 1901 (650 cars sold for $650 dollars each that year) was swiftly followed by Cadillac, Buick (the "Nifty," Model 10), and then Ford's Model N.[34] Between 1900 and 1908, 485 companies began manufacturing cars in the United States. Then, in October 1908, Henry Ford made the car a real mass-consumable commodity when he introduced the Model T. Two years and three months to the day later, the opening of the Highland Park assembly line matched mass production to mass consumption. In 1908 the Model T cost $825 for the "Runabout," $850 for the "Touring Car"; in 1912 the Runabout, offered at $575, first dropped below the average annual wage in the United States. By 1916 the Runabout cost $343, and the touring car $360. As America entered World War I, Ford was building three-quarters of a million cars a year; by 1927, when production ceased, sales not only in the United States but all over the world, particularly in Europe and throughout the British Commonwealth, exceeded fifteen million. By then, the coupe sold for $290. In 1906, 1,708 cars were sold in the United States, by 1929, there were over twenty million cars on the roads of America.[35] Mass motorization, beginning in the United States in the pre–World War I years and catching up in Europe in the twenties and thirties with the Morris Oxford (1913) and the Austin Seven (1922) in Britain, the Peugeot Bébé (1912) designed by an avant-garde painter turned car designer, Ettore Bugatti, in France, and Hitler's notorious call, in 1934, for the mass motorization of Germany with the Volkswagen, was well in place before World War II.

The design of these cheaper mass-market cars focused much more on the experience of driving, and on the effort demanded of the driver, than on the outward appearance of the car as a consumer commodity. The Model T, for example, was lighter and tougher than luxury cars partly because it used new vanadium steel, pioneered in French racing cars: the turn to what car advertisers termed "performance," and away from the beauty of the commodity object, meant that the appeal to the buyers centered on the power of the engine, the speeds the car could attain, and its durability in attaining them. The Model T had a new three-point motor suspension, improved arc springs, enclosed transmission, and a detachable cylinder head. It had four cylinders, twenty horsepower, a hundred-inch wheelbase, and weighed 1,200 pounds; its ratio of weight to power was much better than any predecessor, and with its high-bore engine, it was a flexible negotiator of bad roads and gradients, required less gear shifting, could take much abuse, and was relatively easy to repair.[36] At the same time, it was relatively noisy, clanking and rattling: one joke had it that "when my Ford is running at 5 mph, the fender rattles, twelve miles an hour my teeth rattle, and 15 mph the transmission drops out."[37] This resulted from the not overly neat joinings and rivetings of the many metal pieces, as well as from engine noise; drumming on the potholed roads, the Model T sounded as tinny as it appeared. In further contrast to the richly varnished colors of the luxury cars, in a final cost-cutting measure, all the early Model T cars were coated in black enamel. (One of the more famous observations attributed to Ford: "Any customer can have a car painted any color he wants as long as it is black.")[38] Commodity aesthetics were forgone in this, the grandest commodity, in favor of savings, and the focus was kept firmly on the driving experience itself.

Or rather, what the first mass-produced cars represent is an ultramodern — and ultramodernist — phenomenon: perhaps for the first time (following the bicycle, here as in other ways a harbinger) the deployment of machine aesthetics in a consumer commodity. This car would be a machine for "experiencing in," as opposed to merely living in, and form would resolutely follow function, even if this entailed exposed machine parts, openly visible metal seams, a perceived awkwardness in the overall proportions, and a sacrifice of comfort to performance. Some historians of the early days of motor production, such as David Gartman, are apt to criticize the Model T and its ilk as ugly: "a drab dreary machine devoid of decoration to relieve the monotonous expanses of metal . . . [on which] the high flat roof with straight pillars make[s] the car look particularly clumsy."[39] He sees this ugliness as the all-too-visible evidence of the dehumanizing work on the assembly lines that produced such cars, where "detail workers" made or assembled separate parts of the machine without any vision of the whole. Such judgments are dubious, however, because the aesthetic standards to which they appeal are those of the curving lines of the vastly more expensive custom-made cars. Cars such as the Model T were cheap; they were common; but their disjointed, loose-limbed, spindly, or stubby appearance was a glorification of the object's status as truly popular machine.

In the 1914 Model T Touring, for example, this machine quality is expressed in features such as the uncompromising height of the mudguards above the wheel, the length of the steering stick, the exposed suspension beneath the engine, and the ostentatiously stark arrangement of the four unwieldy lamps jutting out from the bonnet. Such motorcar designs represent a key moment in twentieth-century machine aesthetics, which would see its flowering in the steel-and-glass architecture of the sixties and seventies that flaunted its mechanical innards. In the first year of World War I, such goggle-eyed, metal-rod design, a crisscross of metal parts, bespoke the buyer-owner's decision to engage this new machine in an act of hard driving at speed. The owner could glory in the toughness of the machine and the difficulties of managing it. The Model T would most commonly be referred to as a workhorse, with jokes about the Tin Lizzies' clanks, noises, and limited powers. The aura that developed about this particular commodity, then, was one that stressed how luxury had been forgone in favor of hard work, contact with an actual machine, and exposure to a real experience of driving. (Some of the luxury cars were driven by their owners, but their prestige lay with remoteness from any driving experience — that was left to the chauffeur.) This car had to be driven hard, and it was not comfortable: an ethos of rugged contact with real experience by means of the machine underpinned the first mass-market cars sold to the consuming public. The public proved thoroughly susceptible to this message: Ford's commercial empire, and the industries associated with it, such as oil and rubber, enjoyed such phenomenal growth in these years that they enabled the United States to become the dominant commercial power in the world. The automobile, it has been claimed, not only made America mobile but also powered the industrial expansion that made the United States the world's prime industrial power.[40]

The cheaper cars' underdog machine aesthetics, then, corresponded to the disjointed nature of their assembly line production, but they also represented the purchaser's decision to counter the pallid monotony of his or her work life on such assembly lines with a vivid, visceral experience of driving a hard-biting machine. The machines in the factory could enslave you; these commodity machines, on the contrary, held in their stark machine quality the possibility, it was suggested, of making you free. In Henry Ford's argumentative biography *My Life and Work*, published as early as 1910, he speaks knowingly of "the terror of the machine"; he is referring, however, not to the cars his workers made but to the arguments, which he attempts to counter, that repetitive work on his assembly lines producing those cars is demeaning, dulling, and counter to the desires of any reasonable worker. Take Ford's catalog of the potentially dulling features of assembly line work; imagine their opposites; a list of the pleasures of driving is what emerges. Ford insists:

> The average worker, I'm sorry to say, wants a job to which he doesn't have to put forth much physical exertion—above all he wants a job in which he does not have to think. . . . I have not been able to discover that repetitive labor injures a man in any way. I have been told by parlor experts that repetitive labor is soul as well as body-destroying, but this has not been the result of our investigations.[41]

The car driver—and Ford is quoted as expressing wonder at the idea that "our very own workers will buy automobiles from us"[42]—appeared to want from driving the opposite qualities to those Ford describes in the earlier quote: an experience in which the worker was prepared to exert himself forcefully, where he was called to make constant snap decisions about everything from braking to changing gears, where alertness was constantly demanded, in view of the ever-changing road conditions, obstacles, traffic, weather, and other drivers. There is repetition in driving, but it is always repetition with a difference: every time the driver accelerates, it is a slightly different experience. Decisions about acceleration, braking, speed, and direction are all made the responsibility of the driver. Driving at speed, then, becomes an experience opposite to that of work in the Fordist factory. Ford himself is only occasionally good at describing this experience of driving; more often he speaks sunnily of the car's benefit of allowing families to enjoy the leisure of a country picnic. Yet the way in which his list of the possible drawbacks of the monotony of assembly work — which he defends — uncannily reverses precisely those pleasures which the purchasers of his cars seemed to seek opens this possibility: these buyers were seeking, through driving, precisely to reverse the monotony of their Fordist working lives.

It is just such a concept of "therapeutic leisure" that is advanced by materialist historians to account for the rise of "leisure industries" in this period. This notion, in a manner different from standard accounts of consumerism and commodity fetishism, attributes to the worker-consumer and leisure pursuer a modicum of autonomous will: the increasingly put-upon worker seizes upon country drives, team sports, and hobbies to salve mind and body abstracted by the Fordist workplace. Note, however, that it is a poor kind of autonomy: in this schema self-directed action is permissible if the subject is deemed to be making up for a lack which only the theorist truly perceives. If the worker subject fully understood his position, the implication runs, then he would surely relinquish the dehumanizing work itself rather than attempt to compensate for it in restorative leisure. In this account, the modern worker is engaged in a desperate to-and-fro struggle with the capitalist machines: dehumanized by them each weekday at work, he counters their ill effects by driving off in the leisure machine, the motorcar, on "free" weekends. The early boosters of mass car sales, notably celebrity bosses such as Ford himself, and the rabid new industry of car advertising, the auto magazines, and even a mass of new travel accounts happily touting "motor-tours" — Edith Wharton's *A Motor-Flight through France* (1909), condensed like many such books from an earlier series of magazine articles, is a good early example — all employed versions of this logic. In various tonalities, it became their guiding rhetoric and the organizing trope of their wonder narratives about the motorcar. For workers as drivers, as the Lynds' research in Muncie, Indiana, for example, showed, the association of car and "Sunday outing" was important to their sense of automobile ownership. (This same ritual would become a staple of petit-bourgeois everyday life in Europe after World War II, to be bitterly satirized in Godard's crash-and-burn film of 1972, *Weekend*, and even more comprehensively in Jacques Tati's madcap *Traffic*. In *Traffic*, mechanics on a weekend outing to an auto show cannot get service at roadside garages because everyone is watching on television the bobbing car of the ultimate twentieth-century Sunday picnic outing, the first landing on the moon.)

The notion of therapeutic leisure, while valid, accounts for only part of the attraction and aura of the car for the ordinary purchaser, just as the glamour of the car as rich person's consumer commodity par excellence does not quite account for it either. What this rattling, hard-driving car offers is an intensive experience of driving. Offering a new and intense experience, the car was the most important example of a series of commodities (the bicycle had led the way) which sold themselves as a means of escape both from the facile pleasures of mindless work in factory or office, performed for others, and from cheap consumption of products made en masse. This was not just therapeutic or compensatory but a search for action, for new experiences. Machines as commodities—Singer sewing machines, Steinway pianos, Raleigh bicycles, Ford cars—twisted the standard consumerist imperative because the commodity promised that commodification would be overcome. No wonder that, intuiting the value in this commodity machine, architects such as Le Corbusier soon valorized the machine as the means for recovering social values and beauty itself. This intuition also underpins the hyperbolic manifestoes of the Futurists in their boosterism of kinesis and the modern machinery that propels it.

What the car and its forerunner, the bicycle, achieved, in the era of consumerist simulation and monotonous work, was to make velocity, in itself a form of unproductive expenditure, the sign of a life lived more intensely. Henry Ford's assembly line had been set up precisely to produce cars *faster*: this kind of speed reduced costs, made more cars in the same amount of time, and thereby made for bigger profits. This assembly line speed, its proponents preached, was achieved by bringing machines to the aid of workers; the workers were merely organized more efficiently in conjunction with the welding, panel-beating, and paint-spraying machines, so that they themselves did not necessarily each have to work faster. Ford himself is keen to stress that for many of his workers, "no muscular energy is required."[43] Car driving did not require much muscular energy either, but it required constant mental and even emotional alertness and nervous expenditure. Such expenditure was best savored when it was in excess of any social need. True, doctors and then farmers were among the first groups to buy mass-produced cars in the U.S. Midwest: doctors to go on their rounds, farmers to travel to market towns. Commuting from the suburbs to work, which the car, after the tramways, made possible, soon became the principal journey of most drivers. Nevertheless the pleasure offered by the car in driving went beyond its use value, into the realm of privately and intensely experienced surges of energy and alertness that were absolutely excessive of any social need. The power to speed along the highway, in any direction one chooses, is a limited one, but it offered the opportunity for a time at least to escape the shallow pleasures of buying commodities and the dreariness of working under orders. In other words, in increasingly controlled lives, it presented technology as the agent of excess.

Further, this seizing of a limited opportunity to engage in excessive private behavior (with public consequences) was not planned by the first car builders—in the way, for example, as has been claimed more recently, that car designers arrange for the machine's "planned obsolescence"—but rather was an expression of a need which seized upon the automobile once it was offered for sale, and to which sellers of the car soon catered. That the pleasure of driving at speed was formulated by the drivers themselves, that it was articulated *from below* rather than foisted via advertising or propaganda from above, is shown by the almost uncanny way in which comedy was associated with popular accounts of driving from the beginning. We saw the laughter in the eyes of the woman in the Dodgem car in Frank's photograph: this approach to driving and speeding has always characterized popular versions. The Model T, dubbed the Tin Lizzie, was the butt of countless jokes about its rough-and-tumble dependability, jokes which made it all the more beloved. Such popular, easy comedy itself hints at this object's significance as somehow excessive. As we saw earlier, many of the earliest popular experiences of technologized speed, such as the Coney Island roller coasters, had occurred in the comic, excessive, and proletarian carnival of the funfair. The funfair, the working masses' version of earlier holiday carnivals, gradually became focused on rides and speed as the nineteenth century progressed. Starting with the revolving carousel in the 1860s, the spectacles, such as freak shows, and the tests of skill, such as rifle ranges, were gradually marginalized in favor of rides that culminated in the roller coaster and the Dodgem car. The origin of the mass delight in speed at the funfair also hints that the popular use of speed would relate to its possibilities for excess. Having begun in a jokey, carousing atmosphere of holiday, the speed experience would keep a residue of the comedy in its origins.

Nowhere was the comedy at the heart of speed's thrill more enthusiastically celebrated, drawn out as spectacle, and teased into farcical narratives than in the new invention that came to replace the funfair as popular entertainment in the era of consumerist simulation and became wildly popular at the same moment as the motorcar: the movies. Early movies were obsessed with cars: see early film reel vignettes such as the parade of rich cars in 1905, or the newsreels of the Vanderbilt Cup races from 1904 onward. So many early movies not only focus on cars but make speeding cars the basis of their plot changes and linger on scenes of speed as thrilling in itself that it is as if film as a form from the first intuited a connection to automobile travel. In the spatial logistics of the movies, a seated, stationary viewer watches a moving kinetic image; in the logic of driving, a seated, moving driver watches an apparently moving, but actually still, scene; this correspondence meant that early movies became for their audiences an education in the logics of driving, even as they whetted desire for the automobile by explicitly focusing on its pleasures. There are specific correspondences between the form of the medium of film, in the way in which its symbiosis of technology and representation is received by the viewer, and the union of technology and human skill as it is monitored by the driver driving an automobile. Teasing out these correspondences, we can elaborate a taxonomy of the kinds of perception and excitement offered secondhand by watching a film and firsthand by driving a car. I will do this in a moment, examining the kind of early caper film in which the car itself as a glorious machine is featured very much as the star—the fetishized object as kinetic force. First, however, I want to explore how the thrill of driving, and the presence of the motorcar, came to be represented in some of the writing of the period, and how, here too, its presence came to have a profound effect on how writers wrote.

Driving Texts

Film became the dominant narrative medium of the period when the car went from technological breakthrough to mass commodity; fiction slid in importance as a social discourse. It was in two of the fiction genres—first, appropriately, in children's literature, and then, in a mode fast becoming minor because of its limited readership, high or serious fiction—that the car intruded most forcibly. An immensely popular novel for children in the style of Lewis Carroll's *Alice's Adventures in Wonderland*, Kenneth Grahame's *The Wind in the Willows* (1908) features a plot that turns on the character Mr. Toad's obsession with the newly invented motorcar; Toad is addicted to the experience of driving. Such unabashed enthusiasm for cars, comically yet enthusiastically described, was countered by "serious" fiction, where a reticence to come to terms with the new speed technology was evident. As late as 1925, we find Virginia Woolf in *Mrs. Dalloway* singing the swan song of that mainstay of high modernist urban fiction, the flâneur, a resolute pedestrian in the "walking city." In the image of the ominously closed, possibly royal car that haunts the opening of Woolf's novel, she presents us with the intrusion of the forbidding new machine in all its alienating terror.

Car speeds had been invading and altering literary form in texts by the most serious authors for some time, even if they first showed themselves in ephemeral, occasional pieces. Beginning with a reading of Edith Wharton's *A Motor-Flight through France* (1909), one can see how instant views, a succession of scenes, and a generally speeded-up perception render a travel account that, in its fragmentary, scene-upon-scene character, relays to the reader the variety and the thrill of this new kind of "motor tourism." In *The Wind in the Willows* one long section, which transmits the enthusiasm for automobile speed in the early years of the twentieth century, matches car and "character": automobilism could literally drive one insane. In *Mrs. Dalloway*, the car, technology as phantom, ominously shadows the flâneuse on the London streets. It forces the novel's reappraisal of the flâneur narrative — the tale strung out as an account of an urban promenade — that had been a staple of modernist literature. It is in the unlikely purlieu of Wharton's protomodernist travel narrative, nevertheless — first published serially in the same year as Grahame's tale for children — that the effect of automobile speed radically invades and begins to transform the very weft of fictional discourse: the accelerated and haphazard new rhythms of observation made possible by the car tour, the surprises, snatched visions and unexpected detours that car tourism offers, make for a fragmented, scattered, even rushed quality in Wharton's narrative. In the coming years, this kind of kinetic prose would be reformulated in further modernist narratives not consciously concerned with travel or technology, at times speeding up the rhythms of modernism.

Grahame's novel is a significant moment in the arrival of speed technology into literature because it shows how a character could be converted to motorcar speed merely by observing it. Early in the novel comes what is perhaps the most brilliant description there exists of the excitement of people on first seeing a speeding car:

Far behind them they heard a faint warning hum, like the drone of a distant bee. Glancing back, they saw a small cloud of dust, with a dark center of energy, advancing at them at incredible speed, while from out of the dust a faint "Poop-poop!" wailed like an uneasy animal in pain. Hardly regarding it, they turned to resume their conversation, while in an instant (as it seemed) the peaceful scene was changed, and with a blast of wind and a whirl of sound that made them jump for the nearest ditch, it was on them. The "Poop-poop" rang with a brazen shout in their ears, they had a moment's glimpse of an interior of glittering plate glass and rich morocco, and the magnificent motor-car, immense, breath-snatching, passionate, with its pilot tense and hugging at the wheel, possessed all earth and air for a fraction of a second, flung an enveloping cloud of dust that blinded and enwrapped them utterly, and then dwindled to a speck in the far distance, changed back into a droning bee once more.[44]

Clearly here is one of the luxury cars of a rich early motoring enthusiast, a vehicle lined in "rich morocco." This opulence, however, is nothing compared to the excitement of the car's speed as it passes. This speed is portrayed as a force greater than the forces of nature, so great that it is barely perceptible, with the car altering from a "dark center of energy," to a barely seen glitter of glass and tense driver, to, in a moment, a speck on the horizon beyond. A force, nevertheless, which "possessed all earth and air for a fraction of a second," an apocalyptic apparition, omnipotent, whose terrifying speed boggles the powers of perception of observers and, as it turns out, thrills them with its power. The cart in which sit the three observers of this scene is wrecked, the others are furious, but Mr. Toad—comically, as befitted accounts of car culture in many genres—is besotted:

> Glorious, stirring sight! . . . The poetry of motion: The real way to travel! Here today—in next week tomorrow. . . . Oh bliss! . . . . And to think I never *knew*! All those wasted years that lie behind me, I never knew, never even *dreamt*! But *now*—but now that I know, and now that I fully realize! What dust clouds shall spring up before me as I speed on my reckless way! (43–44)

The attraction to speed felt by Toad is presented first as comic infatuation, and soon as an addiction. Mr. Toad of Toad Hall is the rich gentleman of the novel, a paunchy W. K. Vanderbilt of the Thames valley. He can afford numerous large bright-red motorcars in which he speeds about, he involves himself in "smash-ups," he exasperates the traffic police. When his friends try to restrain him, he grows listless and ill; escaping, he steals a car from an inn yard, is arrested and jailed, escapes, and caps his adventures when, dressed as a washerwoman, he succeeds in again taking the wheel and driving at an insane speed in the very car he had stolen before. All this driving, the mainstay of the plot, is presented in a setting of bucolic Thames-side country; in this nirvana Toad's speed infatuation is reckoned his latest craze. The desire to drive fast is imagined as an addiction, an emotional force and an almost physical need, and the subsequent basis for all of Toad's behavior. It is rendered as a passion which he cannot himself control. This is presented comically; Toad does no real harm to others, and the novel is no parable of rural conservation; it never reaches the point of confronting this techno-addiction with the older way of life represented by the countryside, the slow river, and the homebody natures of the others. In fact, in the novel, the nostalgia for nature and home matches the excitement about speed. Yet because the motorcar adventures are the stuff of much of the drama in the novel, the car has vitality, comedy, surprise, and adventure on its side. Toad's addiction is what renders him purposeful, and this addiction is to speed. Cars at speed take over a text that is cast as a rustic tale, offer it a plot, and explain the actions of the central character. Grahame's novel turns out, in its innocent fascination with the new speed of the automobile, to be offering an intense swan song to narratives about rural peacefulness and homeliness. As such, *The Wind in the Willows*, even as it is fascinated by speed, is also the first major satire of automobile fascination, a minor but forceful genre in subsequent Western fiction that would encompass novels such as the Russian Futurist-expressionist Ilya Ehrenburg's *The Life of the Automobile* and reach a crescendo in 1973 with J. G. Ballard's novel *Crash*. Ballard's psychotic driver Vaughan is the successor to Toad, in a Thames valley now strewn with motorways and lit with a lurid neon glow.

"Serious" fiction of the early twentieth century proved much more circumspect in depicting automobiles and their speeds. Travel books like Evelyn Waugh's *Remote People* (1930), for example, suggest the increasingly blasé attitude toward the automobile; although Waugh details a series of automobile trips over hair-raisingly rutted roads in the mountains around Addis Ababa, he expresses no interest in speed in itself: it has by now become fully and merely functional for the sophisticated, resourceful writer.[45] In American novels by F. Scott Fitzgerald, Sinclair Lewis, and

John Steinbeck, cars of all sorts are described: the focus is generally on the make and marque of the car as a handy signal of the class aspirations and resources of the driver. (In chapter 5, I consider how the car crash works as a trauma in *The Great Gatsby*.) In literary experiments of these years, the car returns as a point of anxiety, a harbinger of urban change which upsets the delicate equilibrium of the city being described. It needles narrative rhythms in books that seem to lack the means necessary to represent it.

In Joyce's *Ulysses* (published in 1921, set in 1904), Leopold Bloom, Dublin pedestrian, is at one point blinded for a moment by the sun reflected off a passing car's windscreen.[46] Critics have noted that this is one of the novel's very few factual errors, for there were no cars in Dublin in 1904. (The city did, however, have a modern system of electric trams, often noted by Bloom, whose noise is celebrated in the opening of the "Aeolus" episode.) That Joyce brought into his novel a car that would in fact not arrive until later in the city, however, might be seen as part of the novel's witty retrospective game of prophecy: when the novel was being written between 1914 and 1921, cars were much less rare in Dublin. If *Ulysses* contains within its panorama a foreboding of the city as it would become, crammed with cars and congested with traffic, then consider also that it implies an elegy-in-advance for the figure on whom urban movement in *Ulysses* and most of the great modernist novels is based: the turn-of-the-century urban pedestrian, the flâneur. This figure, celebrated in Walter Benjamin's *Paris, Capital of the Nineteenth Century*, is the star in almost all the great modernist fictions, from Mann's *Death in Venice* to Musil's *The Man without Qualities*; the flâneur haunts the works of Franz Kafka and calls, "Let us go then," to open T. S. Eliot's *Prufrock*. Roving the streetscapes of these labyrinthine texts, he epitomizes the anxious and alienated modernist urban subject, and his relentless walking, his veritable dromomania, is the key trope of his nervous, restless refusal to feel at home. In chapter 1 we saw how the new popular forms of the 1890s and later, such as detective fiction, inspired a horror of the home in the new mass readership: for a more highbrow audience, the flâneurs of avant-garde modernist fiction were the counterparts of, and complement to, this same avoidance of the home as haunted, plagued, terrifying. Yet by the 1920s, when many of these texts appeared, the trope of frightening home had lost its novelty in popular writing. The flâneur too, it turned out, was a threatened trope. Perhaps this figure's swan song, in fiction in English at any rate, came in 1925 in a novel which both imitates and conjures with that of Joyce: Virginia Woolf's *Mrs. Dalloway*. The novel announces flânerie's failure as governing trope of modernist subjectivity with a flâneuse heroine's unnerving vision of that new invader of city streets and transformer of city dwellers and their relations, the motorcar.

It has been argued that the flâneur or flâneuse is in some circumstances a figure potentially at odds with the dominant and newly massified consumer culture, the culture which burgeoned in the years when most of the novels featuring these figures are set.[47] As a wandering, directionless walker, he or she exists at a tangent to the driven, compulsive behavior of the avid consumer. The flâneur was attractive to modernist writers, therefore, as a figure who could be used to explore ways to articulate the countersign to consumerist contentment. This should not blind us, nevertheless, to the ways in which the flâneur was *the* prototypical figure of consumer culture as it had been constructed in the "walking city" of this period. Turn-of-the-century consumerism, like new-century modernist narrative, was constructed as a matter of walking, whether from one plate-glass shop window display to the next or through the panoply of wares in department stores. In the new mass consumerism, the consumer subject was hailed as a stroller who could stop, shop, buy. Distractible walkers, the flâneurs of the modernists, despite their various degrees of anomie, are exhibiting the prototypical behavior of the new era of mass consumption, and their celebrated angst may often be read as a sublimation of consumerist desire. Consumption as window-shopping was cast as an affair of strolling to view the wares of the city. From this it follows that what one might call, literally, the *pace* of a modernist flâneur novel, as well as its tone and concerns, manages to mimic quite accurately the pace—leisured, whimsical, diverted, anxious—which consumerism as pedestrian choosing demands of those who buy. Further, many of the literary strategies used by modernist writers in portraying flâneur figures and their consciousnesses—sudden cuts from one scene to the next, a lively nebulousness and challenging obscurity, an uncertainty about point of view, a refusal to make one unified personality the focus of the narrative—all mirror states, strategies, and attitudes that members of the new consumer masses were expected to adopt for shopping to be a pleasurable and diversified activity.

Consumerism, however, once it took off, was bound to have a history, one that meant that the pedestrian consumer would only constitute a moment in a longer continuum. This initial stage might be thought of as contemporaneous with the moment of the plate-glass window—first used in shop fronts as early as 1860. It was in the final decades of the nineteenth century and the first decades of the twentieth that consumer behavior in cities was expected to consist chiefly of walking along a shopping street, looking at the wares temptingly displayed behind the plate-glass windows of each shop, and then choosing which to enter and buy. Already other mass-consumer protocols were being developed — as in the idea that people could shop from catalogs, tapped profitably by Sears, Roebuck and Co. in North America and by the Bon Marche in Europe. The arrival of the motor-car in the twentieth century not only choked city streets, making the stroll to window-shop less pleasant; it also accelerated the search for alternative protocols of consumerism. The jaunty, diversified, and fragmented pace of the older flâneur consumerism, which involved a leisurely, if at times anxious, interplay of the stroll and the gaze, provided the template on which flâneur figures could be shown in modernist texts with a similarly playful interplay of the scene, the thought, and then another, different idea; this was now threatened by the very commodity, the car, that was being sold as a prime object of consumer desire. In this sense, the urge to accumulate commodities was overwhelming itself. This conflict, brought out in the clash of flânerie and car culture, is explored in the opening pages of *Mrs. Dalloway*.

Just as the appearance of politics in a novel has been described, by Stendhal, as resembling "a pistol shot fired in the middle of a concert," so too the arrival of the motorcar on London's streets in *Mrs. Dalloway* is announced initially as "Oh! a pistol shot in the street outside."[48] In these pages, mostly narrated through the heroine's sensibility, Clarissa Dalloway, upper-crust wife of a member of Parliament and recent convalescent, is shown gaily enjoying her genteel flânerie and shopping expedition on Piccadilly and Bond Street, in London's poshest shopping area. Although there is much refined, witty attention to the modulations of Clarissa's finer feelings — to "the waves of that divine vitality which Clarissa loved" (9) — and to her nostalgic youthful memories, this is intermingled with a straightforward account of her window-shopping, at Hanchard's bookshop, at an art gallery, before "one roll of tweed in the shop where her father had bought his suits for fifty years; a few pearls, salmon in an icebox" (15). Here the modernist recourse to stream-of-consciousness observations, the flitting from one thought to a slipping, half-adduced, half-reported memory, the reception of impressions, is perfectly matched to the pace of Clarissa as privileged consumer pedestrian; and the sensation of pleasure she receives from the goods in the glossy shop windows is of a piece with the equally ephemeral pleasures of her memories and present concerns. Into this lightly spun, fragilely balanced idyll—while Clarissa is buying flowers—the car bursts like a pistol shot. It comes as harbinger of all that is ominous. Fittingly for Clarissa's class position, it is a car of extreme luxury, driven by a chauffeur, its windows covered by curtains:

> Passers by who, of course, stopped and stared had just had time to see a face of the very greatest importance against the dove-grey upholstery, before a male hand drew the blind and there was nothing to be seen except a square of dove grey. (19)

Just as the motorcar in Grahame's *The Wind in the Willows* emerges as a point of energy from the landscape, Woolf's car here seems to focus the whole energy of the cityscape with itself as still center:

> Everything came to a standstill. The throb of the motor-engines sounded like a pulse irregularly drumming through an entire body. The sun became extraordinarily hot because the motor car had stopped outside Mulberry's shop window; old ladies on the tops of omnibuses spread their black parasols; here a green, a red parasol opened with a little pop. Mrs. Dalloway, coming to the window with her arm full of sweet peas, looked out with her little pink face pursed in inquiry. Everyone looked at the motor car. Septimus looked. Boys on bicycles sprang off. Traffic accumulated. And there the motor car stood. (20–21)

It is the first fully dramatic moment in the novel; this is signaled by the first gap in the impressionistic flow of the text, which comes immediately after the pistol shot sound and the florist's apology for it to Mrs. Dalloway. Yet this break, a white space on the page, the rendition through absence of the car's energy-centering stillness, also signifies the text's reticence about representing a milieu focused beyond Mrs. Dalloway herself. To this broader world, the car, as it were, ardently draws the text's attention. What the story suggests is that there is a famous person—a member of the royal family, perhaps, or the prime minister out shopping—concealed in the vehicle, and that the street at once becomes awash in rumors about the identity of this ghost in the machine. In the succeeding pages, we are shown "the motor car with its blinds drawn and an air of inscrutable reserve" (23) being observed, and inspiring emotions of awe, nationalist loyalty, and even reverence for its presumed occupant in a series of characters who up to now have been, and continue to be, strangers: Septimus and Lucrezia Warren Smith, one

Edgar J. Watkiss, a poor flower-seller named Molly Pratt, rich men at the window of Brook's Club, and a crowd outside the gates of Buckingham Palace. The intrusion of the car, it seems, demands that multiple characters get their moment in the narrative; crucially, this is also the moment when the book's second key persona, the shellshocked veteran Septimus Smith, is first mentioned, when both he and Clarissa, in the first moment after the backfiring shot, look at the car simultaneously. Since the story of how these two sensitive, somewhat disturbed Londoners do not quite meet but how their lives nevertheless do tentatively touch becomes the fragile thread on which hangs much of the novel's narrative, the uncannily still car exists as the sole mediator of the relations between these strangers in the urban crowd.

For Marx the commodity as a fetish mediated and interfered with the real relations between people: here the car (unlike the pearls or the painting which Clarissa has seen in the shop windows) is not itself a commodity for sale—so that the gaze of many different people upon it might possibly (although it does not, in the end) bring people together. The narrative is keen to portray this shared look as a relation built on a shared ideology, in this case of nationalist loyalty, as people assume that the car contains an important national figure. The skeptical joke, then, is that, quite possibly, the car does not carry such a figure; it might, were it not for the spectral hand drawing the blind, even be empty. If so, the car episode becomes a tragicomic one that testifies with grim irony to the hollowness of the iconography by which the ruling elite of a modern, technologized state indoctrinates its subjects and exercises its power, as well as to the gullibility of those it addresses. This irony is underlined, when the most faithful subjects, waiting at Buckingham Palace, miss the car as they are diverted by an airplane overhead, a plane skywriting an advertising slogan which no one can really read. The new tech toys—car and airplane—might appear to have the potential to give the novel a more democratic and broader impetus, to have it attend to a greater cross section of the citizens of the city than a stream-of-consciousness focus would allow, and to grant the potential for them to cross paths as the basis for some kind of community. Rather, they only serve, *Mrs. Dalloway* insists, to further underline the citizens' alienation from each other.

We should not, however, be diverted by the text's cynical account of the hollowness of the state's appeal to its people, for that narrative, suggestive as it is, by no means fully contains the car's effect on and in the text.

Mrs. Dalloway, narrating in the car's slipstream, shows it to be a device that could potentially bring these metropolitan dwellers closer together but instead cements their separateness. The car that arrives with the report of a pistol shot manages to throw the text's representational ambitions wide open: just as it precipitated a series of shocks in the rhythm of city life, the car generates a crisis in the text's confidence in its ability to show modern urban sensibilities in conflict and collusion. Puncturing the rarefied enclosure of Mrs. Dalloway's stream-of-consciousness world, the car shocks the novel into trying to delineate tentative ties and gaping differences in the mass of lives that interact in the city on that day.

Why does the text choose the car as the object with which to announce such a crisis? Since the motifs it represents are backed by the skywriting airplane, the new technologies are featured here as intruding, almost fearful omens. But of what? Up to this point, Clarissa and the text have syncopated the clash and noise of London traffic to the pedestrian and consumerist flânerie that she enjoyed: the car's pistol shot represents the point at which this rush of traffic, of buses and cars, and of anonymous people of all sorts, becomes intolerable, so that it marks the beginning of Clarissa's retreat back into her home. Yet, as we have seen, the novel accepts the challenge of narrating the car's effects; it can only do this, however, by imagining the car's occupant and then implying that the car in fact possibly has no one within. Layering these ironies, the text implicitly reads the car (as, for example, an antinationalist might read a flag) as a hollow symbol, the reverence of which is a foolish delusion. Given that much of what we have heard up to this point is Clarissa's stream of consciousness, we might suspect that this reading is the product merely of her imaginings, so that we could distance ourselves from it. It is as if the novel itself almost begs us to cast it in doubt. To agree that the car is a hollow symbol of the state, when, after all, Clarissa might just as well have thought its occupant was a film star, visiting millionaire, or a mobster out shopping, runs counter to a text now eager to imply that Clarissa (and the other car-gazers) desperately wanted there to be someone in the vehicle. Given this need, they must dream up such a figure rather than come to terms with the car and its culture, even if this is a culture of frightening anonymity, as opposed to, as the novel shows us, a culture of foolishly wishful nationalism. In this rereading, the car becomes the joking allegory of a *deus ex machina*, but one without even the comfort of the controlling figure within.

The empty car is a stark, ghostly, roving, and robotic presence that bespeaks a profound sense of urban meaninglessness and nullity. It's a premonition of an uncanny trope that would later appear in some urban legends and B horror films: the car racing through the streets without any driver or passengers at all. Woolf's version of the gray, roving, empty car at once joins in all the anti-automobile discourses of the day—on their dangers, the need for speed limits, their evil, in President's Wilson's terms, as symbols of a vastly rich leisure class—and breathtakingly supersedes them. It casts the car, its very luxuriousness shown in tones of gray, as indeed a pistol shot killing off the old order of privileged consumer-driven flânerie over which the urban strollers had some control and from which they might derive a capricious if tenuous pleasure. As Clarissa retreats homeward (to a home that certainly has some of the blanched quality of the drawing room of Conrad's "intended" in *Heart of Darkness*), the first pages of *Mrs. Dalloway* read as an account of the final outing of the flâneuse as shopper. The car scene epitomizes this modernist text's embrace of an anti-automobile rhetoric of the day, but heightened to more thoroughly existential ends. In the simplest materialist terms, this was appropriate, for the car was killing off flânerie in London and beyond in precisely this period. By the late 1920s, the department stores of Los Angeles had begun to move to the suburbs and turn their main entrances away from the street pavements of Wiltshire Boulevard and on to the parking lots behind.[49] The earliest "out-of-town" shopping complexes catering to drivers and disavowing pedestrians were built in California in the 1930s.[50] New protocols of consumerism built around the automobile, beyond the interplay of flânerie and the gaze of the window-shopper who was "just looking," were already being invented. As the narrator in *Mrs. Dalloway* explains:

> The car had gone, but it had left a slight ripple which flowed through the glove shops and the hat shops and tailors' shops on both sides of Bond Street. . . . Choosing a pair of gloves—should they be at the elbow or above it, lemon or pale grey?—ladies stopped; when the sentence was finished something had happened. (25)

The passage invites us to ask what that something was, and the text rushes on to assure us that it was the thought "of the dead; of the flag; of Empire" in this post–World War I decade (25). Perhaps. But behind these thoughts, the "slight ripple" felt as the car, and its novelty, confronts and rushes by the culture of consumption in the old style is the shiver caused by the intimation of that culture's disappearance. What the novel stages in its opening pages is a yoking of flânerie, the modernist *topos* for the exploration of urban subjectivity in all its variety, and consumerism. What it stages, rather wistfully, in its insistence that the car signifies merely nationalism while allowing us to wonder at the adequacy of that analysis, is the demise of flânerie, the most characteristic modernist trope, once it enters into collusion with consumption, the most characteristic behavior of modernist bourgeois culture. The car is the marker of modernist narrative's refusal to align itself with post-flâneur modernity. This demonizes the relatively new (in 1925) machine both as modernity's alienating apotheosis and, because the text shows the car as the machine whose qualities cannot be spoken within the modernist flâneur dispensation, as the point at which radical new protocols of narration must come into play. The car marks the threshold at which Woolf's novel ceases to be expressionist and becomes cubist.

Woolf's flâneuse text, happier to annotate the flâneuse's stream-of-consciousness perceptions than to cross over to other narrative horizons, simply extends, in her portrayal of car culture, this monitoring of consciousness; thus the novel can ironically show it filling diverse minds with a groundless nationalism. It forgoes the chance to dissect the new car culture. This task was taken up in other kinds of texts: the first travel narratives reporting on trips in motorcars, the near-hysterical announcements of the Italian Futurists and their British fellow travelers such as Wyndham Lewis in *Blast*, the more techno-revolutionary utopians among avant-garde artists in Russia—and by Woolf herself in her more audacious novel *Orlando*. The Futurists are a special case; here I want to consider how car culture, once embraced, commandeered the styles and stirred up the perspectives of travel writing. My example: Edith Wharton's collection of travel essays *A Motor-Flight through France*.

Early travel narratives describing motor trips sketch the code of manners for a kind of behavior—mass tourism—that was turning landscape and leisure into consumer commodities. At the same time, they were grasping to represent, in new ways, what they sensed was a new experience— the pleasures of motor travel. Far from fearing the car as a symbol, they are keen to celebrate it as glorious possibility. Eagerly participating in car advertising and propaganda, motor-travel writing was another branch of promotions such as early car shows and the races for the Vanderbilt Cup. It was in accord with propagandists' (such as Henry Ford's) delight at the idea that a car allowed unhealthy city life to be abandoned for therapeutic leisure on country lanes. These books also acted as tourist promotions;

journalist-authors and "bright young things" such as Evelyn Waugh were prepared to write about their travels when subsidized by tour companies. (This commercialism allied them with the burgeoning guidebook industry, one of whose most famous series, the Michelin guides, was published by the French tire company.) As studies of tourism from Dean McCannell's work to that of Pierre Bourdieu make clear, tourism, of perhaps all modern activities, represents the commodification of experience itself.

Tourism stages a thirst for new experiences. Yet it offers these experiences at the cost of always ensuring that they are safely commodified in advance. The tourist paradox is that in tourism's search for exoticism and difference, difference is always cut off at the root. Hawking pre-viewed wonders, travel books are paeans to the most pervasive consumerism that modernity offers—they commodify the landscape as spectacle. The more apparently "adventurous" they render (in advance) their hero-readers' faux adventures, by borrowing the now shopworn trope from fin de siècle tales of derring-do that had already been undercut by, for example, Conrad's desultory ironies, or the more "exotic" their reported discoveries, the more they stand for fetishized commodification; this fetish magic works precisely by convincing the consumer that she has accessed something not merely "purchased" or mundane. The pressures on *A Motor-Flight through France* in these terms are therefore intense: the text is inescapably a tourist brochure in disguise, a catalog of the delights not of specific commodities, and not merely a list of the commodified charms of hamlets, vistas, châteaux, and medieval churches throughout France, but a description of life itself while on holiday as commodified experience—as "lifestyle" rather than any form of unmediated living.

Apart from opening with the point that "the motor car has restored the romance of travel" because it has freed us from the railway's "bondage of fixed hours and the beaten track" (1), Wharton does not belabor the delights of automobilism here. Rather, she exemplifies them in her prose. For this is *fast* writing: skimming, moving smoothly from observation to observation, detail to detail, at times jittery and prone to distraction, always ready to move on and mightily satisfied with its progress. Every guidebook is awash in names and places, but here this tendency to list is exaggerated into a flow: in the countryside, hamlets and towns appear in the distance and disappear behind the car's viewers about every four lines: L'Isle sur Tarn, Rabastens, Albi, Carcassonne, Castres, Narbonne, Nimes . . . When the tourers break their journey to explore a town, the language and pace of views flashing by, as seen from the automobile, is kept up: it still jumps about trying to keep pace with the authorial eye now trained by the automobile perch to practice the quick look and no more. The piled-on place names and impressions insist that beneath the tourist's joy of looking is the joy of fast moving — and that the writer, and reader, must strain to keep up:

> From Nimes to the Mediterranean the impressions are packed too thick. First the Rhone, with the castles of Tarascon and Beaucaire taunting each other across its Flood, Beaucaire from a steep cliff, Tarascon from the very brink of the river; then, after a short flight through orange orchards and vineyards, the pretty leafy town of Saint Remy on the skirts of the Alpilles; and a mile to the south of Saint Remy, on a chalky ledge of the low mountain chain, the two surviving monuments of the Roman city of Glanum. They are set side by side, the tomb and the triumphal arch, in a circular grassy space enclosed with olive orchards and backed by delicate fretted peaks: not another vestige of Roman construction left to connect them with the past. Was it, one wonders, their singular beauty that saved them, that held even the Visigoth's hands. . . . ? (125)

This is writing that is out of breath, writing energized by the pleasure of the fast and definite look that names, notes, and moves on; it is writing on adrenaline. It offers deft impressions, no more. There are observations but no contemplation. Compare this to Clarissa Dalloway's rhythmic, jazzy, but pedestrian reverie sixteen years later. In Wharton's travelogue the progress is transformed by the presence of the new machine, the motorcar. The car, as toy of rich people, plays perfectly to the consumerist trajectory of the travel book; its shimmer as luxury accessory enhances the holiday's snob appeal. That the characters are touring in a motorcar radically alters the tempo of the text. Rather than juxtaposing a steady and tempered succession of sights with reflections on each, as does the early flâneur passage in *Mrs. Dalloway* (in doing this, Woolf's novel owes more to the model of the tourist gaze implied in John Ruskin's *Stones of Venice*, for example, than it does to travel writing like that of *A Motor-Flight*), Wharton gives us a torrent of sights in fast succession, a swift series of scene changes and a text where we must always be prepared for surprises. Yet these surprises are all within a narrow range of the types expected in travel writing: notable ruins, quaint churches, jagged and fretted mountain ridges. No real alterity gets spotted in the fast-forward framing of the visible, despite the expressed love of the exotic common to all travel writing. Given this, it is not the variety of the scenes that is really exciting but rather the underlying sensation of fast movement — the excitement of speed. *A Motor-Flight through France* is not simply a text that gets down as prose the rougher brush strokes of impressionist art, but (in a style which, in its unconsciousness, surpasses the all-too-self-aware experiments of the group) a Futurist text avant la lettre.

Tourism, as an invention of modernity that commodifies what it markets as new life experiences, follows the protocols of consumerist behavior. Tourism's protocols are very like those of shopping. As with shopping — think of Miss Honeychurch of E. M. Forster's *A Room with a View* (1908) in Santa Croce without a Baedeker, for example — tourism is chiefly practiced as flânerie. It is often described as a matter of pedestrian strolling, with frequent stops to inspect, and above all to gaze upon, the monument or art object. That art object then becomes the substitute for, and in its supposed authenticity the guarantor of, the value of every salable commodity. After this gaze at art, the buying of the souvenir reconciles the tourist to the primacy of commodification. The tourist gaze, then, has its own complicated protocols, especially when aided by amateur photography, for example. It is this gaze that is shattered in Wharton's book, and the kaleidoscope turning is a function, literally, of seeing through the windscreen of a car. This early attempt to delineate the joys of the particularity of motor tourism offers scenes observed so fast that the contemplative, reverential moment is radically condensed and the juxtaposition of often incongruous differences is what grabs our interest in the text. Speed of looking makes for surprises, dislocations, the celebration of difference, and the glamorization of shocks as pleasant and stimulating. As the car zooms toward a sight, so does the writerly eye: this textual perspective is composed of zooms and withdrawals, in a textual counterpart to a kind of composition that was just then finding its forte in a whole new medium: film. This is speed writing in the era of car technology, a new shorthand of visual "telegraphy." It was a fast notation of the experience of a "niftier" (the word was first used in the United States) kind of seeing, which replaced the older contemplative gaze of the first stage of consumerist tourism with a variegated rout.

Even more important than its shocks and quick changes, which mark it as thoroughly modernist prose, is its character as a version of *unmediated* writing. What the text attempts to do is to report immediate impressions of scenes in a highly energetic prose. (Impressionist painters' use of the blurred outline to paint some of the very sights which Wharton describes is also related to the blurred outlines of such scenes as seen from a speeding train or car.) Its obscurity, its shock tactics, its mad juxtapositions do not sell themselves as an attempt to shock the reader, to unsettle her, to confuse her out of her complacent slow contemplativeness and comfort, as so much "shocking" prose and painting have been said, in various ways, to do: it would be an exaggeration to claim that this new kind of writerly glamour marks a subverting of earlier norms, certainties, or styles. Rather, it presents its shocks and sudden scene changes as notably pleasurable improvements on the slower, more sedate progress of earlier kinds of "just looking." Keeping its shocks on this side of the threshold of obscurity, it advertises the pleasure of speed-shock narrative, a quick look, and the rat-tat-tat of succeeding impressions. It brings us back, in other words, to adrenaline: here is a text where fast tourism is brilliant because it is adrenaline inducing, exciting in its speed and variety, a novel thrill.

It suggests the transparency of its prose with its flow of place names, followed by a phrase or sentence only of impression. This transparency, the refusal to "get in the way," to come as little as possible between the reader and the scenes the author saw, a refusal if possible to let the words tread on the experience, is the textual counterpart of the consumer's desire, when rehearsing the elegantly "natural" protocols of consumption, to find the act of consuming one to be supplemented with unmediated experiences. These are the experiences which are induced by, and in turn induce more, adrenaline. Wharton's text therefore is naive in the most modern way: its simplicity, its embrace of the actuality of the shock of the new, offers a new descriptive machinery where unmediated experience itself is presented as something that can be known by its production of a thrill, of adrenaline, of a shock which produces a sensation not only in the imagination but in the very body of the reader. Sensation fiction, the thrillers written in the Victorian period to pass the time (of waiting, while being carried) on commuter trains, a special consumer product invented to satisfy a niche market in late-nineteenth-century writing for the newly literate masses and a precursor to the detective and thriller genres, is here deployed in a new way, so that it reaches its limit in travel writing that offers sensations at speed to provoke a bodily *frisson* not at the sight of another hamlet or medieval *eglise* but as a sign of life intensely lived.

Filming Speed

Wharton's book was written a decade after the showing of the first commercial film, at the time when films were becoming the chief mass entertainments of every city in the Western world. Film's shadowy light pictures appeared to offer the unmediated access to the gaze that books such as *A Motor-Flight through France* proposed as a literary and experiential good. With its repertoire of zooms, camera angles, long shots, and close-ups, film had at hand a repertoire of shock tactics performed at speed and without warning which worked like sleight of hand but, like Wharton's text, remained, as mass entertainment, well inside the threshold to the obscure. Film's light effects, its instant transpositions from one perspective to another and from scene to scene, also generated excitement and incited a rush of adrenaline in the viewer. As visual medium, film fitted perfectly into the protocol of consumerism that involved the reverential gaze, but its newness too made it seek new experiences. From the start, it was fascinated by the car. It was as if film intuited that this technological medium for moving at speed, and film's own technologically accelerated picture sequences, had in common the capacity to generate similar excitements in both drivers and viewers.

The new moving images of film specialized in showing the joys of the new vehicles at speed. The camera could be stationary, assuming the perspective of Kenneth Grahame's shocked characters at the sight of their first car. It could be mounted within the car, giving the views through the windscreen: in the filmed *Jim Hurst Tours*, viewers could imagine that they were inside a car looking out on the streets of Chicago and Berlin. Or it could move alongside the car, setting up the filmic conditions for the first car chase. Film is moved through a looping camera to produce a stream of images; when the movie camera films movement at speed, it is as if the medium itself and the way it works are being brought to the attention of the viewer by being replicated in the subject matter of the picture itself. Filming a racing car, film draws attention to itself: a tight symbiosis of medium and material. The way in which film became a mass medium meant that its origins too were in the fairground, the mutoscope and the peep show, not far from where, on the roller coaster, the masses were granted early experience of the new speed thrills. This promoted the car's affinity to comedy — and jibed with film's immediate coupling of comedy and speed. Film's apparently unmediated gaze could illicit a physical, adrenaline-rush reaction — a reaction that appeared to closely approximate the frisson originally generated by the events represented. It could involve the viewer in the somatic quality of the experience shown much more handily than could even the jazziest modernist writing. Film took the strategies of sensation fiction, and the ploys of fairground comedy, and from the beginning wrapped them around plots that involved racing cars. Very often the climax was that staple of film action, the movie car chase.

The car chase may be the most characteristic scene in film, and it has been so from the beginning. Early silent films, such as *A Runaway Match, or Marriage by Motor* (1903), directed by the British director Alf Collins and produced by Gaumont, for example, recast the oldest romance plots as modern, technology centered, and thrilling by featuring the car chase to raise the tempo of a lovers' intrigue. In *A Runaway Match*, about a father who disapproves of his daughter's love match, the camera focuses on his car chasing after the lovers as they drive at speed to a minister. This may be the first car chase on film; it already uses point-of-view shots seen from the perspective of both pursued and pursuing automobiles.[51] Car chase scenes mean a focus on the new technology of the car, by the new technology of the moving camera, as a means to transmute ordinary narrative suspense — the excitement about what will happen next that was the basis of the detective story's addictiveness — into a format that induces a bodily sensation in the viewer. They are par excellence those moments when a medium, based on technology that enhances the power to produce modulations of the gaze, proves that it can induce in the viewer a visceral and extended affect. Movies, too, are commodities, with a price, that are meant to be consumed; often their technologically mediated looking looks on other consumer commodities, including cars, to co-opt movie viewers into the pleasure of consumption and to persuade them to buy. In moments such as those of the filming of speed — particularly in the simple palm-sweating seconds of the car chase — however, the motion picture's mechanical reproduction of the intense experience, brokered and enhanced by technology, creates a bodily sensation. At these moments, it truly makes its viewer sense excitements to be experienced rather than have her gaze at commodities to be purchased. This is a medium that forgoes any vestige of aura in favor of inciting a thrill. It finds that thrill in movement, more often than not, in the swoosh of a speeding car.

A Race for a Kiss (1904), for example, is another of the earliest films to stage the minidrama of adrenaline, transgression, and personal power that can be played out around breaking the speed limit. This short sequence is the first to show a speeding car being flagged down by a policeman, in the scene which closes the film; the film's opening dramatizes a race between a horse ridden by a jockey and a driver in a car. For this velocity to be dramatic, the speeder has to be shown as victorious over the horseman, and then transgressive of the law. Here speed is imagined as exciting only when it participates in a larger drama: a struggle against the old order of horse power, against the law, a race for a kiss. In the decade that follows, while the narrative frames of the spectacle of speed are inevitably refined, complicated, and played for their multiple possibilities (the challenge, the race, the chase, the prize), the circumstances nevertheless come to matter less as the filmic possibilities expand for rendering the essential speed experience. These possibilities arise from technological changes and camera strategies: the mounting of the camera behind the driver's shoulder, cutting and editing techniques that show off the velocity of the vehicle in contrast to the stationary, unwitting spectator by the roadside, the close-up of the driver's face behind a dulling windscreen to suggest at once the swishing effect caused by glancing *at speed*, and the terror, concentration, and exhilaration evident in the driver's eyes. Even more compelling: the shot of the car approaching at speed to scare the cinema spectators or, even better, the training of the camera either on the passing scene or on the ground beneath or immediately in front of the car, which, flying by in a blur, makes the reality of velocity inescapable. Pure speed cinema, shorn of all narrative framing, might be impossible: the illusion of cinema (itself a moving image in the projector that pretends to stillness on the screen and is presented in a still frame) always depended on a degree zero of absolute complicity between moving camera and moving image never being reached. The narrative could be presented as evidently false and conventional by being cast unapologetically as one of a number of highly recognizable genres. Consider speed's effect in comedies and the gangster film. It the caper films, elements of both these genres were bound together, with plots fueled by comedy and confrontations with gangsters that were obviously and repetitively generic, so that the thrills and spills of the overcrowded police car could become the heart of each film's experience. In the caper film, the laughter and suspense generated by the mock narratives could be rendered as warm-up acts for the real experience that was being offered—the lovingly photographed, although simulated, experience of speed itself.

It is striking, then, that these films concern surrendering control, giving up or failing to achieve purposefulness: the opposite to the dramatic trajectory of *A Race for a Kiss*. Take, for example, the Keystone film *A Lover's Lost Control* (1915). Here pleasure itself is cast as surrender of purposefulness and order. More, the film contrasts the pleasures of being lost in consumption—it opens in a department store—with those of the car chase. It offers three sequences: a comic scene of confusion and disarray in the department store, the chase of the hero's car by the police, and—characteristically for a Keystone caper—the plunge of both police and chased car into the ocean. In this short film, the terms of the adrenaline-driven comedy that we witnessed in Robert Frank's photograph of the Dodgem car couple are laid out. Consumption of commodities and the speed experience are presented in tandem to imply that speed may be the culmination and superb intensification of the experience of commodity consumption. Or rather, since the film's scene of buying in the department store descends into a comic riot, what is suggested is that consumption pushed to its utmost intensity, to the moment when it becomes transgressive breakdown, finds its outlet in the thrill of the car chase. Evading the police by driving fast, moreover, makes speeding into lawbreaking, a defiance of the state's order. The thrill of the lawbreaker adds a modern folk heroism to the thrill of velocity. The film's confrontation of order and transgressive speed is resolved—without injury—when both chased and police cars catapult into the ocean: to the cheers of the audience, the kind of narrative of speed and heroic lawbreaking that would soon be taken up in the earliest cartoons resolves its contradictions in a comic invitation to celebrate disaster as a dream of the ultimate speed thrill, a lapsing out beyond the torque of the vehicle and the drag of gravity altogether.

Here adrenaline is being summoned up in the cinema spectator by the twin spectacles of consumption so intense it is transgressive, and speeds so fast they are thrilling both in their lawbreaking and in their own right. But the adrenaline-driven tension dissolves, effervesces, and suffuses the audience, the chasers, and the chased alike in a technological bath in the ocean. As the cars plunge, the threat of the car crash is comically overcome; the audience's assumption that transgression is impossible in modernity, that the chased will always be caught by the police, is answered by the sight of the vehicles plunging. This plunge into the ocean celebrates speed as at one with the forces of nature, unknowable, unfathomable, as a means of achieving union with such forces, driving into a medium where the rules of weightiness, traction, torque, and all the realities that hold one down are overcome.

Blur: Rapid Eye Movement and the Visuality of Speed

We find ourselves in fact faced with the exposition of a world where IMAGE =
MOVEMENT.
—Gilles Deleuze, *Cinema I: The Movement Image*

Speed itself is nothing apart from the world of three dimensions . . . but it has
proved itself in one phase or another to be perhaps the most vital element in human
welfare. Its command invests individuals with such a large measure of what seems
to be power that, when it is compassed in a fresh and unexpected manner, as it has
been by help of the motor-car, men are liable to the illusion that there is a singular
bliss in mere speed by itself.
— *Times* (London), October 17, 1911

The boundaries between things are disappearing, the subject and the world are no
longer separate, time seems to stand still.
—Ernst Mach, quoted in Paul Virilio, *The Vision Machine*

In 1917 Matisse painted *Le parebrise, sur la route de Villacoublay* (The
Windshield, on the Road to Villacoublay), which shows a stretch of road
seen from a car windscreen (figure 8).[1] It is a thoroughly unconventional
painting of a standard impressionist subject. In retrospect, Matisse's impressionist painterly method has come to stand for aura-laden, formally
composed sympathy for nature and affect; here, however, he makes clear
that his viewpoint is ultramodern: an observation post invented by a new
technology. From the car's interior, he looks out from a vantage point that
suggests forces rather than affects, rigid lines rather than roughened edges,
and, instead of a Benjaminian aura, the values of precision, the specifica-

FIGURE 8. Henri Matisse, *Le parebrise, sur la route de Villacoublay*, 1917. Oil on canvas, 15.25 × 22 in. The painting belongs to the Cleveland Museum of Art, bequest of L. C. MacBride. Courtesy of the estate of Henri Matisse.

tions of the engineer, and the welded connections of metallic constructions. He might as well have painted the sky, as the more consciously technophilic Robert Delaunay did, in *The Red Tower* (1911–12), through the girders of the Eiffel Tower.

Matisse's painting, as well as others, such as *Route a Calmart* (1916–17), results from drawings he made on a long car trip in 1916. The car journey excited him because he came to think of the windscreen as a "mobile balcony,"[2] a novel version of the fixed frames, such as windows and mirrors, he favored in many of his works. This painting shows the characteristic interest of his art in framing nature as view; here, rather than a balcony door frame in Nice, nature is framed by a car window. Yet the price of mobility in this painting is a radically unsettled quality. Nature is framed by technology, but not necessarily contained by it, for in the painting (a frame within a frame), the world of fields and hedges exists off to each side, disappearing toward the edge of the picture. It is as if no frame, once mobility becomes a factor, can contain: the aesthetic decision to allow us only part of a view is brought to the fore. Other strategies unsettle any assumption that this is an unmediated representation by the painter-viewer. The central scene of a framed road ahead is a stark exercise in classical perspective: this road, its banks, and marshaled lines of trees all converge at a point in the distance that complements the viewing point of the artist and the viewer before the scene. Cutting across this receding progress, however, is a fragile but insistent line in the middle of the canvas. It is no more than the realist representation of the split in early windscreens made by two sheets of glass. It imposes on the neatly framed perspective, however, a line that corresponds to the line of the horizon in many conventional landscapes but occurs here close to the viewer, so that it jarringly cuts up and dislocates the view. It offers a precise alternative to the line of the horizon. (The real horizon line, only vaguely suggested in the painting, crosses the endpoint of the perspective higher in the scene.) Further, below the windscreen frame but within the picture, Matisse displays the top of another, prior drawing, possibly of the same scene: a shadow of the painting within the painting itself. What appeared at first as an uncomplicated scene of a landscape viewed through a windscreen emerges as a series of mediations on framing and painting whatever landscape one sees.

Le parebrise, sur la route de Villacoublay really shows us at least three paintings—the overall work, the scene framed by the windscreen, and the painting or drawing which juts into the picture at the bottom of the canvas. They each draw our attention to the multiple complexities involved in the act of looking, and of editing, through the framing of what one sees. And this self-consciousness is generated in the first place by the shock, for the painterly world of Matisse, of this specific viewpoint—from within the automobile. This in turn alerts us to the ultimate source of the painting's uncanny, restless quality. As the painting-within-the-painting rests against the car's heavy wooden steering wheel, we are made aware that the car's driver is missing from the scene. The driver and the painter (who is also missing but is presumably sitting in the back seat) are in a sense equated. And the car, as the absence of a driver makes clear, is not moving. The "mobility" which excited Matisse is denied him at the very moment of creation. One senses that it is the frustration generated by this immobility which energizes the work and makes an apparently simple landscape so strange and arresting. The unexpected congruence of nature and technology may be what renders the painting, considered formally, with its numerous arrangements of parallel straight lines, almost a premonition of Piet Mondrian's yellow, red, and blue grids in, for example, *Broadway Boogie Woogie* (1942–43), another painting about traffic. More unsettling: the stress on a mobile viewing post which now is forced to be *still*. It is as if the painting's cross-slashed perspective, composed of its slipping subviews on each side (it is a triptych for the age of technology) and its smaller painting propped where the driver should be driving, posits itself as the final moment, in modern perception, of a gaze that can be wholly still. Its uncanny stillness begs us to consider how a scene in movement, at speed, might appear.

We have seen in chapter 3 how the car, as the most luxurious and expensive commodity, proffered itself not merely as an object to be acquired but also as a mechanism for the overcoming of its own commodity inertia, in that it granted the purchaser access to a radically new experience. Here we will examine the specifics of which this experience consists. By "experience" here I mean that which is apprehended by the body, through its senses, as a new or more intense sensation or affect (rather than that which is thought, as a new idea or paradigm). "Experience" in this definition is that which exceeds the deadening reification imposed by commodity fetishism, defined by Marx in chapter 1 of *Capital* as the state in which the relations between people are mediated by commodities and replaced by the relation between the subject and the commodity itself. Experience here is posited as a physically apprehended sensation that, by short-circuiting cognition (and hence consciousness) nevertheless potentially possesses a utopian or even political quality: in its novel excessiveness, it has the chance to carry the experiencing subject beyond the all-congealing network of commodification and toward a level where critical praxis might be possible. Such new versions of experience, enabled by the automobile as new technology, turn out to center in the first instance around vision and the sense of sight.

"Rapid motion through space elates one," as the young writer James Joyce in his short story "After the Race" observed.[3] The subject of this chapter is how people saw in new ways while they experienced this novel level of technically induced elation. To represent this new kind of seeing, painters, photographers, film directors, and others developed images that at times tentatively, at others bizarrely, worked to represent the reality of this new sensation. Seeing while physically moving at considerable speeds was not new: Wolfgang Schivelbusch has described the new kinds of looking possible, since the mid-nineteenth century, through a train window.[4] Both high and popular art forms were fascinated by the possibilities of looking at speed. Proust in *À la recherche du temps perdu* and Woolf in *Orlando* dwell on the delights of looking while journeying in the automobile. The Royal Academy painter and designer of car-racing trophies Hubert von Herkhomer claimed that "the pleasure [of motoring] . . . is seeing Nature as

I could in no other way see it . . . one picture after another delights my artistic eye."[5] At least from the moment that cars began to be enclosed and could move at average speeds of fourteen miles per hour and more, seeing through the windscreen of a moving car was considered a novel, even incredible, kind of experience.

The automobile offered the eye new challenges. This novelty was enhanced because of the parallels between the human gaze from a moving machine and the advances, during the same period, in new machineries of representation. If the still camera and still photography match the age of the railroads, then the movie camera and moving film match the era of the automobile. Further, just as people were getting their first opportunity to look from moving automobiles, high art began to take an intense interest in the possibilities of technology to enhance the human gaze. While this interest had numerous outcomes, from the Futurists' fascination with automobiles to Francis Picabia's 1915 portraits using automobile bolts and pistons for *291*, the journal founded by the photographer Alfred Stieglitz, cars and their culture also became an artistic subject. The apparently mundane act of looking either from the vantage point of a moving car or out of a car window became in the early twentieth century a characteristic gesture of a radical reevaluation of human looking aided by technology. This new look, in turn, was at the center of a reevaluation of the relations of the human body and machinery — particularly machines that moved bodies at speed.

Windscreen Teletopology

Matisse's painting comes from one of two new subgenres of images characteristic of the first years of the twentieth century, both of which owe their existence to the invention of the windscreen. First there were views from behind the window, of the world in front; conversely there arose another genre of views from outside the car through the screen to those seated within. The glance into the car, as we shall see, explored aspects of the driving classes as subjects; views through the windscreen from within offered a more radical opportunity. They could represent new ways of seeing made possible by the new velocities of motion — of the gaze in movement.

To reconstruct a windscreen teletopology, we need to recover the sense of shock felt by the first drivers. This shock has since been lost to us, as bodies and senses adapted to the perceptual challenges posed by the new technology. One might object that this initial shock was lessened because automobiles only gradually came to be capable of the kinds of speeds at which the act of looking from a moving vehicle could be so strange as to be shocking. Numerous accounts of the road and countryside "whizzing by" however, not least by Henry Ford himself, suggest that even passengers in cars traveling at fifteen miles per hour felt the novelty of speed looking. Thus the act of seeing at fifty miles per hour, which people were soon being called on to perform, must at first, especially for the driver, have been nothing short of traumatic. This gaze-at-speed presented itself as a limit gaze: that is, as an effortful, stressful, and willful act at the margin of the humanly possible. This speed looking highlighted the limits of human vision, and even the fragility of the act of seeing. This jars with the Enlightenment certitude of the reality of the observed object, on which the long nineteenth-century tradition of realist representation, and scientific observation as a whole, had rested. (Before the windscreen and enclosed car, the elaborate goggles of the first drivers, masterpieces of Victorian mass production and among the earliest techno-bibelots, testify to how stressful this new looking was.) The car's windscreen, along with the still camera, the moving camera, and other technologies of the ocular which came into widespread use at the beginning of the twentieth century, were symptoms of a new phase of modernity where technologies pushed their users toward their perceptual limits. In doing so, they made those users question the value of their own corporeal perceptual efforts in assessing what constituted reality in space. Any presumed correspondence between the tangible or the visual and the actual could be put radically into question. To look while traveling at speed, as unsettled perceptual limit work, was to become aware that to believe one's eyes was increasingly untenable, and that what constituted the material real might be put into question as well.

This occurred first because the viewer through the windscreen of a speeding car was presented with an unprecedented succession and variety of scenes, a massive sensory overload of roads, nature, structures, people, written signs, others. With all this flashing before her, the viewer had the task of editing, choosing what was important, ignoring the rest, and re-stitching scenes into a narrative that would, in turn, make sense of the confusing mass of scenes that followed at every succeeding moment. This newly violent variety of looking was altogether excessive when compared to the certitudes of the look which composes its (single) scene by means of perspective. A perspective-composing look demands a contemplative time, dependent on the fixity (real or implied) of the viewer. This allows her to locate, in the scene, a fixed point within it, which is the mirror image of her own presumed if unspoken fixed vantage point outside it. This fixity allows her to imagine herself, once the scene has now been composed in tacit relation to her own now-central subject position, as mistress of all she surveys. ("Everything I see is in principle within my reach, at least within reach of my sight, marked on the map of the 'I can,'" as Maurice Merleau-Ponty brilliantly summed up the logic of this unassumingly hegemonic perspective-directed gaze.)[6] To look while driving at speed, on the contrary, with the look which exists now at the limit point of the human possibility to see, was stressful, and could entertain no such certainties. Rather, what was needed was an editing system, and what was brought into play was a version, improvisational and always unsure, of sampling—that is, choosing here and there, in split-second successive decisions, what appears important before the eye makes contact with a new element in a new scene. For the anxious driver, for example, the solution might be to focus with a determined effort in creating a perspectival point on the road ahead, so that all detail to the left and right is edited out or survives as a mere blur. This blur, whatever the strategy used, will constitute the sign of the limit of visibility in speed viewing. Blur signifies that excess or waste scene that is excluded by the viewer-sampler. Through blur, this excess of the seen still intrudes itself and declares its presence as a kind of forced unconscious, and its message is that to observe at speed is always to run the risk that the scene(s) will decompose. Scenic overload so intense as to threaten scenic decomposition, all countered in the moving subject by an improvised sampling: this is the new, tentative quasi logistics of the automobile gaze.

To this desperately unpredictable, always potentially shocking protocol of the speed look there is added a further uncertainty, one alluded to even by Matisse, a painter intent on raising anxieties about the effects of the juxtaposition of interior and exterior space, when he painted the countryside from within the uncannily stationary interior of a closed car. This is the uncertainty, promulgated by the presence of the intervening windscreen, about whether anything beyond it has a material existence at all. Once the view is framed by the metal of the pillars, the possibility of recomposing it within the terms of a perspectival arrangement is granted, but this possibility turns out to be an illusion, given that, in a moving car, the view that is framed is being constantly altered. Yet this teasing possibility, which invites us to recompose the view as if it were a representation, thereby suggests to us that what is beyond the screen might *merely* be a representation—that is, a virtuality with only a mimetic relation to the real. One might assume that this constant exposure to new scenes, which occurs when looking as one moves at speed, would move the subject closer to that which is seen, and so make the real more tangible. However, the reverse is what occurs, because, at least within the confines of a closed car, the viewer is at all times separated from what she sees and invited, by the framing of the windscreen and windows, to conceptualize the visible as a representation. This makes for a continual othering of that which is seen, an acknowledgment, simultaneous with the look, that what is seen is not part of the (moving) position which the self inhabits. The gaze through the windscreen is always unavoidably a heterotopic look, which harbors in this inevitable othering a suspicion that the framed scene is virtual rather than real. (At this point, remember Jacques Derrida's definition of *différance* as "archi-writing—this interval is what might be called spacing.")[7] In this gaze which presupposes différance, any certainty about the reality of what is seen is radically put into question, and the possibility that it might merely be a memory, or a mirage, or a dream, or any version of virtual image, is ever present. The windscreen then is very close to the movie screen and even the television screen.

The view through the windscreen of a moving car therefore turns out to be a radically bifurcated experience. On the one hand, the shock effect of multiple images that appear to rush up close and then zip by on either side seems to offer a new kind of sensory immediacy, a contact between the viewer and the scene that is more intense, because faster, than any previously imaginable. Paradoxically, however, the same view turns out to be constructed around a new kind of distancing, a glance that is always framed in advance, which offers the sensation of looking into a scene of which one is not a part. The windscreen, by denying the chance of other kinds of contact, suggests that the scene outside might exist only as a virtuality. These two notions—of intense closeness and of ethereal possible virtuality—are present at once as clashing, opposed elements of the viewer's experience of this novel gaze. Seeing, within this technologically prostheticized framework, in other words, is possible only within a dialectical structure, in which the claims of experiential immediacy and illusionary virtuality are counterposed. These counterpoints correspond to speed's appeal to a newly intense experience on the one hand and the mass marketing of the car as desirable commodity on the other. The act of looking as intense exposure to multiple stimuli is at the center of the speed sensation as a radically new, pleasurable experience; the anxiety (and reassurance) that what is seen is merely a simulation befits the fact that the car is a new kind of consumer commodity. It is a commodity which offers both to mediate all lived experience and distance it from what is felt at the same time as it appears to make experience more immediate.

These two trajectories, in turn, neatly map onto two famous, and contrasting, accounts of what it means to live in modernity. That the gaze from the auto offers a new level of intense, shocking visual experience makes it a star exhibit in the modern milieu described by Max Weber, that world of shocking, overstimulating, mechanical, hyperabstracted, and fatiguing urban life that is the lot of the modern city dweller. Georg Simmel, in "Metropolis and Mental Life," described, in terms easily applied to the experience of seeing from the automobile, how "the psychological basis for the metropolitan type of individual consists in the intensification of nervous stimulation which results from the swift and uninterrupted change of outer and inner stimuli . . . the sharp discontinuity in the grasp of a single glance, and the unexpectedness of onrushing impressions."[8] That Simmel here begins with vision in his adroit description of sensing in a speeded-up environment simply proves Martin Jay's contention that vision is the primary sense in modernity, even at the moment when the hectic quality of modern life was considered by Simmel and others to be placing more dignified versions of sensing under threat. Yet this anguished, nervy narrative of the low-level brutalities of urban life in the twentieth century existed side by side with a counterstory which dwelt on modernity's endless capacity, on the contrary, to suffuse its denizens in a dreamscape of narcotic images. This version is perhaps best exemplified by the notes of Walter Benjamin in *The Arcades Project*, in which, although he speaks of shock as that moment where people come into consciousness of the reality of the dreamscape in which they move, he sees modernity as the triumph of *Vergnugungsindustrie*, the pleasure industry, with the commodity, casting a new kind of mythic aura, as its cynosure. This is the forerunner of the "society of the spectacle" memorably anatomized by the situationist Guy Debord, for whom the spectacle as dreamscape is capitalism's ploy to reenchant the alienated existence of the bedazzled consumer, as a means to deny him any real agency:

> The more [the spectator] contemplates, the less he lives; the more he accepts recognizing himself in the dominant images of need, the less he understands his own existence and his own desires. The externality

of the spectacle in relation to the active man appears in the fact that his own gestures are no longer his, but those of another who represents them to him.[9]

When this bewitched spectatorship is the activity that precludes the subject's active agency, this version of the entrapment of the modern gaze on a virtuality, a dreamscape which disables subjectivity, would seem the opposite of the version proposed by Simmel of the hyperstimulated and, for Simmel, thereby more intelligent modern spectator.

These two accounts of modernist looking are not, however, mutually exclusive. To the extent that they are opposed, they lead to two contradictory accounts of a modernist, technologically enhanced gaze; the fascination of both with the novelty of the new milieu nevertheless renders their conclusions on the agency of the modernist subject surprisingly compatible. When Simmel describes how the urban cosmopolite, confronting repeated shocks, develops a hard carapace of dulling indifference, he comes close to imagining that varied, successive series of visual stimuli as a spectacle in Debord's negative sense. Conversely, when Benjamin describes in his essay "On Surrealism" how the "profane illumination" of the realm of dream images produces a level of such mass enervation that it leads to a communal bodily tension, his language of corporeal overstimulation is uncannily close to the more matter-of-fact urban sociology of Simmel.[10] The extent to which either writer works out what his account implies for any given subject's political agency has been hotly debated by commentators since; the need for a politics of the gaze is clearly an issue proposed, at least implicitly, in the writings of both. Likewise it suggests itself at once when we return to what could have been a prize exhibit for each author's method: the new act, apparently so simple, of looking out the window of a speeding car. The new speed gaze from the moving car brings each of these opposing versions of modernity into urgent, immediate confrontation.

This new gaze is both lived, physical experience and consumer pleasure at once. It is a vivid example both of Simmel's overstimulation and of Benjamin's reenchanted spectacle made possible by capitalism. Can a look at the ways in which this new gaze was described or represented suggest that one account is more valid than another? If they do so, what does this new look imply for the agency of the subject who enjoys this gaze? The speeding car offers the possibilities of a novel gaze that overcomes perspectival looking. Does this engender in the rider or passenger new possibilities of action, that is, an agency that could properly be termed political; or does it immerse that subject more deeply in the dreamscape, offering merely an illusion of the freedom which car advertisers have from the first attached to this technology of personal speed? Or perhaps it is possible for the modernist subject to sustain a reaction to this new gaze as both hyperstimulation and narcotic dreamscape at once, playing one against the other, or zapping from one to the other, in a new grammar of perception which short-circuits evaluations of the authentic and inauthentic and proposes a new rhythm of sensation to navigate space and its multiple scenes. Here I consider a series of reactions at the time to speeded-up seeing in order to examine the versions of agency they imply.

Bergson through Futurism

The great philosopher of these vivid unsettlings of the visual by the new possibilities of movement, who theorized them at much the same time as they occurred, was Henri Bergson, just as his most brilliant reader, writing a half century later around the moment when electronic rather than merely mechanically aided looking and viewing had become commonplace, was Gilles Deleuze. Bergson's usefulness for our purposes comes from the way in which, particularly in his early work *Matter and Memory*, he retheorizes the human subject's sense of her occupation of space in light of the more complex relation between (mental) image and memory. New ways of looking, among them technologically enhanced means, had influenced Bergson in rethinking the "mental image," the notion of the "mind's eye."

In Bergson's work, Simmel's sociological mass observation, it might be said, is carried to its theoretical conclusions, to the point where the totality of the subject's perception of space is put into question. In the course of Bergson's discussions of the meaning of movement and flux, a whole new conception of space is implied. This reimagining of the notion of space in philosophy found its counterpart in the same period in a similar, and more popularly influential, review of what constitutes space in scientific terms, notably in the work of scientists such as Einstein and Bohr. If Bergson's philosophizing, however, begins as epistemology and becomes metaphysics, then the work of the artists he influenced, particularly the Futurists, shows its limitations as a means of reimagining the problem of whether the speed gaze is stimulation or dream immersion, whether it enhances the possibilities of active agency or haplessly submerges the subject deeper in the

Vergnugungsindustrie of capital. Some Futurist production reminds us of the profound political dangers of overzealous applied Bergsonism, in that it was used by the Futurists in their support of emerging and then triumphalist Italian Fascism. Nevertheless aspects of Futurist experimentation and research can be recuperated, I suggest, to teach us not only that a too-avid Simmelian reading of modernist stimulation can foster empty fantasies of power, but that the stimulations of the speed gaze can only be dealt with in relation to the materiality of the perceiving body, its sensations, and its dreams.

Bergson suggests that space can no longer be thought of as an abstract, always already existing ground or plane on or across which movement takes place, or as an empty surface which precedes the objects that occupy or traverse it. That conception of space is a useful abstraction produced by the logic of a particular protocol of looking and image making — a regime of visual composition which, for Bergson, is thoroughly questionable.[11] Claiming that "abstract space is, indeed, at bottom, nothing but the mental diagram of infinite divisibility,"[12] he posits instead the notion that it is movement which generates space. Movement, therefore, is not simply a progress through this abstract plane, which can be known only when mapped as a succession of momentarily held positions, but instead a play of tangibilities, especially images, a matter of pragmatic action rather than contemplative, static positions, and a fluctuation of emergence, intensities, extensity, and becoming, rather than a matter of Cartesian gridded space to be mapped or known.

Bergson reimagines space as an entity dynamically produced through motion rather than an abstraction that must always be thought to precede such motion; space, to use his own term, is *an unfolding*. His bravura account of its continuous creation is strikingly analogous to the epistemology of the contingent, often traumatic windscreen gaze that I described earlier. That gaze too unfolds new spaces continuously; reacts to some of them much more intensely than others; is always directed to action (in continuing the journey) rather than to static contemplation; values the continuous emergence of new scenes, sensations, reactions, and connections; and, given its radical contingency and unpredictability, seems primed to put any certitude about the spatial real into doubt altogether. In these terms, Bergson brilliantly disposes of the idea of "place" — which could be defined as the aura-laden glorification of one of those static points of contemplation on the old Cartesian grid. His celebration of this reimagined "unfolding" space of an active, ultra-intense subjective perception is very much in keeping with any account of the relation between subject and space as this relation is being renegotiated once the subject becomes a viewer in a technological prosthesis which moves her physically as she looks.

Bergson's account is in keeping with a celebratory description of this new technologically driven gaze. He concludes his extraordinary exposition by claiming that what is needed to enable a proliferation of intensities is a return to the actuality of immediate, lived experience.[13] The philosopher, feminist, and theorist of space Elizabeth Grosz, in a compelling rereading of Bergson through what she terms (in a footnote) the "bastardized, anal reading" of his work by Gilles Deleuze,[14] chooses to depart from his thought at this point, instead designating a play of virtualities and actualities in search of the restoration of becoming (i.e., becoming other-than-itself) to both space and time.[15] This is indeed the point at which the Bergsonian analysis turns to advocacy and must be treated warily, for Bergson's account of how motion unfolds and actualizes space, while brilliantly evocative of the potential implications of shifting perception in the machine age away from the logic of what might be called homogeneous vision, only implies some greater immediacy and, to use my term up to this point, a more intense experience. His version pushes us to accept that the alternatives to the Cartesian gridded conception of space and hence movement are *necessarily* utopian, liberating, or in some sense elemental.

In the first, closely argued chapter of his Bergsonian analysis of film technique, *Cinema I: The Movement Image*, Gilles Deleuze makes two extraordinary claims for Bergson: first, that he transformed philosophy by turning it toward the issue of the new rather than the eternal, to ask, "How are the production and appearance of something new possible?" and second, that what Bergson aims to do is "to give modern science the metaphysic that corresponds to it, which it lacks as one half lacks the other."[16] Newness gets delineated, then, within the sphere of a metaphysics, and this metaphysics is focused on movement. As Deleuze explains succinctly at the outset, movement for Bergson is "distinct from the space covered, . . . is indivisible, or cannot be divided without changing quantitatively each time it is divided. . . . Movements are heterogeneous, irreducible among themselves" (1). Bergson's movement is not reducible to mapped instants in (conventionally conceptualized) space or time, for if you map it as two near-instantaneous points in space, as Deleuze notes gleefully, "It will always occur in the interval between the two, in other words behind your back" (1). And this mobility which occurs "behind your back" is the famous Bergsonian *durée*, which is then thought of as a whole "which implies that movement expresses something more profound, which is the change in duration or in the whole. . . . To say that duration is change is part of the definition. . . . Now movement expresses a change in duration or in the whole. Movement is a translation in space. Now each time there is a translation of parts of space, there is also a quantitative change in a whole" (8).

Movement, conceptualized as the durée, is here nothing short of change, and hence, it appears, the engine of history itself. Yet this durée, as Deleuze also notes, is a metaphysics; he subsequently terms it "a spiritual reality" (11). As such, it can only act on *relations* — and relations are always external to the terms of objects themselves. Bergson's philosophical broaching of the new, then, while it appears to promise an account of how movement — especially fast movement, speed, velocity — can be the basis, first, for a reconceptualization of the spatial imperatives which underpin Enlightenment rationalism, and subsequently for a new account of historical development itself, needs to be treated with extreme circumspection by any critical theory which takes a materialist reading to be the goal of its intellectual investigation. For the materialist critic, the durée remains at best an unduly optimistic term to delineate the potential of movement and speed.

Bergson's *Matter and Memory* was published in 1896 and is thus almost contemporary with the appearance of the first commercially produced motorcars. Its "shifting of the soul this time from the brain to the motor" (the phrase is Paul Virilio's, from another context)[17] might be thought of in part as expressing the optimism regarding speed technologies implicit in that moment. It is in the writings of his most avid disciples, the Italian Futurists, and in particular the early manifestoes by F. T. Marinetti, especially the famous Futurist Manifesto, which appeared in *Le Figaro* on February 20, 1909, the assorted pieces published in France as *Le futurisme* in 1912, and the more cogently elaborated discussions of Umberto Boccioni, especially his *Technical Manifesto of Futurist Sculpture* of April 1912, however, that, famously, the automobile is the explicit symbol of the new speed culture, and fast movement's potential is celebrated not merely theoretically but also as a pragmatic and tangible experience. Futurism today is perhaps most remembered first for its brutal misogyny and second for the movement's reprehensible advocacy of Italian Fascism. What I wish to show here is that its members' initial, enthusiastic pre–World War I investigations, in moving from the theory which fascinated them to a working model of the subject-artist's relation to technologies of speed, caused them to confront implications in the theory which, at best, betrayed its limitations as the basis for any kind of politics whatsoever and, at worst, displayed the ease of its deployment in favor of groups using brute force to seize power.

The Futurists' first assumption was that the force of movement and speed needed necessarily to be embodied. From the start, Marinetti was interested in speed not in the abstract, and not as an element "always behind your back," as Deleuze claims that Bergson represents movement, but only as it was embodied in the clamoring, active artist himself. The often ridiculed opening set piece of the Futurist Manifesto of 1909, where Marinetti and his friends are shown feverish in the face of "our ancestral ennui on opulent turkish carpets," which Rayner Banham assures us is not a pastiche of a decadent novel of the period,[18] far from being merely self-promoting, is the absolute prerequisite for the stark list of resolutions which follows. Showing the young artists' unease with their bourgeois milieu as a fever-inducing restlessness, and deploying a battery of frustrated action verbs — "awake all night . . . constellated . . . trampled . . . arguing to the limits . . . blackening . . . sweat . . . ferret" — as a means to kindle similar sensations of impatience in the reader, the manifesto's opening implies that the desire for movement at speed, rather than being aroused by the sight of "locomotives that hurl forward at insensate speed," was instead merely assuaged by such sights. That is, this desire for speed was already inherent in the artist as subject even before the new locomotives arrived to inspire him. For the Futurists, the durée is imported into the psyche and recast as a subjective trait. When the young Futurists become drivers of their automobiles, an activity described, appropriately for the period, in terms of riding a difficult horse, this speed is realized:

> We drew near to the snorting beasts and laid our hands on their burning breasts. Then I flung myself like a corpse on a bier across the seat of my machine, but sat up at once under the steering wheel, poised like a guillotine blade across my stomach.[19]

Here the verb change is crucial: the language of frustrated action — "I flung myself like a corpse" — which amply suggests a temptation to lapse into decadent languor, is renounced at the moment of contact with the car, which causes the Futurist to primly "sit up at once." Even here, however, it is the subject's own will which matters; Marinetti (perhaps inspired by another major influence, Walt Whitman) infuses Bergson's ideas with the self-aggrandizing impetus of Nietzsche's will to power. Some years later, nevertheless, Marinetti, in one of the pieces published in *Le futurisme*, would repudiate Nietzsche's superman as the holder of an all-too-classical pedigree.[20] The verbs grow more active, the tone more declamatory, as the Manifesto progresses: the message is that the Futurist must embody speed, then use it. This Futurist artist is quintessentially a driver of an automobile, turning the speed he embodies into a force for revolutionary change. Compare a relief sculpture of 1884 by the proto-Futurist Milanese painter and sculptor Medardo Rosso, *Impressione d'omnibus*, for example, with Marinetti's rapturous account of his friend's driving at dawn.[21] In Rosso's work, the four omnibus passengers who are represented, even if a Rodin-like roughness in the rendering suggests the blurring effect of people glimpsed only for a moment, are all shown as stiff with the boredom of modern mechanized life even if they are traveling at (relative) speed: the person carried at speed, rather than the driver, is, it appears, truly powerless. Marinetti's young racers, in contrast, actively and furiously wrestle with their powerful cars as a means to realize their energized selves. In taking into their own bodies the speed that marks their subjectivity (they live most fully when speeding), they display speed as a force. Thus for the Futurists, speed was "spiritual" (to use Deleuze's term regarding the notion of movement in Bergson) only when it was a force, that is, a form of violence which, embodied in each of them, aggrandized each personally. The Futurists' self-centered realism about speed transforms the transcendental tendency in Bergson into a Nietzschean program of will to power achievable by harnessing new technologies of personal speed. Their texts teach us that movement will first be experienced as embodied, and as a force which transforms the subject's energy into new and unprecedented power.

The second immediate lesson of early Futurist writings and experiments is a more general version of the first: if speed is embodied as force, then it invariably inheres in, and is only exhibited through, matter—often through the medium of the human or animal body. Speed's inevitable materiality seems a Futurist given. It is thus appropriate that the finest Futurist artist, Umberto Boccioni, was a sculptor, one who in works ranging from his much-discussed *Forme uniche della continuità nello spazio* (Unique Forms of Continuity in Space) of 1913 to his now destroyed *Espansione spiraliza de muscoli in movimento* (Spiral Expansion of Muscles in Movement) of 1912,[22] and in his careful, complex readings of Bergson ("Absolute Motion + Relative Motion = Dynamism," 1914),[23] was obsessed with the perception of dynamic movement, but only as it could be discerned in moving objects, or, almost invariably, in moving bodies. Typically, a Boccioni sculpture displays a form, such as a human body, contorted and tweaked along a diverse series of planes. These diverse planes suggest force vectors that cut out beyond the form itself to intersect with every plane in space outside it; note, however, that its strange vectorality works for the viewer only because she implicitly compares it to a realist body that is, as it were, hidden in the folds of this de-composed and abstracted flesh. Boccioni followed Rodin in believing that sculptors should work to represent the movement of a figure between two poses; it was in representing this version of the durée that the artist betters the photographer, who, as in the case of the pioneering "movement studies" of Eadweard Muybridge and Étienne-Jules Marey, can in fact only "capture" movement as a succession of still images.[24] Movement imagined in this way is a force within a material figure. In this sense, Boccioni's work resembles the early accounts of car speeds by observers on the roadside, astounded by this new force hurtling by.

The career of Giacomo Balla, the most notable Futurist painter, moves from portrayals of people, swallows, small dogs, and machines at speed toward more fully abstract versions of speed sensation. His *Penetraᵹioni dinamiche d'automobile* (Dynamic Penetrations of an Automobile) of 1913 (figure 9) might be taken as a limit point of the representation of realist forms in his work: here the speeding automobile is barely discernible as a thin outline veering off to the left of the canvas amid a rich torrent of heavily shaded force vector lines which, meeting at sharp angles, denote speed force. Look closely: an initial set of lines, more symmetrically posed, meets at what turns out to be the focus of the painting: a point corresponding to the center of the car's steering wheel. Even in this almost abstracted representation of speed's force, speed is embodied in a physical form. Likewise it is a mistake to see Balla's more thoroughly abstracted speed representations, such as his *Spessori d'atmosphera*, painted in the same year, as abstractions in the sense in which that term is used, for example, about the sculptures of Russian Constructivists of the same period such as Vladimir Tatlin, or the paintings of El Lissitzky. Despite the intensely suggestive series of circles and succession of parabolas of this work (one of four made to illustrate a promotional text by Boccioni, *Pittura scultura futuriste*, all of the originals now lost), which registers the blur of speed superbly, these precise painterly gestures were themselves the result of obsessive and exhaustive experiments by the artist into how the perception of speed

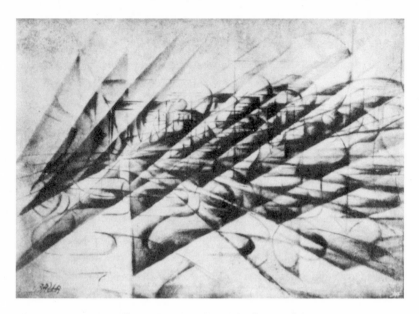

FIGURE 9. Giacomo Balla, *Penetrazione dinamiche d'automobile*, 1913.
Courtesy of the artist's estate.

can be represented—in this case, into how speed effects the perception of
light. They are representations of specific forms, however attenuated: the
painterly task is still the making visible, as accurately as the brush can, of
forces whose energy emanates from material objects. These are studies of
the limits of perception which it is necessary to reach to see speed; they
resolutely focus on a dynamic, but still existing, materiality.

One might claim, then, that despite the bombast and determined self-
promotion of the manifestoes, there is a relative lack of theoretical or representational ambition in Futurist writing or artistic production: the group
could only theorize speed as a force embodied in a human subject, and only
represent it as a force embodied in the material world. But if their project
appears now as a narrowly and, as Futurist political affiliations would show,
dangerously modified Bergsonism, one may assert that the artists' attempt
to "apply" the philosopher's ideas, and their easy marriage of them to
Nietzschean and Whitmanesque versions of selfhood, mainly exposed the
limitations of the transcendental thrust of Bergson's notion of the durée.
The Futurist Manifesto and paintings perform the valuable task, for our
purposes, of returning the issue of movement at speed to the experience
of this movement by the human body, and of insisting that the representation of such speed effects can only take place as forces in relation to ob-

jects, matter, and the material world in general. At the limit point of Balla's painterly investigations, moreover, we see him arrive at an examination of the ways in which such new experience of the material world is knowable through seeing; his task too is an attempt at a new teletopology for the mechanical era.

This sensation, as the frantic idealism of both the philosopher and Futurists indicates, was consciously available, however, only as a limit experience: ready to slide into the transcendental realm, on the one hand, or manifest itself as physical force — so that it could be dangerously available for the most brutal and retrograde populist politics — on the other. That is: Simmelian trauma as the basic experience of modernity was recast by the Futurists, in the case of the subject's interaction with new technologies of speed and with the motorcar in particular, as force that enhanced individual will to power; the Benjaminian version of modernity as dream immersion, likewise, is recast in Bergsonian mode as a more or less spiritual delineation of the relations between moving objects. If we place Bergson and the Futurists in their historical contexts and imagine the effect of their respective polemics against the background of a new barrage of mostly more lowbrow discourses — advertisements, comic books, car magazines — about the new technologies of personal speed and their effects in this period, then we can see that both were avant-garde in bringing the issue of movement and speed into their respective fields. Each could only articulate movement as a limit discourse, one on the cusp of consciousness and the expressible, one liable at all times to an expressiveness that challenged the experiential.

Articulating Blur

This limit discourse of speed was, in relation to vision, balanced on a further paradox: while movement at speed promised that one would see more — a multiplicity of scenes replacing other scenes in an endless parade — the short time available to look at any one scene meant that the faster one moved, the less one saw. Hence *blur*, the effective erasure of the visible, became the dominant trope for representing the sensation of what was seen at speed, from a car, in the years between Bergson's *Matter and Memory* and the Futurist Manifesto. While Bergson in philosophy and the Futurists in painting, sculpture, and polemics were recasting the issue of speed as, respectively, a new antimaterialism and a new applied Nietzschean and reactionary protopolitics, a mass of artists, reporters, and writers were intuiting their own versions of how what is seen at speed might be represented. For them, as we shall see, variations on blur could annotate a hierarchy of responses to, and perceptions registered in, speed seeing, in ways which could make the new activity of driving seem both a "romance," old-fashioned, embedded in nostalgic narratives of quest, heroism, and status, and a shockingly modern, up-to-the-minute practice in which nothing less modern than new kinds of perception could be sensed and understood. Many of these artists and writers were employed to promote the fascination with what came to be known as automobilism and as such had a vested interest in casting it as a romance. What is noticeable, however, is that the romance narratives (as in, say, the account of an endurance race or in the cloying copy of car advertising) almost always give way to excited attempts to render speed as an altogether new experience—and especially to show the novelty of seeing at comparatively great speeds.

In these renditions—as one would expect in any accounts where the limits of the available resources to describe any sensuous experience have been reached—versions of synesthesia proliferate. Accounts based on one sense are plundered to convey the newly intense experience of the other one in question. Such transfers are also short-circuited, however, by a paradox of speed seeing: while one apparently sees more, the fastness of multiple exposures means that in fact one sees less. Into this representational impasse, where what apparently is available is an excessiveness (of images) but what in fact is opened up is a sense of lack (of those massed scenes unseen), artists and writers imported varied accounts of how a new kind of prosthetic seeing operates, how this new kind of seeing recalibrates the relation of the eye to the other sense organs as well as to memory, emotion, and thinking, and how, in this recalibration, reordered models of the human subject as agent were being thrown up. This subject as agent might not lapse into either the repeatedly shocked figure described by Simmel or the modernist dream-sleeper evoked by Benjamin but would juggle shocking image changes and the effects of overexposure with dream-inducing images. This varied work of looking would be orchestrated in a synesthetic complex which could radically recast the prostheticized subject.

Such a figure could not be teased out in terms of old romance narratives. Those action dramas, as in the case of pre-Conradian colonial adventurer novels such as H. Rider Haggard's *Allan Quatermain* (1887) and John Buchan's *The Half-Hearted* (1900), depended utterly on the dominance of the eye: the explorer-hero of the imperial romance would be master of all he beheld. The new romance heroes of the postimperialist moment were instead the athletes and mechanics who carried human speed capacities to their limits; for them, the eye was a guidance and direction system (like radar) rather than a precursor and sign of territorial possession. In this regard, there is a suggestive moment in an essay by the author Wyndham Lewis, critic and imitator of the Futurists in Britain, when he discusses what, with perverse and characteristically Futurist bombast, he calls "the Romance of War." Speaking of how, when first brought to the front in 1914, he could see nothing but felt keenly the "romance" of the battle, he comments: "The truth is, of course, that it is not what you see at all, that makes an event romantic to you, but what you *feel*."[25] Lewis here expresses the dilemma not only of war painters but of the artists and writers representing car culture as well, even as he declares the way beyond it: when the eye confronts a lack, the other senses — and the emotions, he implies — rush into the vacuum created. This in turn — and here he is much less forthcoming — begets a new kind of romance, where the tatters of the old tropes of pluck, gamesmanship, and derring-do maintain a precarious and stilted twilight existence as the threadbare emblems of earlier heroisms alongside a new order of synesthetic perception which prioritizes the optimal arrangement of the human body's observations and responses and a monomaniacal self-monitoring in order that the speed attained can itself be overcome. The older narrative machineries could no longer arrange in any recognizable comfort the onrush of images that confronted, for example, the automobile driver; new arrangements, new ways of processing the seen in relation to other kinds of sensing, feeling, and thinking, were incrementally developed so that speed seeing could be understood. Realist narrative proved unequal to representing these new complexes of sensations, its focus on succession and the progress of linear time too sedate for an experience which was to be held only for a moment. Images — pictures, paintings, sketches — which delineate spaces rather than temporalities turn out to be more symptomatic in charting the change in sensory powers. Before speed was described, it was shown. "History decomposes," as Walter Benjamin put it, "into images, not narrratives."[26]

One reason for the relative lack of narratives of speed was a new focus on the present instant, the here and now. This focus was matched by new technologies of representation to record the new sensation of speed — the most important being the camera with a shutter speed fast enough to record a moving object. One can see how this worked in the finest of the early cars-in-motion photographs, those of the French photographer Jacques Henri Lartigue between 1905 and 1912. Lartigue is routinely praised in histories of photography as the originator of the "snapshot aesthetic." As he began to use a hand-held camera in place of his earlier tripod-mounted one precisely to enable him to capture the new sensation of seeing speeding cars, here clearly is a case of car-as-technology itself almost demanding creative innovation in another technologically enabled art form.

In Lartigue's most famous shot, of a car in the Grand Prix of the Automobile Club of France in 1912 (figure 10), for example, the residual romance narrative still holds sway: in the tensed, hunched shoulders and gripping hands of the driver, we have the image of the explorer-adventurer par excellence. In fact, the image's most daring artistic gesture, its drastic cropping so that the front half of the car is cut out of the photograph, focuses us all the more on the driver-adventurer rather than on his automobile. Nevertheless this cropping also signals the inability of any image, even of a camera shot as bold and original as this one, to contain or represent a speeding car in full. The instant, the cropping insists, is all; if it is not "captured," then the car and its speeding glory have escaped. This photograph, the cropping makes clear, is a limit-image. Within the half of the nonexisting diptych that Lartigue supplies us here, paradoxically the car itself appears quite still. However, this stillness is focused on the tense hand gripping the steering wheel: the effort of the hero of the romance of speed, in other words, is the photo's most still point of all.

Presenting this particular imaging of speed, Lartigue's photo is very close to Balla's *Penetrazioni dinamiche d'automobile* of a year later (except that there the car, also cut in half, points in the opposite direction); both are hampered in fully showing the speed effect because they are representing a speeding object from the point of a stationary spectator rather than from the viewpoint of the driver himself. The still spectator, even one with a movable hand-held camera, must, as it were, find his counterpoint in the vehicle's driver, whom he then must also show, mirroring himself, as a still point, without blur. Using the same focus on stillness as the vortex of suggestions of movement, Balla can show a vehicle's movement as abstracted arcs and planes, but only as arcs that radiate from the relatively realistically portrayed car and steering wheel itself. One might claim that an older version of human agency—the heroic idea that the subject is in charge of the speeding technology—is what stills the point at which the hero's hands come in contact with the steering wheel here: the ruling idea is that

FIGURE 10. Jacques-Henri Lartigue, *A Competitor in the Grand Prix of the Automobile Club of France, 1912*. Courtesy of Friends of J.-H. Lartigue, Paris.

human control is what matters. It is also the technology of the camera's eye, however, that is the maker of this point of stillness. The camera eye, faster than the human eye, captures an instant, which it then renders as still. Ultimately the snapshot is unable to show speed as such. How speed *is* shown in Lartigue's photo is through the contrast of the still car body and driver with a series, first, of blurred and second, of angled, elements: the roadway, which exists as a swish of lines in the bottom third of the photo, four or five shadowy spectators, the two poles or trees are shown as blurred. The spectators, poles, and even the car's rear right wheel are shown at an angle; they seem to trail backwards. The blur is the result of the camera eye's focus on the moving element, the car, which—in opposition to what a viewer's own eye perceives—it shows here as still.

If, for the viewer of the photograph, the still car stands for the single, "captured" instant, then its blurred elements—which to a human viewer of the race, conversely, would be the clearly visible, because stationary, ones—stand for time as more than an instant, time as duration. It is by a savage and preemptive reversal of actual human perception, then, that the camera produces the image of speed. In this mode, the camera image suggests that those elements which we see as blurred are not important, are only background to be dismissed, in favor of a vivid focus on speed experienced in a moment. Such a focus on the instant — which was taken up by artists such as Robert and Sonia Delaunay with their theory of "simultaneism" in Paris in the same years — reads speed as the intense experience of every single instant. The camera's technology of seeing presents the point of most intense speed as the point of visual clarity, that is, as its most wholly unmediated realism. In the snapshot, clarity stands for movement captured in an instant. The new technology of speed perception could only present its viewers with speed as a force lived in the moment; thus it bolstered the notion that speed could offer an intense, because moment-to-moment, experience.

This particular reversal of the logic of human perception also suggests that this focus on the instant dematerializes time. Time, duration, is the element represented in the photo by the blurred roadway and the rest. (The durée is indeed here always behind one's back.) Nevertheless the photo's point of clarity — car body and driver — its realism, catches the eye only because it contrasts so blatantly with the blur in the rest of the image. In a still photo of a stationary car, for example, such clarity would be omnipresent and unremarkable. Overcoming the blur of time to savor the clarity of the split second — all enabled by another machine — becomes the pro-speed message of this logics of technological perception.

This is enhanced in Lartigue's photograph by what one critic has termed "the strange leftward tilt of spectators and poles."[27] This angularity, achieved because, experimenting, Lartigue jolted his camera during the shot, sets up a series of vectors in the photo — for example, where the lines of the imaginary bases of the poles meet the line of the uprushing ground — which resemble the Futurist marking of arcs and angles to represent sensed speed. They create a series of arrow points in the composition, all of which point the way to the car's forward movement. They mimic, and reverse, the forward thrust of the human or animal torso in racing mode because here the human figures reach backward while the car leaps forward; in this way, they too represent a residue and the demise, however formalized, of the old narrative of speed as heroic endeavor. But they also make for a distortion, a knocking sideways of the poles and figures already blurred: these figures, merely standing to look, are registered now as shadowlike rather than material. Each person, as a figure of the spectator, is a mirror version within the photo of ourselves. We find the reflection of ourselves within the photo disconcertingly askew, mockingly half-erased into shades. Our passive looking, as well, is mocked here, while the one who experiences the speed, the heroic figure accorded the intense point of clarity, is alone granted the respect of realistic depiction.

Cast between these opposites, close to the center of the photo, is an evocative, uncompromisingly ungainly bundle of circular forms — the spare tires, the tank emblazoned with the number six, the moving wheel itself. This wheel, with the smudge of light at its center, which is both half-blurred and half-tilted, like most of this vorticist composition, struggles between the photo's mass of blur and its particle of clarity, suggesting a raw, undefined technology that is merely functional and wholly at the service of speed. The wheel as pure speed is also a reflection of the camera eye, looking back coldly. It manages to be blurred, tilted, and clear at once, as it looks into the lens of the camera. The people, speed's viewers, and even the driver, speed's servant, are all peripheral to this central wheel as eye, and whether shown through realism or stilted blur, the point is that they can merely work to keep up with the "pure" speed of the technology itself. In this image, in which the wheel-eye faces the camera eye, one technology is shown as congruent with the other. It is the surface speed technology itself, that wheel in complicity with the camera eye, that steals the photograph.

We, as viewers, disconcerted before the cropped car and the dizzily tilted vortex of the wheel eye, can, it is implied, hardly see technology's speed: we are exposed as unequal to it, needing to reach further levels of intensity, and of tenseness, to appreciate it. Given, then, that images of technological speed would advertise the human viewer's inadequacy, it was inevitable from its earliest depictions that any simple romance narrative of the speeder as hero would fall away. In the work of early commercial artists, such as Ernest Montaut (1878–1909), who has been credited with pioneering many of the devices conventionally used since to convey automobile speed in images, from blurring backgrounds to bending the car bodies and showing the front wheels larger than the rear ones, as well as using "speed lines" to indicate the vehicle's swoosh through the air,[28] it was the machine, not the driver's heroic form, that was the star. This was speed as a force beyond Simmelian trauma: it was the force of the machine at work.

The logic of the car and its driver, however, as opposed to that of the train and its passengers, was that the human subject would prove equal to — and, more, exert power over — the machine. The motorcar, in other

FIGURE 11. Ernest Ford, "Climbing Snaefell: A Driver's Outlook (All he sees is a little strip of road 100 yards ahead)," *The Motor* magazine, 1914. D. B. Tubbs describes this as "a vivid impression of a Vauxhall at the 1914 Tourist Trophy in the Isle of Man."

words, would enter into a symbiotic relation, as machine, with the human subject and, in doing so, would render that subject more machinelike, less likely to be traumatized by technology, less likely to be carried beyond the levels that his senses can comfortably perceive. We can see the logic of this being worked out in the copy and the drawings in the early car-racing magazines and "motoring papers"; in Britain, these included *The Motor*, *The Autocar*, and *The Car*. One dramatic kind of image, instead of showing a racing car from the viewpoint of a roadside spectator, gave the view of the road as seen by the car's driver. A vivid example by Ernest L. Ford, showing such a view from a Vauxhall in the 1914 Tourist Trophy in the Isle of Man, is captioned "Climbing Snaefell: A Driver's Outlook (All he sees is a little strip of road 100 yards ahead)" (figure 11).[29] Beyond the tightly gripped steering wheel there is barely more to be seen than a vortex of swoosh lines. Here, when the viewer of the drawing identifies with the driver, the driver's tensed hands and the way speed severely limits the field of his vision signify the desperate struggle of the human subject in extremis to match the technological wizardry he apparently controls.

One of the most famous of this generation of commercial, magazine, and poster car artists was the Frenchman René Vincent, who worked for

L'illustration and for Michelin and Citroën into the 1930s. In much of his work the human figure is rendered smaller and smaller and at times forgone altogether. For Vincent, the surging car, ready to fly off the road resplendent in its technical force, is king.[30] By this point, representing the thrill of driving is given up in place of a hymn to technology as a Benjaminian dream. The car posters of Vincent and others were often designed for billboards, a new form of advertising itself meant to be seen for an instant by people driving by. The cars portrayed on the billboards are commodities, yes, but commodities that exist not only as objects but as forces. Such forces, the image implies, overcome the inertia of the commodity and allow it — seen for an instant, a vortex of arrows and blur — literally to melt into the air. They promise to make the spectator overcome altogether any lingering sense of the inadequacy and anomie generated in the face of the commodity form. In the popular art of the car in the decades after Lartigue, the Futurists, and other experimentalists, we see a gradual desertion of the representation of human inadequacy before the machine, as the art deco artists come to glory in the dream force of the machine itself.

In the same years, however, one can trace the persistence of images of drivers ensconced within cars as a kind of armature. In these scenes we are asked to look not with the driver out through his windscreen but rather in through the windscreen at the face behind the hands gripping the wheel. This genre of car images was also pioneered by advertising, where consumers not only needed to be tempted by images of the car as dream commodity but at times also to have comforting versions of themselves as drivers reflected back at them from poster or page. These head-on shots are never simply images of the driver as hero in the old romance mode. For one thing, the perspective often places the viewer in an ambiguous, threatened position: that of facing the dangerous oncoming vehicle. Second, some of the most striking images are thoroughly abstract, such as A. M. Cassandre's poster for the Triplex-Sicherheitsglas company of windshield makers of 1930, which in a burst of unabashed and brilliant cubist portraiture shows an abstracted, helmeted head and two blank eyes behind a rectangular sheet of glass above a massive steering wheel (figure 12).[31] When the images conform to realist conventions, they often show the driver as uncannily remote, as in a painting by A. E. Marty for a Citroën poster, *The Citroën Woman in the Place Vendome* (1924) (figure 13).[32] Here the stylized headlights, half-seen steering wheel, side windows of the car, and even the woman's eyes compose an abstracting pattern of half circles. This is a pop version of the

FIGURE 12. A. M. Cassandre, *Triplex*, 1931. Colored lithograph, 47 × 31.5 in.
Courtesy of the Cassandre Estate, © Mouron.Cassandre (www.cassandre.fr).

FIGURE 13. A. E. Marty, *The Citroën Woman in the Place Vendome*, 1924. The painting was used for a Citroën poster. Courtesy of the artist's estate.

cascading discs of Robert Delaunay's painting *Homage to Bleriot* (1914), in which the aviator's aircraft is celebrated in a flurry of discs and circles inspired by the circle of the propeller. In Marty's painting, this renders the woman's face immaterial, remote, and abstracted too. Marty's image also evokes the genre's most striking novelty: many of the drivers are women. As the new driver, the New Woman has replaced the heroic male.

There has never been a shortage of women as objects of the male gaze in images of cars intended for a male audience: one of the most vivid early images of the speed force of a motor vehicle, an advertisement for the Automobiles Richard-Brasier, Gagnates de la Coupe Gordon Bennett 1904, signed by C. Bellery des Fontaines, places a strangely androgynous figure, presumably a woman, as part figurehead, part speed ghost, before the engine grill of a car itself reaching from a ghostly ocean.[33] Car "bodies" and women's bodies, in some of the most blatant uses of the female body as lure, have, since the moment when mass advertising and the mass-produced automobile were both invented, been displayed side by side. To this cornucopia of male heterosexist kitsch and the blatant exploitation of women, the image of the woman as driver, especially as seen through a windscreen and from a viewpoint where the car she drives presumably is close to bearing down on the viewer, presents a subtle challenge. In painting the driver (rather than the passenger) as female, it offered an image of the new woman as the proud possessor of a new, cool, subjectivity. Popular "car art" in particular played a major role in fashioning the twenties "new woman."

This figure of woman in the driver's seat was seized on by women eager to represent themselves as newly empowered. The iconic image here is Tamara de Lempicka's noted *Autoportrait*, commissioned in the mid-twenties for a cover of the German woman's magazine *Die Dame* (figure 14). In this forceful work, the conventional blurred lines that had been used by Rene Vincent, George Ham, and others to signify automobile speed, and which could not help but infuse their subjects with suggestions of ethereality, were replaced by a cubist arrangement of triangles and triangular vectors to imply smooth, deliberate, and engineered movement. Within this movement machine, the woman — whose face occupies no more than the top right one-sixteenth of the canvas — empowers herself by wrapping her body in the armor of the amply delineated massiveness of the machine's metal covering. In this work's perspective of the sideways glance, moreover, the viewer is positioned as a pedestrian standing by the side of the car (or possibly as the driver of another vehicle), looking at the driver from outside. She for her part looks neither at the road ahead nor at the viewer. This is the epitome of the Weimar *Sportlerin*: beneath her helmet cap, her look, really, is a kind of sneer. Here is the new woman as driver: independent, wealthy (driving her own large car), *au fait* with, and part of, moderne angularity and scale. Painted from the side but *in situ*, the car makes her a warrior. And mass culture duly noted its accord between speeding and its version of the New Woman: the term *fast* came into vogue in the twenties for this version of modern femininity.

And yet . . . the Sportlerin's averted eyes, far from being riveted by the new demands of speed, looking neither into the distance nor into the future, rather seem languorous with older memories of other seductions cast in the monotonous and repetitive cadences of leisure. This self-portrait was commissioned, note, for the cover of a magazine, for a relatively new kind

FIGURE 14. Tamara de Lempicka, *Autoportrait*. Courtesy of the artist's estate.

of pop-cultural document that worked to recast its women readers to themselves as consumers of commodities and so could not help but commodify and objectify women themselves. This cover art advertises both car and woman as desirable commodities, the formidable allure of one reinforcing the other, so that the heightening of the forbidding qualities of both is mostly a ruse to englamour them further, within a fashionably masochistic matrix, as objects to be desired. Compare this painting to the Lartigue photograph: the rotating wheel-eye, oscillating before the viewer's gaze, which centers Lartigue's photo is replaced here by an elegantly nonaerodynamic rectangular door handle. This device, secret but central in the broad expanses of empty space at the bottom of the picture, turns the issue of representation away from how one looks and sees (as in Lartigue) to how one enters and whether one can. Behind her locked door, at her car window, this fast Sportlerin remains, despite the steps made in the emancipation of women and their assumption of new roles, still the courtesan in her boudoir. Or rather, a representation which evidently aims to show a new kind of powerful woman turns out to be still trapped within the codes of a visual narrative which had for centuries shown women as entrapped and objectified.

This image is comparable also to the mass of even more bombastic Futurist car art: it too could only show technology as grand in a new way by displaying it as an attribute of the human body, so that it co-opted car technology to show the power of the male body just as de Lempicka does the female. Like her, in doing so, it found itself trapped in conventional narratives of (in its case male) adventurous purpose. The Futurist work stands, in the practice of representation, for the failure of Bergsonian idealism when it came to be turned into images that could not, it appeared, make their point fully without reference to bodies — and then could not help but glorify those bodies in terms that were lamentably pre-Bergsonian. So too de Lempicka's self-portrait, along with other more popular images that worked to celebrate the New Woman as car driver, could not help but short-circuit the more ambitious representational tasks of the new pop-cultural images of the car — to render up before our eyes the architectonic shifts of a whole new visual experience — in an all-too-jolly representation of the new woman, images which turn out to be much less radical than they seem. As any materialist theory of historical development is aware, new forms of production, artistic and otherwise, contain within them broad traces of previous forms (so that the first cars resembled horse-drawn carriages, for example). In the work of middlebrow artists like de Lempicka, however, it is as if the avidly pursued aim to render speed is sabotaged when they insist, first, on showing how speed technology's strength can be measured with reference to the power of the human body and, second, on displaying with shopworn narratives of gender empowerment the glamour of corporeal speed. When such new power as the human subject as driver might possess turns out to be cast within representational narratives of embodied movement which predate the new technology, the images, for all their gleaming chrome and swoosh of speed, turn out to be old-fashioned paintings of human exceptionalism or determination. Bodies, again, betray: the trace of past formations in these images of the new is borne on the human body itself.

Car art, in other words, to be truly new, had to jettison older models of representation of the human subject or leave them out altogether: this latter strategy, indeed, is the shocking novelty of Matisse's car painting. The most revolutionary car art was that which refused to depict a human figure, but without denying his or her existence; on the contrary, she was, as it were, brought back into the painting from around the margin and placed in front of it as the heavily implied viewer. Again, Matisse's *Le parebrise, sur la route de Villacoublay* of 1917 stands as a lesson here. When the image is what the driver sees, the viewer and driver are one, and both are dematerialized because they are outside the picture. This suggests that the power of the new technology in calling up in its users a novel regimen of sensation could not be shown through older generic images of the moving human form, but could acutely be suggested by showing a space in which the human figure was somehow uncannily absent. A body, in Deleuzian terms again, "without organs." Showing the space around the implied body to suggest a missing body, however, is not to announce a quasi-apocalyptic "death of the subject," or a subject puffed out like a candle flame by the superpower of speed technology. Instead it challenges the implied viewer in order to call up, in the problematic act of looking, a new, more complex notion of the relation of new intensities of sensing, especially that of sight, to a sense of self. By removing the human figure from the picture and thus denying the viewer the relatively easy task of sympathetic self-identification (or otherwise) which could be accomplished by endowing that figure with older narratives of empowerment or servitude, the figureless image asks us to invent a new kind of self-consciousness and sense of selfhood that could jibe more coherently with the new sensing protocols of technology-enabled speed.

Such work, in turn, has to be portrayed as pleasurable to incite viewers beyond the worn certainties of the old narratives. It is the traces of such pleasures and promises that we will search for next.

Adrenaline, Technoscopics, Tension, and the Ganzfeld

The most important contribution to our knowledge of the active principle of the suprarenal gland . . . is from Dr. Jokichi Takamine who has isolated the blood-pressure-raising principle of the gland in a stable and pure crystalline form. . . . To this body . . . he has given the name "Adrenaline."
— *American Journal of Physiology* 5, (1901): 457

When you drive in Paris at night, what do you see? Red lights, green and yellow ones. I wanted to show those elements, but without necessarily situating them the way they are in reality. More like the way they appear in memory? Red stains, green yellow gleams passing by. I wanted to refabricate a sensation using the elements that compose it.
— Jean Luc Godard, *Jean Luc Godard par Jean Luc Godard*

The value of the Futurist and pop-culture images of early cars and drivers may be to show that we can never imagine a body with organs, or an eye without a body, for very long. What a look at the celebratory images of the car as would-be adventurous toy in mass culture proves is that the tendency of many of these representations toward showing the human body only succeeds in lumbering them with the old baggage of conventional narratives of human figuration. Thus it might seem that car images without bodies — whether in Matisse's *Le parebrise, sur la route de Villacoublay* or in Ernest L. Ford's magazine drawing of what the driver of the Vauxhall in the 1914 Isle of Man Tourist Trophy could see from behind the car windscreen — might offer the best chance of imagining any new regime of seeing to which speed gives rise. They excise from the image conventional tales of ambition and "drive" with which a portrayal of a forward-leaning driver might have encumbered their pictures. Unlike the very possibly passengerless car of Virginia Woolf's *Mrs. Dalloway* — another car that lacks a body — they focus on what the unseen driver herself would see while driving with concentration. They suggest the eye of a presumptive driver by showing us a version of what she sees or would see. In doing so, they conceptualize the seeing eye as dismembered, as not needing the viewer's body. Over against them, the heroic images from pop culture, which cannot quite let the body disappear and instead fix it in a way that paralleled the advances of stop-motion photography, insist that this disembodying of the eye is impossible, that it can exist merely as a representation's conceit. They insist on the importance of the symbiotic relation between the human body and the car and insist that it is only in mediating this relation that the eye can function. In this insistence, I suggest, pop culture once again trumped high culture in its understanding of new technology. The problem with these Futurist and pop-cultural bodies in cars, however, was that they tended to still be shown within old (or Nietzschean) paradigms of heroic human endeavor. They showed bodies of heroes. What had to be achieved (and what was perhaps intuited by images that omitted the human body in representations of the car) was a new paradigm for imagining human energy in the face of technology. Human energy, however, was also being thoroughly reconceptualized at this very moment.

In St. Petersburg, the first statue of Lenin which many travelers to the city saw showed him standing atop an armored car. (Appropriately, both for the changes sketched in this study as well as for Russian history, the statue stood before the Finland Station.) Discussing this statue, the poet Joseph Brodsky comments:

> The very idea of carving an armored car out of stone smacks of a certain psychological acceleration, of the sculptor being a bit ahead of his time. As far as I know, this is the only monument to a man on an armored car that exists in the world. In this respect alone, it is the symbol of a new society. The old society used to be represented by men on horseback.[34]

In the twentieth century, a stone car replaces the stone horse that elevated and commemorated the heroes of earlier regimes. The new hero is elevated atop an automobile. The pathos that draws the poet's drollery — the immobile stone car deadening forever the very speed for which the car might be valued — draws our attention, nevertheless, to the fact that the car's scale defers to, and refuses to surpass, the scale of the human body. Part of the appeal of the car in offering the power of speed to individual subjects is that its scale aimed to match their bodies. In the earliest years of car production, as cars stopped resembling the outmoded carriages whose dimensions had been planned around those of the horse, cars grew lower and smaller. Soon, the faster the car, the smaller it was likely to be. The design of cars as objects was devoted to imagining how the car body might wrap elegantly and con-

veniently around the human bodies within it. The new science of ergonomics developed around car design; the curves of seats and dashboards followed the body's curves, while the car body's own curves mimicked those
of the most beautifully stylized human bodies. This was not a machinery
that awed with its massiveness, as with the electric turbines and steel mills
of the 1920s, nor was it a technology whose miniature quality delighted, as
with the transistors of a half century later. Rather, the car was scaled to the
human body, suggesting in its human scale that it might be a partner to it,
deferring to human height, reach, and comfort. It implied that its mechanical power worked in tandem with the bodies' locomotion.

While hand and gear shift, foot and brake lever, appeared synchronized,
it was in the interface between the human eye and the car as viewing mechanism that the mutual dependence of machine and body was most evident,
and most fraught with tension. There have in the twentieth century been a
remarkable series of theorizations of human and mechanic seeing (magis-
terially surveyed in Martin Jay's *Downcast Eyes*). These culminated in Guy
Debord's exposé of the power of spectacles of capitalism in *Society of the
Spectacle* and Michel Foucault's mapping of the omnipresent disciplinary
gaze of panoptic modernity in his *Discipline and Punish*. This rush to theorize the gaze makes clear that the new mechanical kinds of looking, in suggesting that there was much more to be seen, and that there were scales and
speeds of seeing beyond what the human eye was used to, had an effect on
human consciousness as unsettling as had earlier discoveries in optics such
as the telescope. This unsettling, we may speculate, may even have threatened the standard Enlightenment assumption that the eye is the primary
sense, the sense to be trusted unequivocally. I suggest that when, at the turn
of the century, the automobile brought on the possibility of speed vision,
a vision which had been presaged by the view from the train window, in a
machine which obviously was not a camera (although it was soon rigged
as a camera mount), it posed a new, radical challenge to this sense of the
primacy of human vision. It did so in ways that went beyond those of any
camera, which after all was controlled by its user, and it did so for masses of
people. This challenge was suggested by the car's scale. One might think of
the car as a huge camera, in which, as in the camera obscura of the Renais-
sance, the human viewer had to climb inside. When the movement-speed
of the car-as-camera took over, the instrumental relation between human
user and seeing machine, which left the human subject in control, was less
evident. Further, there was no end product to be studied, no photograph,

no moving film: the view from the windows and in the multiple mirrors of the closed car presented itself as process—a process like streaming video. This camera obscura in motion pushed human perception to its limits: a thrilling stress test of the driver's vision. Driving, moreover, made clear that this stress would be shared by the other senses as well.

Jonathan Crary, in *Techniques of the Observer* (1990), discusses how nineteenth-century advances in the understanding of physiological optics, that is, of how the eyes work in the human body, which in turn were influenced by the invention of the camera and other technological aids to sight, laid the foundations for the disavowal of conventional perspective which became the hallmark of modernist representation, not least in photography itself. He notes that as the eye's powers were developed, studied, and explored, the eye was separated from the other senses and considered in isolation, and this "autonomization of sight . . . was the historical condition for the rebuilding of the observer fitted for the tasks of 'spectacular' consumption."[35] The new scientific and technological regimes of the eye and its accessories, in other words, laid the foundation for the particular kind of desiring gaze—the gaze of the consumer on the magical commodity—which was becoming the crucial glance that could make all the dreams come true in modern capitalism. Many of the new technologies, perhaps especially the movie camera, and their associated discourses worked to isolate the sense of sight from the other senses.

Consider for a moment the movie as the early-twentieth-century endpoint of this development: film's—especially silent film's—telling of stories to the eye only was complemented by the strange heterotopia of the movie theater, where groups of people sat in (apparent) isolation in a darkened room, their eyes alone held by the light dancing off a screen, their other senses left in abeyance. However, when one considers how sight was newly deployed by the driver of the motorcar, invented at the same historical moment, the case for the isolation of sight seems much more open. Far from dismissing or dulling the other senses, what the moving automobile did was to demand that the driver deploy her whole body, and every one of her senses, beginning with the sense of sight. The eye sees a pedestrian race across a dangerous curve looming ahead; the foot presses hard on the brake, and the hand shifts gears. The unpredictable, continuously altering scene that is taken in by the driver's eye—that scene of close-ups, zooms, and long-distance shots, with its multitude of changing elements so numerous and varied that the driver's eye must constantly edit—then turns out to be so exhilarating and stressful at once that the whole body behind the eyes must be brought into play to keep the viewer in control of the situation and make it safe for further viewing. The turn to the body in representations of driving, whether for self-glorification in a twist of the old heroic style, as with the Futurists, or for advertising enticement, as in the case of the new car advertisements, brings home to us the notion that the delighted eye within the moving automobile must always be backed up by a body. It brings home to us, in other words, the truth that was being progressively elided, as Crary brilliantly shows, by the other new envisioning technologies, especially film, which had dissociated the eye from the other senses of the body.

We have already examined how the car's curves and its embrace of the newest kind of ornament showed it off as the paramount commodity and the alluring object par excellence to catch the deepest-pocketed consumers' desiring eye. The car also offered itself, in driving, as a route beyond the inevitable frustrations of consumerist desire, in that it granted an enhanced physical, that is, embodied, experience. As it turned out, this experience centered in the first place on the satisfactions, excitements, and challenges offered to the sense of sight. But while much modernist innovation in the area of optics, as Crary points out, enhanced sight but also autonomized it, separated it from the other senses and abstracted it, the sight excitements offered to the driver, *au contraire*, made it clear that sight could function only in relation to the body as a whole, and particularly in relation to the body's mechanical powers. In the driver's seat, one's movements were certainly limited: note that car seat design has been much more innovative than (even as it inspired) the modernist chair design for office and home by Le Corbusier, Eileen Gray, and Ludwig Mies van der Rohe in the twenties and thirties. This seated driver was not, however, a passive consumer; instead, eye was called on constantly to coordinate with muscle, particularly with the senses of hearing and touch, if the reality of the experience was to be felt safely and to the full, when the machine's power lent itself to the frailer mechanics of human mobility. In this pleasurable, continuously variable work, in contrast to passive consumption that employed only the autonomized gaze, what was demanded, as eye relayed its message to muscle and coordinated the reactions of the other senses, was *alertness*. Alertness took on a new valence as arbiter of the best of life itself in this period.

In 1901, exactly at the historical moment we are discussing, Dr. Jokichi Takamine isolated adrenaline as the blood-pressure-raising substance produced by the pituitary gland. In the accounts of the clinical effects observable in the human body of the increased production of adrenaline, the older adventure narratives of human action compete with a tentative emerging discourse which would delineate the signs and jiggings of a "normal" alertness in the excited human body. The older narratives centered on the well-known account of "fight or flight": confronted with a threatening situation, the story went, the human organism, its system primed to excitement with a fresh and instantaneous dose of adrenaline, would choose her newfound energy either to struggle or to flee. This story plants a rationalist belief in the availability of choice even in the trickiest of situations, at the heart of a moment in the Darwinian narrative of species struggle. (It also implies a pre-Bergsonian sense of space in which to make this choice.) The newly discovered body substance gets to be placed at the service of quick, but reasoned, choice. Adrenaline allows you to choose faster. Notably, in this narrative adrenaline is read as an aid to speed, both as physical movement ("fight . . .") and as mental agility (the speed of human response). Choice need not anymore be the result of the kind of contemplation (now reckoned, comparatively, as slow) that makes rational thought thrive; choice, with adrenaline, can now be instantaneous. This instantaneousness also renders the choice intuitive, however, and the notion of human intuition, a quasi-spiritual feeling which had always had its adherents among the champions of sensibility, in the theorists of the sublime, and in the romantic poets, might now seem to be reinserted in the medico-scientific narrative of human response. Almost, but not quite: adrenaline, as it came to be described, diluted feeling (which, like contemplation, was best indulged in slowly, at leisure) in favor of a marshaled alertness, a decision-making speed that killed any kind of slowing-down doubt in favor of physical-body-evidenced decisiveness. What was going on in accounts of new discoveries such as adrenaline was a subtle, improvised, but nonetheless radical imaginative rewiring of the human sensory and decision-making processes with a narrative which idealized instant and decisive response. The best person was henceforth to be not the one who thought out the choice rationally to make the best decision, or felt its possible consequences most intensely with the most profound feeling, but the one who left the least possible time between seeing, choosing, and acting, whose response was speediest.

The car, coming to the roads at the same moment in which adrenaline was discovered, became the test machine in which human subjects were examined for the speed of their reflexes in response to a succession of varied stimuli. It became the vehicle in which one could test one's own reflexes in these terms, enjoy the test, and derive pleasure from speeding up the rate of one's responses. This enhancement of the coordination of eye and limbs did not occur only in car culture at this moment; the precise management of human movement was becoming an obsession in a number of fields. Taylorism, the quasi science that pushed for more-efficient workplaces through the micromanagement of human motion, conducted numerous studies of how the human body as machine might be harnessed more simply to do more work. The soon-to-be-vast new scientific discipline of psychology was populated by figures such as George W. Beard, A.M., M.D., whose *A Practical Treatise on Nervous Exhaustion (Neurasthenia), Its Symptoms, Nature, Sequences, and Treatment* was reprinted five times in New York between 1888 and 1905. If alertness and instant coordination of the eye and limb were to be the most valued traits of the human agent as machine, then neurasthenia, or "nervous prostration," could result when this coordination was practiced too much and too intensely. Dr. Beard's first criterion for a diagnosis of nervous exhaustion also focused on the way in which this disease, like its cause, was speedy: "The symptoms of organic disease are usually fixed and stable, while very many of those of neurasthenia and allied states are fleeting, transient, metastatic and recurrent."[36]

The cardiac "palpitations, twitching of the muscles, spinal tenderness, weakness of the eyes, insomnia . . . and involuntary emissions" were all readily understandable as the overexertions effected by the human organism to make itself react faster in tandem with its speed machines. These symptoms were the body signaling to its owner that it could not compete with the speed of the machine. In neurasthenia, Beard claimed, reflex action increased: the limb reacted before the eye saw, and the key claim of rational choice was surrendered altogether. Taylor dreamed of even more smooth coordination of eye and limbs, and Beard warned of reaching the limit where such coordination broke down because it was too fast to be bearable. Later Gestalt therapists would focus on a moment when external movement became for the eye (as opposed to the whole organism) simply too fast to be discernible. They charted a moment when the viewer would break down the sight barrier and behold, instead of distinct objects, a murky haze named the Ganzfeld by the psychologist Wolfgang Metzger in *Optische Untersuchung am Ganzfeld*. (This research would be taken up again in the age of Mach 2 supersonic speeds and space travel.) This could lead to a "complete disappearance of vision for short periods of time," a sensual journey not into blindness but beyond the limits of the gaze.[37]

These dreams of a speedier body put to better use, fears of the effects on that body of such speed, and notation of the moment when speed overwhelms the eye before the mind can send its message to the limbs, along with a plentitude of other discourses,[38] mark the emergence of what Hillel Schwartz has termed the "distinction between the body one *is* and the body one *has*."[39] It is a new concept of the body as motion machine, a concept developed by considering that body in contrast to the new speed machines. The apparent collusion of human body and car meant that the automobile became a chamber in which the human body as machine might be subjected to self-experiment, pushed to its limits, taught to enjoy being as fast as the machine itself. The car was a unique new machine that offered to the body much prosthetic power and left that power in the hands and feet of the body itself. This power was mediated by, and controlled with, the human eye. Watching the road ahead, reading alertly the endless array of signs on the broad and featureless masterpieces of modernist engineering that were the motorways (and it is remarkable how much written signage is necessary to direct the motorway driver), editing out the extraneous and unnecessary, avoiding seeing the swoosh on each side by focusing on an ever-changing spot ahead, never going quite so fast that one breaks the sight barrier and enters the Ganzfeld but pushing to higher speeds to enjoy the sensation of eye and limbs under stress: these were the joys of automobile nervousness. Deploying human and machine power to complement both, the driver's look flashes in staccato-jazzy nervous-glance rhythm. This is the quintessential modernist gaze. It alerts the body to a new level of nervous energy and presides over a new regime of looking that, far from dissociating the eye from a sensuous existence, hails the entire body to energize itself with the eye's energy. This is a new corporeal regime where eyes and bodies in tandem with machines are called on to be fully alert. The distractible eye maintains its focus by coordinating the reactions of the other senses and the propulsion of the limbs, all to brace the body over the machine.

The eye in speeding is shown so much more: in one car journey, it sees more scenes which change more often than in any film, and in return the eye must energize the body to continue the force of the spell of this envisioning. In debates about the nature of work, especially about the new Fordist assembly line, this frantic activity was often seen as tragedy; think, for example, of the overworked subaltern laborers tending the subterranean machines in Fritz Lang's film *Metropolis*. In the car, however—in the realm of relative autonomy, and often leisure—the machine-body was thought of, when it was considered at all, as empowering, easy, a comforting stimulation. The speeding, closed automobile, with eyes staring from its windows straight ahead, sold vision of a new demanding kind as a fine alertness. Driving, as quintessential new everyday activity invented in the modernist moment, modeled alertness as a behavior pattern that would not only delight and reanimate the eye itself but cast its magic luster, in the form of that new energizing adrenaline, through the limbs and other senses. The driver's alertness outfitted her as a subject for whom both fight and flight—the options of the ultrafast, struggling human—could, as she moved forward to progress while fleeing dull slowness, be one and the same, decision and desire.

Actually, if the *accident* is solely *what occurs*, and not, like *substance*, *what is* . . .
— Paul Virilio, *Open Sky*

The essence of modern technology is by no means anything technological.
— Martin Heidegger, "The Question concerning Technology"

With driving, very soon, came the searing reality of the crash. The various authorities differ on when the first car crash occurred. Most cite the case of Margaret Driscoll, a poor woman crossing the road in South London in August 1896, when she was knocked down and killed by a speeding car. Others refer to Mr. H. H. Bliss of New York, who on September 23, 1889, while assisting a woman passenger from a trolley car, was struck by an electric taxi.[1] The historians' refusal to agree alerts us to the reasons why they feel the need to discern an original moment. It seems important to fix the first car accident not because accidents involving traffic were by any means unknown before the invention of the motorcar; Charles Dickens, for example, when writing *Our Mutual Friend*, had been deeply traumatized when a train in which he was a passenger derailed in the Staplehurst disaster of 1868. Because each car accident was presented as a small-scale horror, however, rather than a spectacular disaster, their full effect, it appeared, was more likely to be grasped only en masse; thus the search for the first. In 1900, when 400,000 pedestrians a day crossed the broad Place de l'Opéra in Paris, sharing the road with 60,000 vehicles and 70,000 horses, no fewer than 150 people were killed by horses and trams in the French capital. (In that year, two were killed by cars, the same number as by bicycles.)[2] Yet because car accidents have, since those first, become so common and so everyday, recuperating the specific horror of each has, strangely, been tougher, given what is taken to be their quotidian inevitability.

How, then, to know the crash? The statistics can astound us, the horror of a specific crash move us, but connecting the two has proved difficult. The crash as a small-scale, domestic horror is graspable, but it is then cast less often as part of a mass tragedy than as the individual effect of some chance determination—an accident. Individual crashes, unless they were "pileups" or killed a celebrity, lacked the stupendously mass tragedy of the kind that could be sensationalized in the penny papers. Perhaps the most shocking of all twentieth-century accidents involving a betraying technology and furious speed, for example, occurred in the north Atlantic fog on the night of April 14, 1912, when the *Titanic* sank; 1,552 passengers were drowned. In the following year, 1913, in the United States alone 4,200 people were killed in car accidents. (Now almost 40,000 die annually in car crashes in the United States.) It has been estimated that up to thirty million people have died in car crashes in the twentieth century. Each year of the twenty-first century adds at least a half million more.[3] The cumulative figures are shocking, yet the slow accretion means that the mass media only rarely sensationalize them into a broadly felt scandal. The car accident is an intimate kind of disaster. It touches individuals, a personal tragedy. Newspapers do comment on what is the almost willful refusal, in the name of the car's convenience, to ignore the cumulative tragedy of its accidents. This casts the crash, each time it occurs, as a crisis involving a few people, and car crashes are described in narratives broken and remade on the scale, very much, of the domestic novel. The specific car crash's representation is measured to the scale of individuals; this has made such representations fertile testing grounds for the traumas, neuroses, and crisis rearrangements of individual subjectivity, responses to the accident's arousal of terror, horror, and fear. Taken cumulatively, car crash statistics point to mass slaughter. Yet the two discourses veer off from each other: between the personal and local nature of a given crash and the magnitude of the overall reality, the connection is remarkably seldom made.

Car crashes are a twentieth-century phenomenon. This new occasion of fear soon became, for the commuter listening to the traffic report, an almost quotidian experience. Nevertheless there is a sense in which the crashes remain unspoken, hovering beneath the horizon of the field of vision of public culture. Here I will trace the ways in which narratives and images of the car crash did find their way into public discourse during the century. Each of these discourses, I suggest, represents a veering off from the actuality of the crash itself, a displacement, to different degrees, of its fearful reality. An avoidance? No doubt. But also a willful refusal to be terrified, and a trusting to chance, even when the odds are heightened in the conjunction of human and technology.

This split originated in descriptions of crashes in the first years of auto-mobilism; these descriptions went through a series of stages. In the first, when cars were bought as indulgences by the rich and were marketed as a technology of adventure, the crash was often treated as comedy, a hilarious "spill" that brought the driver up short against a heifer or a sycamore. Once fatalities began to be reported, this came to be countered by a discourse of social control, of the regulation of car speeds with speed limits, car road-worthiness through inspections, and driver preparedness through licensing. This brought the state to bear relentlessly on its citizens as drivers: the most common scene of the average citizen's encounter with the state's apparatus of law and order soon came to be the traffic stop. This discourse of social and statist control, and the language of its opponents, was soon countered by a less common, yet startling, often self-consciously artistic discourse of the car crash as a version of a violent apocalypse. In Filippo Marinetti's Futurist Manifesto above all, the moment when the Futurist hero crashes his car into the "divine mud" of the ditch marks the climactic conjunction of new technology and cyborg subject in a brutalist apocalypse of modern-ist energy. These celebrations of the car crash as glorious victories of the new, in turn, found their counterparts in a discourse that might be termed "crash analysis," which only came fully into existence in the mass car and freeway culture of the post–World War II boom, when the terrors, traumas, and necessity for callousness in the face of the ever more common car crash were explored with a bitter but fascinated scrutiny. Examples of this genre include Jean-Luc Godard's anti-Gaullist film *Weekend* (1967), and a line of thinking which culminated in J. G. Ballard's novel *Crash* (1973), which Ballard accurately characterized as "the first pornographic novel based on technology."[4] Although these texts take us into the second half of the cen-tury, because of their value in comprehending a cultural issue that was de-veloped at least a half century before they were written, I include them here. Ballard's extraordinary, notorious novel is a searing exploration of the nexus of a sadistic sexuality, violence, late-modernist selfhood, and crash culture. These texts come out of the first broad movement, influenced by the rise of environmental and consumer activism and the mass motorization of the European bourgeoisie, to critique car culture. Their satirical critiques are hedged with a kind of awe before what they have tracked down as the dangerous technology's fascination. Ballard, for example, needs to reassure his readers by means of an introduction that "the ultimate role of *Crash* is cautionary, a warning." One wonders.

This quartet of discursive protocols of the car crash — crash as comedy, crash as arena of state control, crash as apocalypse, and crash as awed critique — has variously processed twentieth-century impressions of automobile accidents as public information. They also annotate the nuances of the accident as intimate trauma and personal experience. As personal, local trauma, the car crash marked a new category of experience that the modern subject needed to absorb, an event where reality, as unexpected and unwelcome phenomenon, violently intruded on the will-to-simulation implied by life in a (relatively) abundant consumer culture. Earlier, we looked at how the new automobile culture of personal access to thrilling new speeds became broadly implanted so quickly in modern life because it offered access to a certain real of physical, thrilling experience, in a new order which more commonly offered the comforts of simulation as the reward for consumption. The car's access to speed for its driver marked it as a new kind of reward in consumer culture, a guarantee that that culture need not be wholly about garish appearances. If the consumer cornucopia was to be sensational, the car implied, then it could be sensational in the fullest sense of inducing sensations of excitement and real participation in natural life for its customer practitioners. Yet the offer of heightened physical sensation and corporeal excitement, promised as the experience of driving a car, was only offered through consumerism — at its simplest, the car, which enabled the experience that appeared to transcend consumerism, was itself a consumer item. Further, the sentient experience it offered — the thrill of personally speeding — was bracketed as a leisure experience: it offered no real new power to the driving subject. This, of course, made for its joyous supplementarity; it was outside the usual run of the simulation-besotted culture, and this was the guarantee of its reality. But this bracketing of the joy of speeding as an end in itself, as a possibly dangerous social act, a leisure activity, and as an activity without value in the sense that it did not contribute in any new way to the subject's empowerment, meant that to drive at speed was, yes, *experience*, but experience (like the tourist's gazing at a sight) that was trapped within consumerism's simulative parameters. The very fact that film (a simulation, inscribed on light) could, as we have seen in the case of such a prosaic sequence as *A Race for a Kiss*, induce a similar sensation, could make the palms sweat and the neck arch as the viewer participated in a simulation of the speeding experience of the car chase, proves that experience in this physical, bodily sense was increasingly reproducible by the newest technologies that enhanced consumerism's protocols of simulation as its siren call of desire. Yet if to drive at speed is a thrill that, cast merely as leisure, is held hostage to consumer simulation, the moment of the crash, of the traffic accident, becomes a gruesome interruption in this reveling in the happiness of the purchased machine.

The accident becomes a frightening reminder that a reality of the frail body and its capacity for hurt and dismemberment lies behind the salespeople's promises of happiness. As such a jolt, the accident is the punctum, the interruption of the speed experience operating under the sign of simulation, by a physical real that offers itself too as the reality of the desire for speed. The crash is a tragedy involving personal horror, chaos, crushed bodies, and mangled machines; it marks a flash bespeaking the intrusive revenge of the real on a culture whose pleasures are built on the dream of escaping the illusionary world of consumerist simulation while still wishing for its cosseting promised security.

What consumer-based speed culture does so brilliantly is to hint that the terror of the crash is the inevitable counterpoint to the thrill of speed. One reason driving at higher speeds is a greater thrill is because one is putting oneself at greater risk of crashing. The terror of the crash, suppressed while one gathers speed, is the necessary complement to speed's thrill. With the mass sale of cars, people were granted mass access to personally experienced and generated speeds; they were also given a further power, a new potential to inflict damage, hurt, and even kill, on a new scale. They were given a new power to kill—and to do so in the flick of an eye, a moment's inattention, a resolution to go faster in a new direction. If speeding itself was a thrill that was supplementary to the simulation-ridden everyday life of its practitioners, a promise of physical sensation proffered by consumer culture, then its complementary power—to cause a crash and hurt oneself and others—was very much part of a really existing social fabric with specific and grim social effects. This awareness that speeding, itself a self-centered and lonely experience in the standard manner of most consumer activity, could at any moment become social in the grimmest circumstances, at the moment of the real life of the accident, perversely worked to make the speeding experience itself more apparently real. The threat of danger, of the car accident, ever present while driving, the more present the more speed one gained, meant that the speeder had to be constantly alert, to employ her senses more fully, to play a game of keeping within limits imposed by the warning, cautious authorities of the state, while, by doing all these things, enjoying the apparent reality of the speeding experience even more. Speeding fed its sense of real experience on a good quotient of anxiety, inducing an adrenaline rush in the speeding body that was in considerable part fed on fear. Fear, never inadmissible, makes astringent the thrill, the excitement, of driving at speed. This fear, of the accident, is of an event that is social and real. In consumerism's offer to the masses of a physical experience, it ensures that the social and the real are what are presented as horrific. The fear of the real, which induced its avoidance, is cast as a component of the physical thrill of speeding as experience.

These cultural implications heighten the central fact of any car crash, its wretched and wrenching horror. Apart from the world wars, car accidents, from the early days of the automobile, became by far the most common sites for people in developed countries to witness real scenes of sudden death and destruction. That the accident could happen in a moment, wholly unexpectedly, meant that for many the car crash was (and is) Western culture's prime example of the very idea of accidentality, the very example of fate itself. Once the term "accident" came by and large to mean "car accident," then a new setting where the possibility of violent catastrophe could occur to anyone was accepted as a given. The very possibility of the crash posited intense violence as the corollary of the satisfyingly smooth flow of traffic. The speed thrill got to incorporate the "instinct to kill." The chance of a crash made this violence a potential, even likely, event that would touch everyday lives.

This arrival of a new form of violence — of radically life-altering catastrophe — as a possibility into people's increasingly protected lives, was entwined with a kind of frantic urgency because it came about in vivid relation to the new stress on the human organism as a machinelike generator of energy. If *experience* — a recalibrated complex of sensations of the body's material interrelation with the physical world — was what the car's speed offered the driver, then we might search for a series of new sensory possibilities developed to allow the subject access to this experience (we have already explored this in relation to sight). These sensory possibilities were represented in new narratives, representations of the human-machine interface that were concerned with what it meant *now* to be human and sentient. These accounts centered on new discoveries and debates regarding the resourcefulness, usefulness, and potential of *energetic* human action. Key was the isolating, at this very moment, of adrenaline. These new narratives, couched often in either the prose of scientific journals, the dubious write-ups in the "Motoring" sections of the newspapers and car enthusiast magazines, or the emerging pseudoscience of resource management that became known as Taylorism, all told their tales of this new energy glibly, awkwardly, and enthusiastically. They are part of new ways of thinking, often at the margins of official science, aimed at delineating a new rhythm of speeded-up Western human experience. In these accounts of a poised and efficient (rather than manic) energy, the new Taylorized worker, the "man in the crowd" of Gustave Le Bon, newly freed by the eight-hour day, would find much praise for the possibilities of his or her pleasure. Speed, as Aldous Huxley wrote, is the only new pleasure invented by modernity. When one thinks of new narratives within which human experience came to be couched around 1900, one thinks of Freud. There is a case to be made, however, that Freud's limning of new nuances of human secular experience marks the end of a trajectory rather than a beginning: that his recasting of the Greek myths as prototypes of the agonies of modern life experience, for example, represents another, more profound stage in the expression of the bourgeois family romance narratives that had been perfected, for example, by the Victorian novelists, rather than the commencement of a new episteme of knowledge of the human psyche. (Freud's analyses, however, are also readable in terms of the blockage and encouragement of human energies: see his account of human *drives*.) The upsurge of accounts of human energy, on the other hand, offers alternative, if at first glance less glamorous, versions of the new texture of everyday lives in the milieu of what Jacques Ellul would famously term "the technological system."

With this new attention to human energy, spurred in part by the contact of the human body with newly invented technologies, the speed of the car and the demands placed on the driver were, of course, only one example. In this constellation, however, the car crash functioned as a breakdown with an enormous symbolic as well as actual power. For the car crash did not simply involve the breakdown of the new machinery with which the human body interacted (as is the case, for example, with the "crash" — i.e., the mechanical failure — nowadays of the computer) but was a moment when the machine's splintering also brought its human user face to face with extinction. The crash showed up a number of the crucial rules within which the interrelation of human being and machine was to be managed in Western democratic modernity. In the edgy rapport improvised as the key protocol of the human-machine interface, the human was to have *choice* — even to the point of having choice to cause his or her death. At the same time as the subject was entrusted with such awe-inspiring choice for simply interacting with the machine, the interdiction of the unspoken rules, the seizing of the experience of pleasure to an excessive degree — by simply driving too fast, too inattentively, too dangerously — carried with it the most extreme penalty imaginable. Choice was granted, but extreme vigilance and attentiveness were demanded. Speed, the new pleasure of the human subject's psycho-physical regime of *energy*, was proffered as choice (which was thus mooted as the basic requirement for the relishing of pleasure); but to practice this choice and to access this pleasure, the subject was called on to exercise continuous attentiveness, alertness, vigilance, and rule keeping. (And this whole nexus of protocols and behaviors, tendered at the level of each individual driver, as with any ideological construct worthy of the name,[5] was always represented as the most natural code of behaviors in the world.) The new activity of car driving and the access to speed — that sole new pleasure invented by modernity — worked as a dramatization in miniature of the tender balance of choice, freedom, and pleasure on the one hand and censure, duties, and penalties on the other that were to characterize the relation of Le Bon's man in the crowd to both his sense of his own agency and his desire for security and acceptance of control.

We can now map the four discourses of the automobile crash I have outlined onto the matrices of freedom-pleasure and control-penalty which arrayed themselves behind the possibility of the crash and offered themselves as a means to prevent it. The car's driver, choosing her own speed, was no longer by necessity a passenger, as had been the case with tram, subway, and train; this matched the ethos of mass consumerism, where the vast array of commodities in the new department stores bespoke not just an abundance not quite within the individual's reach but the need for the shopper to *choose* from the profusion before enjoying the chosen commodity. This commodity was then granted a tincture of aura, a stamp of uniqueness because it had been chosen (from among all the others) by the buying individual. Likewise this act of choosing validated the buyer's own sense of selfhood; she exercised her freedom to enjoy her own version of pleasure. When the user of the car as mass transit accessed the pleasure of speed by herself, making all the decisions herself about how she moved, then this rite of choice was magnified, even if it was employed in what became a mundane activity, because the choice was not simply about possessing a commodity but a series of choices that promised access to a novel physical experience. The discourse of comedy and jollity that surrounded car crash accounts in the early days of automobilism understood this relation of choice and consumer gratification intimately. In this period, when many drivers were rich hobbyists and thus models of the new consumers, a crash or "tumble" was seen as one of the thrills, portrayed mostly with a certain wryness, of a conspicuous display of the extended free choices afforded the rich. The comic discourse of the crash characterized a dream of choosing the novel experience, of choosing to exercise its possibilities in the wildest, most freewheeling ways—and never having to pay a penalty for it. Rather, enduring the spill, and even driving in pursuit of it, made one a "daredevil," an adventurer; it allowed the rich consumer-driver to show himself or herself as still practicing the protocols of an earlier era when humans proved themselves through activities more dangerous than choosing commodities. That the daredevil act was mostly a game (with, for example, elaborate dressing-up rituals of goggles, driving coats, and, for women, veils) also made it, reassuringly, part of consumerism's more constricted and less heroic regimes of freedom of choice. And there was always the possibility of a fatality—though more likely of a pedestrian, not the driver—to prove that in this search for new experience, authentic physicality had not been forgone.

The ensuing and complementary discourse of state control surrounding the crash could provide the reassurance of security that the posing daredevil craved. From its earliest days, this voluminous and repetitive discourse gave rise to a vast supply of new terms, a whole new language:

speed limits
traffic lights
Belisha beacons
highway patrol officers
traffic wardens
speed-calming devices
national crash tests
crash dummies
roadworthiness
impact studies
driver's license tests

"sig.-alert"
speeding tickets
driving offenses
the Department of Motor Vehicles
Breathalyzer tests
swift-response teams
jaws-of-life
penalty points, and so on

In this new jargon, one can trace, first, the state's enthusiasm for the driver's freedom to enjoy speed as a model for the individual's freedom in a consumer-centered democracy and, second, its anxiety that this freedom needed to be rigidly controlled. (For example, since the invention of the automobile, the dream expressed by state-employed traffic engineers for a traffic system has been this: cars would run automatically on tracks, taking away the driver's control and making her a passenger; car manufacturers invented "cruise control" but inevitably are wary of any system which runs counter to the dream of individual control offered by the car.) There is still much to be written of how the modern nation-state superseded concern for the integrity of its territory with concern for the rate of movement of its people, goods, and money (and of "aliens") within and through that territory: the state as traffic policeman. The state's discourse of the car crash, its rhetorical structure that of the cautionary tale, promises the driver citizen a lavish measure of security within the exercise of a limited but satisfying choice. It guarantees that this choice can be practiced with reassurance. This rhetoric of cautionary warnings brings into the open the spectacle of the crash itself; indeed, it glories in its gore and its obscene wreckage of the physical human body. It makes evident the fact, suppressed by the daredevil game player racing toward speed and pleasure, that in a crisis the human body will be mercilessly crushed by the machine. It always frames this grim spectacle within the textual strategies of reassurance, but it stokes fear of the crash to offer the remedy of its own version of security as state control. Flaunting the crash's brutality, the state ensures that the very fear it has fostered and worked up will be reinscribed as the not-quite-suppressed unconscious of the pleasure of choosing speed in the first place. Calling on its citizens to make their own choices as drivers if they wish to access speed's thrills, the state concurrently decrees the constant monitoring of such speed thrills in the name of alertness and vigilance. The good citizen as driver always exercises agency as choice but forgoes most of the potential pleasure that choice suggests by "driving safely" and also by being vigilant: alert to his own dangerousness, he must also be wary of the threat posed by others. The possibility of pleasure is in this way incited, but this pleasure is at once decreed excessive: defensive alertness, rather, is represented as the proper demeanor. The energy that the human subject, interacting with the machine, is expected to exhibit is channeled away from excessiveness (although the possibility of indulging in such excess is always upheld as a dream deferred, a road mirage) and routed into the more prudent grooves of constant alertness. This subtle and complex balance of control is guaranteed by brandishing before the citizen-driver the gruesome spectacle of the crash scene, where the bloodied victims and wrecked chassis bespeak the dangers of excess.

The victims also offer testimony, however, to the occasional brutality of chance itself, its callous unforgivingness even of the always alert and well-energized human subject. If *energy* (as alertness) is the required value of the human subject as participant in the technological system, and speed's thrill is the reward granted by technology-driven commodity culture for a life of energy alertly dispensed, then it is fully appropriate that, in a society in which most death is hidden and its rituals erased, the shocking, sudden spectacle of death in the car crash should be unveiled randomly, periodically, and publicly as the apotheosis of speed culture. It is Paul Virilio who most comprehensively charts the centrality of energy-driven speed culture to our contemporary concepts of life itself when he discusses the meanings of the word *vif*:

> The French word "vif," "lively," incorporates at least three meanings: swiftness, speed (vitesse), likened to violence — sudden force, abrupt edge (*vive force, arete vive*), etc. — and to *life* (*vie*) itself: to be quick means to stay alive (*etre vif, c'est etre en* vie!).[6]

When quickness means life, its excessiveness, its misuse, means death. The technology is smashed, but this is nothing compared to the rupture of the speeding body. The crash is the end of speed, the completest stop. This might seem as if it were the point at which all discourse ends, at which, with the pleasure of speed transforming itself into unspeakable pain, the discourse of speed would reach the point of the unsayable. On the contrary: around this fraught degree zero of speed discourse have coalesced a constellation of quasi-mythic, almost-thoughtful texts and image sequences, portentous and cavalier by turns, which admirably attempt to unveil speed's deepest meanings for the human subject in modernity even as they sound its victims' requiem. These are texts and films that forgo accounts of the traumas and personal feelings that arise from the family romance plots which are the domain of Freudian and post-Freudian accounts of the modern subject's meaningful existence. Instead they concentrate on the surface textures of modern life, its everyday rhythms, its repetitions rather than its anxieties. At the same time, like every new discursive formation, they bear within themselves traces of the older forms and narratives of meaning; these shadows become the measures against which the rhythms of truly modern life come implicitly to be measured and found wanting. Confronting both shadow text and innovative text, they work as modernist critiques, awash with cool irony. Smashing the suave planes of this irony as it smashes the coldly technology-riven lives of the characters described, the crash in these texts arrives as a kind of truth bearer, an inevitable if repeated endgame, a revelation.

Revealing truths, the crash assumes in these works a glamour, a stylized aura: the texts try to treat it with what Theodor Adorno once termed "the jargon of authenticity."[7] In a world controlled by panopticist surveillance, for example, the crash can represent a moment of the serendipity that the state's eye has striven to suppress. The crash might be chance's, or the driver's, victory over conformist security. In the film *Les tricheurs* (The Cheaters, 1958), directed by Marcel Carné, for example, the young heroine, who wants a white Jaguar, declares, "I wouldn't mind dying like Dean: young, and at great speed."[8] At this point, with the lonely death of James Dean in his Porsche near Paso Robles in 1955, the old tropes of adventure, in discovering new worlds, had all been flattened out into speed dreams; only speed now was adventure, and speed was only truly annotatable as adventure at the moment of its impossibility. In this nihilist formulation, the energized subject could still dream of herself as heroic only at the moment of heroism's defeat at excessive speed. In a further irony, this discourse of heroic martyrdom fits cozily in the nexus of consumerist dreams; remember that chance, serendipity, and shock are all the other side of the coin of the serendipitous choice which enlivens the freedom of the consumer. The shock (of the crash) lurks behind the consumer's freedom; it authenticates it, endowing it with an edge, a cultural unconscious of tragic danger. The car crashes that have transformed celebrity figures into chance's martyrs — Jayne Mansfield, Tom Mix, Nathanael West, James Dean, Albert

Camus, Jackson Pollock, Princess Grace, Princess Diana—grant a buzz of nervous tragedy to lives, and drives, dominated by the careful management of energy. These celebrities' shocking deaths in crashes offer the tragedy of their decimation as the triumph of the dream of escape into nothingness, an escape enacted while they each were in the grip of the thrill of energy's expenditure in speed.

To harness this thrill as a means at least to endow modernist Fordist lives with some meaning, if not as the basis for an altogether novel vision of the possibilities of the subject (and her politics), has, post-Dean, become the goal of scattered science fiction writers, outré film directors and a mishmash of utopian artists. That they have seldom escaped from a fascination before the scene of the car crash and the lurid glamour of its wreckage shows the desperation of their limning of the interface between human subject and technology, as well as offering evidence of their unwillingness to let go of that crucial assumption of modernity that technology might yet save us even as it ruins and lays waste. Paul Virilio, preeminent theorist of this tendency and a commentator prone to read the relations of technologies to humans in more or less apocalyptic terms, notes that the crash, the accident, tells us much more about the cultural effects of the technology than the spectacle of its smooth functioning ever could. J. G. Ballard, possibly the most creative thinker on the human-technological interface in the Cold War era, fashions psychic narratives of sadomasochistic behavior (especially sexual behavior) around the story of technology's breakdown, specifically the car crash. These writers fascinate in part because they refuse the older essentializing accounts of technology as merely instrumental,[9] and as rationalizing, abstracting, deadening, as a counter to the warm "dwelling" of a humanity that might somehow shake itself free of the technical. (This latter, for example, is the version of the modern subject's relation to technology expounded by Martin Heidegger in "The Question concerning Technology.") Thinkers such as Virilio and Ballard begin by taking Heidegger's dualism into account and even work to exacerbate the fears of technology on which it is built. Nevertheless their texts are based on a vision, however terrifying, of the breakdown between the realms of human desire and technological instrumentality. For both Virilio and Ballard, speed is the trope whereby they investigate the ways in which humans use machines as clever devices of interpellation and the gaining of power. Speed for Virilio is the primary trope in modernity of assault,[10] while for Ballard it is the fast route toward an uncanny, made-strange world where characters seem to struggle against the anomie that the technologized milieu they inhabit (Ballard follows Heidegger in his initial assumptions) tends to produce. Speed for both, and driving in particular for Ballard, is a key phenomenon of modernity, the one which shows modernist subjects in their truest relation to the forces of modern power as they are projected in the everyday. These forces, for both Virilio and Ballard, work as a repressed violence. For both, speed is the most vivid force through which this violence is uncovered and made evident. The key implication of the work of both is a shocking one: speed is modernity's violence.

Virilio, in *Speed and Politics*, traces a history of the speed of people and their machines, from the rise of the medieval city state to the post-Hiroshima era of possibly instantaneous nuclear war. He delineates the ways in which relations between velocities, whether human or machinic, effected successive reorganizations of forms of rule. He focuses on the powers exercised by emerging nation-states over velocities. The velocities of arms and armaments, from the slingshot to the cruise missile, underlie for him the history of warfare. Showing how ever faster and deadlier weapons always outpaced the development of faster means of human transport and were each in turn outpaced by the speed of the transmission of information via the media, Virilio arrives at a history of the present in which, for him, the instantaneousness or near instantaneousness of each of the three kinds of movement (the split second of computer communication, the finger on the nuclear button, and supersonic speeds in air transport) has led to a disappearing point where speed itself is more or less superseded and all duration can be canceled out in the zap of an instant. At this moment, he suggests, "penetration and destruction become one"; that is, the speed of transport machines is shown up as part of the tendency toward violent penetrative assault, merely aping the destructive purpose of the superfast new missiles. Speed, in other words, has now revealed itself as violence. He might have dwelt on a vehicle such as the stealth bomber, where the specificity of the space in which it fires its missiles matters nothing, and "all that counts is the speed of the moving body and the undecidability of its path."[11] Such is the state's dream machine of this moment when speed, rather than territoriality, is that which must be controlled in order for the state to keep its power. For Virilio, it is this convergence in destructive mode, to which the history of technology has brought us, that has been foretold by every car accident. The crash for him is a tragically overdetermined moment when speed shows off its destructive and violent capacities, forces of violence that are in turn taken over by regimes of power.

Virilio, in books such as *Bunker Archeology*, a meditation on Nazi fortifications on the north French coast, and *War and Cinema*, on how the film camera shot was improved in wartime, especially during World War I, is a theorist of warfare. One may object that his texts, which read like implicit jeremiads, rework with a lurid poststructuralism the Heideggerian fear of technology's potential for dehumanization. One need not endorse Virilio's discursive alarmism, however, to accept his insight that it is at the moment of the crash, when speed shows itself as violence, that a politics of speed is possible. I suggest that such a politics can be discerned in the successive discourses that have been developed to describe automobile crashes, that is, in the quartet of discourses I outlined earlier.

In the regime of *energy* as the primary evidence of human life well lived which developed at the beginning of the twentieth century and was now encapsulated in the particular sensory actions and reactions demanded of the stressed subject once he was given the opportunity to drive a speeding car, the crash is a punctum, a denial of energy's delights. It reminds one not to misuse one's energy and shows us that in the gravest instance, this energy is powerless and an illusion. If driving stands as one of the most characteristic new kinds of behavior of the subject in late modernity, in that it teaches her how to deploy her energy in ways appropriate to the forces at work in modern life, then the crash is an avowal of a more severe and greater power that lurks behind the pleasures available to this energized subject. Consider the degree and kind of freedom offered to the subject while driving. First there is the freedom to purchase and ostentatiously consume (as leisure) the car itself as commodity, to show off one's possession of the grandest, shiniest (and, year after year, mostly newly fashionable and ever changeable), bauble of the mass market. This freedom corresponds to the simplest level of commodity culture's satisfactions. With new models, different marques, world production ambitions, and new levels of advertising, car sales represent a most intense example of the consumer carnival. With its stress on social status and snobbery, the market for automobiles shows itself as the first stage of consumerism, still deeply cognizant of the class distinctions which in fact were more wholly meaningful in the pre mass-consumption era. This is the version of driving as freedom which shows us the crash as comic "spills."

A more profound exemplar of modern life, however, is the kind of freedom afforded one as a driver: when you drive, you make constant decisions based on ever-changing scenes, shocks, and stimuli. In the name of forestalling the potential crash, this freedom is hedged in by numerous limitations designed by the state in its role as traffic policeman. The state's discourse, first, flashes before us the spectacle of future disaster and, second, promises us security if we give up the most intense pleasures possible of the experience. The state, in other words, would have us as drivers all behave in the same ways—so that here, even though we appear free and hence each unique, is a classic version of the modernist nightmare of standardized, automaton, and assembly line behavior. Reinforcing the fact that we must conform, the spectacle of the crash comes as a terrible warning, so that every crash reinforces the state's power to control and may be the key necessary component in the state's use of spectacle to control our everyday freedoms. (The crash is an advertisement, then, supporting the repressive tendencies of the state.) On the other hand, we can remain contented in the knowledge that our freedom, within limits, is considerable: not only—as exemplified by the experience of driving—our freedom to make our own minor decisions but our freedom to be shocked by an experience which might be new. This is the freedom, with all its possibilities, that is being tackled by writers like Ballard in their exploration of the meanings of the car crash.

Clearly these restrictions and these freedoms can exist simultaneously: they engage with and accentuate each other, and the tension between them reinforces each. The citizen's fear of the accident, fostered by the state, comes to be recast as a more muted apprehension of the state's control itself, into the sense of compliance which makes one obey the rules. This contrasts with the desire for the potential pleasure, that desire nurtured by commodity culture, which taking fuller advantage of one's proffered freedom might bring. This nexus of apprehension and desire structures the subject's "ideal" deployment of the energy which signifies his very life. Energy is thereby cathected into a specific, and more easily controlled, tension. It is upon the shimmering scene of this tension that the modern political subject is interpellated: on the one hand by the repressive apparatus of the state, allied to the capitalist production aims of Fordist efficiency and conformist compliance, and on the other by the hints of free choice offered by the consumption carnival displayed invitingly by commodity culture. The crash lets us know that we can enjoy our freedom to choose commodities, but if we try to have the new at the level of actual lived experience, we may well meet disaster or inflict disaster on others. At the moment of the crash, nonetheless, the state arrives to try to save us. It is the tension between these two competing strands of interpellation that is left to us as our everyday pleasure—of driving, and of living as subjects in modernity. It is a tension which, because it is punctured by the crash, can perhaps only be read critically in all its interpellative power through the contemplation of that moment. The crash, therefore, is a deeply political spectacle.

Moreover, the crash's shock effects, unlike the shock tactics ascribed by critics to much modernist art, do not necessarily lead to a jolting into consciousness or a new sense of critical distance and may actively forestall it. This is so because the crash presents itself as a warning of what may happen again in the future: it orients its watchers firmly toward their subsequent behavior. Within a framework of repetition—crashes follow patterns—the crash as phenomenon is always new, for no two crashes are ever the same.[12] For the Victorians, the topic of energy, and of its lack, was often associated with fear—fear of the potential of energy, or its lack, to provoke global and personal disaster. There was, for example, Lord Kelvin's warning in his essay "On the Dissipation of Energy" (1892) that the heat death of the sun would occur sooner than anyone had imagined. (This prediction would furnish the final image for H. G. Wells's *The Time Machine* in 1895.) Some years earlier, Jean-Martin Charcot's experiments at the Salpêtrière infirmary in Paris on patients showing symptoms of "hystero-epilepsy" had suggested how prone the overtense body is to breakdown and to exhibiting "perversions of sensibility." From the level of the individual psyche to that of the whole solar system, the discussion of energy and the tension necessary for its proper maintenance was wont to be cast in terms of accompanying fears. And these fears—a new nervousness—were built up by developing images of possible future catastrophes that might envelop the unwary or the overexcitable. In this context, the crash could function as a replica, in everyday life, of these anxieties. And like them, by focusing the mind of the observer on future possibilities, it handily diverted its audience from the kinds of attention to the past which might lead to a political analysis—to a course of action embarked on as a community.

Henri Bergson, in *Matter and Memory*, explored how present sensations were enriched and made something more than humdrum reactions (the kinds of activities referred to as "knee-jerk" or "reflex" reactions) when they are mixed with memories. Walter Benjamin, in turn, saw the potential for a politicized apprehension in this account of Bergson's, which Benjamin praised for attempting to overcome the flattening out of all experience in modernity, even as he also pointed out that Bergson, in implying that this kind of reification could be overcome by subjective, personal action, refused any historical determination of memory. The crash, in this context, offers a shock which merely explodes memory, while offering itself as a fearful spectacle which works to influence future behavior. The spectacle of horror, offering itself as a local, intimate kind of spectacle, manages to appear subpolitical, offering only a lesson to the driver to be wary and conform. (Almost all general accounts of crash rates and the like in the media are couched in such terms.) Possibly only when the ratio of coercion and free choice, which takes the measure of the crash now and appears to us utterly natural, is radically altered—perhaps by a technological innovation—will we then be able to more adequately understand the significance of the crash in its political dimension.

The Crash as Comedy

Why were the first car accidents seen as comic? Why were the earliest crashes represented as moments in a kind of joking game? Accounts of the first accidents, in, for example, the *Times* of London, assume a dry, factual tone: the accident was the new thing because of the novel vehicle involved, and sometimes merited attention because of the wealth or prominence of the cars' owners. These earliest accounts modeled their reports on notices of accidents involving horse-drawn transport, bicycles, and trains. Possibly the best-known example of this genre from the beginning of the last century familiar today is the fictitious, but typically recalcitrant, account of death beneath a train that Mr. Duffy, in the act of lifting a forkful of dinner to his mouth, reads in James Joyce's short story "A Painful Case." (The title of the story is taken from the headline over the account of the accident.) The bland seemliness of such reports was challenged by the writing in the new mass-circulation papers, especially as the numbers of cars and accidents increased; these launched campaigns against reckless driving, which culminated in Britain with the founding of the Pedestrians Association in 1929, the important Road Traffic Act of 1930, which abolished speed limits altogether, and the Act of 1934, which introduced pedestrian crossings, Belisha beacons,[13] and a speed limit in built-up areas of thirty miles per hour.[14] If we search for published representations of accidents themselves, however, it is to the stories and cartoons of magazines such as *Punch*, and soon to early film, that we must turn. Here was formulated the strange mixture of class consciousness, the sense of mishap, and outright comedy which mitigate the tragedy of the earliest car crashes.

As one of the pioneers of the mass-market magazine genre, the reading of which was itself a new kind of "leisure activity," *Punch*, aiming like its countless imitators and followers to be snobbish and populist at once, waded enthusiastically into the world of "scorchers," "driving habits," speed traps, chauffeurs, choleric majors at the wheel ("Major Mustard"), "erratic steering," and the whole lingua franca and spectacle of "the Montgomery-Smiths in their motor-car, enjoying the beauties of the country."[15] The new thrill demanded a new language, and magazines such as *Punch*, in on the beginnings of fashion as the mechanism that made lowbrow and mass culture seem endlessly appealing, were eager to jazz up their pages and their circulations by inventing it. *Punch* handled the cycling craze, and then automobilism, as new fashions which (for fashion demands that one must appear blasé about it) it cannot quite take seriously. It pandered to fashion's snobbery by always noting—usually in a shorthand phrase, "Major Mustard"—the social status of each of its characters, all the while appearing to undercut with humor the japes of the fashionable crowd. Along with other "pictorial weeklies," such as *Tidbits*, the French *Illustration* and *Petit Journal*, and car magazines like the U.S. *Motor* (founded in 1903), *Punch* was inventing a new mass-market taste, honing a grammar and a vocabulary nimble enough to excite the consumer-reader's desire.[16] (In 1895 the *Petit Journal* launched a subscription and raised £1,500 to build a monument to Emile Levassor, who died when his car hit a dog during the Paris–Marseilles–Paris race of 1986; the editors described the monument, which still stands at the Porte Maillot in Paris, as "a monument to a victim of automobilism." It is another stone car, even if carved in relief.)[17]

It is striking how often incidents as grisly as car crashes could be mentioned in these magazines. In a signifying code where the protocols of status were being recast from ones based on rigid class distinctions to ones based more simply on the possession of the new accessories of leisure, spills, breakdowns, and crashes of these new accessories were the fodder of *Punch*'s automobile humor. The crash, by being made the butt of jokiness, could be withdrawn from the arena of real alarm and cast instead as the benign, foolish evidence of a kind of mass-market adventure. Nobody dies in these *Punch* cartoon crashes; in the cartoons and illustrations there is never even black-and-white blood. "Spills," as sites where characters renegotiated their place in the revamped class system, were never allowed to become tragic, could never inflict wounds. Rather, they are starred sites where the protocols of a new class — as leisured consumers — are invented in the course of showing them as preposterous, even deluded, but engaging in a delusion of personal power and knowledge which the cartoon finds funny and of which it ultimately approves.

A standard *Punch* car crash cartoon of the early twentieth century shows a driver and passenger crouched in attitudes of shock and horror as a young cyclist into whom they have crashed goes flying through their windshield. The cartoon is titled "So Inconsiderate" and bears a caption of the driver telling his passenger: "Jove! Might have killed us! I must have a wire screen fixed up" (figure 15). The accent clearly is on consumption: the driver is outfitted in goggles and a driving fur coat, both staples of the haberdashery extensively advertised for drivers in the open-car years. The first thought of the driver in the accident — his need for a stronger screen — reinforces with a laugh the consumerist imperative. This shopper's response and its inappropriateness are, however, the butt of the cartoon's humor; his callous carelessness about the flying cyclist's life is the focus. We are not shown an injury, even as the drawing displays a flying body, projected at speed; instead, our attention is drawn by the caption to the selfish gall of the driver. His self-centeredness is what is in the end celebrated. The driver's self-serving insouciance, his downright carelessness about causing harm to others as he dreams up other accessories to buy is both berated and celebrated. Time and again what the *Punch* cartoons celebrate (even as they laugh at the characters who embody them) is this refusal of the driver to allow reality (especially the gruesome reality of a crash) to stop him from forging on. The cartoon becomes an occasion for celebrating the indomitable quality of the driver who outfoxes the accident and literally refuses to see it because he is willfully deluded by his pursuit of the new consumerist leisure. This comic delusion is posited as a necessity and, in its way, the heart of the pleasure of the experience of driving itself. This is wholly in keeping with a consumerist reading of automobilism: focus on the consumable commodities, and problems are rendered nonexistent. With the apparent naturalness of humor, these cartoons paint the consumer automobilist as a weekend adventurer whose laughable delusion is a kind of brilliance. This delusion, it is implied, is exactly what makes the adventure, and the physicality of the automobile experience, safe for consumer culture.

SO INCONSIDERATE

"Jove! Might have killed us! I must have a wire screen
fixed up."

FIGURE 15. "So Inconsiderate: 'Jove! Might have killed us! I must have a wire
screen fixed up!'" From J. A. Hammerton, ed., *Mr. Punch Awheel: The Humors
of Motoring* (London: Educational Book Company, 1908), 191.

If automobilism is to be fostered, it seems, this is the kind of illusion that
must, even as it is being exposed, be sustained.

The delusional imperative was reinforced by the uses to which cars were
often put in the other mass-leisure invention of the day—film, especially
so in a new, briefly voguish genre of "trick pictures," which specialized in
"motor mayhem."[18] These trick pictures are one of the opening salvos of a
long history of the car crash in the movies, where film at once brings us up
close to the reality of the crash and desensitizes us to it. Most of the trick
picture movie reels have been lost and are known only through contempo-

rary descriptions; the sequence of stills shown here, along with the accompanying account of how a trick picture can be made in Frederick Talbot's "Trick Pictures and How They Are Produced," from *Moving Pictures: How They Are Made and Worked* (1912), gives a good idea of the comic delusions of their brand of grotesquerie (figures 16–20).[19] Talbot uses as his demonstration piece a series of stills from a bioscope reel titled *The Automobile Accident*. It told the story of a drunken workman who falls asleep in a roadway:

> While he is sleeping peacefully a taxi-cab comes along at a smart pace, and, not observing the slumbering form of the roisterer, the chauffeur drives over him, cutting off both his legs. The shock awakens the man rudely, and he is surprised to find his lower limbs scattered across the roadway. The chauffeur is horrified by the unfortunate accident, but his fare, on the contrary, a doctor, is not much perturbed. He descends from his carriage, picks up the dismembered limbs, replaces them in position, assists the afflicted man to his feet, and after shaking hands each proceeds on his separate way, the workman resuming his journey as if nothing had happened.

To stage this trick, Talbot explains, one needs simply to substitute, in the scenes showing the crash, the character playing the drunken workman with another, "a cripple who has lost both legs in an accident."[20] It is his fake limbs that are apparently severed, then reattached. Another actor is substituted for the scenes in which the workman walks away. A series of scenes cobbled together in a continuous loop of film (with the casual dexterity with which the crash victim apparently has his legs reunited with his body) sustains the illusion of the worker's magic imperviousness to the injuries of the auto accident. To satisfy "a popular taste [which] demands extreme novelty," as Talbot's guide to making movies puts it, trick pictures such as this one need to show "some scene impossible to picture without sacrifice of life."[21]

Technology, then, presents dying as an art — or rather, film pretends to an expertise that can raise the dead and make the maimed whole. The reaction this film wishes to illicit is the shocked "How did they do that?" and this at the very moment when we might be expected to expend some empathy on the gruesomely wounded man. The technologically manufactured spectacle, in other words, forecloses the necessity of human empathy by bringing to the fore the cleverness of its technical sleight of eye. It allows

FIGURE 16. "The producer giving instructions to the principal actor and his double, the legless cripple. The dummy legs in the foreground." From Frederick Talbot, "Trick Pictures and How They Are Produced," in *Moving Pictures: How They Are Made and Worked* (London: Heinemann, 1912).

FIGURE 17. "The taxi-cab running over the sleeper and apparently cutting off his legs, but in reality displacing the legless cripple's property limbs."

FIGURE 18. "The roysterer after being run over by the taxi-cab sitting up and brandishing his severed limbs."

Both from Frederick Talbot, "Trick Pictures and How They Are Produced," in *Moving Pictures: How They Are Made and Worked* (London: Heinemann, 1912).

FIGURE 19. "Observing the effects of the disaster, the doctor proceeds to replace the severed legs."

FIGURE 20. "The limbs replaced, the patient and doctor shake hands."

Both from Frederick Talbot, "Trick Pictures and How They Are Produced," in *Moving Pictures: How They Are Made and Worked* (London: Heinemann, 1912).

us to understand that such empathy would have been a waste of feeling, for the technology (of film) has the means to make the (apparently) injured whole. (This is the kind of moment in which simulation becomes spectacle, in the scathing sense of that term used by Guy Debord.) The technology of film, the medium here, offers itself also as the magical analogy for the technology that is portrayed: the automobile. The car's cruelties, the film's magic suggests, are an illusion too. Further, as watchers of the film, we identify here with the user of the technology that the film portrays: in this case, with the car's passenger. Appropriately, he is a doctor; it is he who performs the medical magic in the scene shown. What happens *in the film* is that the technology gets to act as the doctor, making the wounded man's wounds not matter.

This magnificently magical illogic of the trick picture laid down the protocols followed in thousands of car crash depictions in films since, from the classic scene in which the car and its passengers fly (sometimes in slow motion) over a cliff to that in which the wild car chase ends in a fireball. It is all, the medium suggests, an illusion, and we as the spectators, at the head of a taxonomy of the powerful that stretches via the passenger as doctor, the car, and the film, have the magical ability to make the wounded whole. And because we always know that it is an illusion, it's a joke too, inducing a fear-tinged laughter. The humor that imbued so many representations of the first car crashes represents, as such, a sordid conspiracy of the refusal to tell the truth on the part of new technologies—a conspiracy that we can lay at the door of consumerist imperatives. To choose, to buy, to see: all these new powers refused to be tamped down by the sense of danger and, on the contrary, were enhanced by it.

Yet this laughter too has a utopian aspect. What we must remember was that the showing of the crash was a new thing, in that the car crash itself was a novel phenomenon. Just as we can read the fascination, in the eighteenth century, with the insane (as in the fashionable tours of Bedlam hospital) as a complex part of the reaction to the demands of the Age of Reason, and as we might read the Victorian fascination with the colonial "native" as a component of the imperial imaginary, so too the twentieth century film's obsessive portrayal of the crashing car is part of the complex reworking of this century's relation between technology and the human subject. In all three cases—the insane in the age of the Enlightenment, the native in the age of imperialism, and the car crash victim in the era of technology—the image of the victim of the new development was transformed, through the specific rituals of gazing developed in each case, into a spectacle of grotesque laughter. This laughter cruelly others the victims and, in doing so, works as a secular ritual which affirms the viewer's refusal to be part of that othering. In the case of the car crash victim as spectacle, as in each of the others, that refusal is possibly wishful thinking. To the extent that it is not simply fearful, nervous laughter, however, it is unlike those earlier moments in the history of seeing as scapegoating in that the viewer cannot quite forget that in this case the other might become the self in a moment — "by accident." The semantic shift whereby the disaster in the car came to be called an "accident" until, as is the case now, the very term "accident" is virtually synonymous with "car crash" is telling. It suggests that what is at stake in the laughter before the early movie spectacles of the car wreck was a reappraisal of the very notion of accidentality, now that technology had intervened forcibly in it, that governed the human subject's sense of agency. The car, as commodity, posited itself not only as an object destined never quite to fulfill the subject's desire but as a prosthesis which accentuated, through the sensation of speeding, the buyer's sense of lived experience. Guaranteeing that this machine intensified subjective experience was the end fact that it also offered the subject the possibility to annihilate others — or the power of self-annihilation. All this "by accident": to have intense experience in the era of techno-consumerism, in other words, one had to concede in advance a change in the ratio of the self's agency and outside forces. To feel through oneself the greater power of the machine, one had to gamble. Calling what might happen an "accident" implied that "chance" alone operated as cautionary control of one's lived thrills.

Yet although car culture — as with the Futurists — might have fostered quasi-Nietzschean dreams of a new stage in the subject's heroic battle with fate in pursuit of the will to power, more prosaically, it was in the sphere of the state — in the enforcement of national traffic laws — that the quotient of power, chance, and accidentality was endlessly debated. The second, better-known discourse of the car crash is that of the state's traffic rules. The state's legal apparatus and "rules of the road," determined, you might say, to wipe that laugh at the spectacle of the car crash off the faces of its citizens, nevertheless did not do this necessarily by showing them some more realist or vivid image of the crash. Rather, it showed its astute appraisal of what was really at stake in the new culture of its citizen drivers by inserting its discourse at the level of delineating chance. It showed its capacity, well beyond that of the citizen on her own, to measure rates of accidentality and then worked to offer its own kinds of reassurance by marshaling notions of liability, blame, and insurance. In making the car crash a concern of the state, it moved it from being a butt of laughter to being a matter of statistics.

Traffic Laws

When Margaret Driscoll, in London in 1896, became the first person to be killed by a car, the coroner concluded the inquest with a commonplace staggering for its lack of foresight. He said he hoped that such an incident would never happen again.[22] (Since then, in Britain alone, it has happened more than half a million times.) Blatantly wrong and blatantly optimistic, the coroner's observation nevertheless turned out to be uncannily characteristic: it set the tone of the state's discourse on automobiles. First, it shows the functionary attending at once to numbers: he is—even if hoping for a negative result—thinking statistically. Second, by asserting its singularity, he shows himself to be thinking of the car crash as an "accident," that is, an event ultimately beyond human and state control, which, when it comes, will always appear aberrant, an event blamed, finally, on chance. These two assumptions, together with the statement's naiveté, offer a template of the state's discourse of speed control and its consequences. In subsequent decades, the idea of the death rate, a concept foretold in the coroner's comments, would come to govern governments' policies on speed.

Paul Virilio, in *Speed and Politics*, has written vividly of how the state must be reconceptualized not primarily as the guardian of the national territory but as the controller of the movement of its citizens and others through that territory: the state as "traffic cop." Clearly it is in the state's role as regulator of traffic speeds and flows that the average bourgeois "law-abiding" citizen most frequently comes face to face with the state's police power, because it is in traveling at speed, on the public roads, that a citizen is most likely to break the state's laws—to speed. In urban studies from the polemics of Jane Jacobs to those of Mike Davis, a consistent theme has been how different urban constituencies have used the diverse public spaces of streets, crossroads, and squares; they can be transformed in a gesture from the route of an army's triumphal parade to the scenes of revolutionary clashes. Less thought has been given to the social and cultural role played by routes through the national territory, although since the novel's beginnings in picaresque tales such as Smollett's *Humphry Clinker* (1771) to

Jack Kerouac's *On the Road* in post–World War II America, novelists have consistently celebrated the open road as the site in which to glorify the freedom-hungry individual's desire to test the limits of the liberal, rationalist state. As the democratic nation-states developed their extensive networks of surveillance, control, and interpellation in the second half of the nineteenth century, founding standardized systems of policing, schooling, and tax paying all undergirded by extensive bureaucracies, the roads, as public space that was open to all classes, became sites where the powers of these new state networks came to be actively contested. With the open road as an arena where hegemonies might be contested, the rise of the private motorcar, and the assumption from the start that motorcars would be allowed to use the public roads, played a crucial role.

In 1934, a pamphlet by T. C. Foley, *The Pace That Kills* (price one shilling), published by the Pedestrians Association, the advocacy group which supported the rights of people traveling on foot on British thoroughfares, opened with the following observation:

> In 1830 a distinguished British statesman, William Huskisson, then President of the Board of Trade, was knocked down and killed by a railway engine at the ceremonial opening of a new track between Manchester and Liverpool. This dramatic demonstration of the danger to life and limb of the new form of locomotion shocked the country and the lesson was not lost. Railway trains were compelled by law to run on private tracks from which the public was excluded. . . . It is interesting to speculate what the effect on the evolution of the motor car would have been, if Mr. Gladstone in the Nineties, had been killed at a demonstration of one of the new "horseless carriages." Would the new method of locomotion have been banned from the public highway and motorists forced to build private tracks?[23]

The use of the public way by any kind of vehicle is a right granted implicitly by the state; this is the logic underlying the state's assumption of its role in policing traffic. In Britain as elsewhere, the national legislation on automobiles did mediate between the different interests of road users — the private motorists versus the carriage drivers, whose horses were now likely to be frightened, the private drivers versus the drivers of omnibuses, trams, and trains, hauliers and drivers of wagons, farmers and drivers of livestock, and all of these versus pedestrians.[24] With the Motor Car Act that came into effect in the United Kingdom on the first day of 1904, replacing the

Locomotives on Highways Act of 1896, the state, in a move which would become characteristic, offered private drivers the incentive of speed as it imposed controls and increased regulatory oversight. The speed limit was increased from fourteen to twenty miles per hour, while from now on all cars were required to be registered, for a one-pound fee, and all drivers needed a driver's license, to cost five shillings. The next full-dress piece of motoring legislation did not come until 1930, when, after massive lobbying by the Automobile Association, the minister for transport Herbert Morrison offered to put the nation's trust in "decent motorists" and removed the speed limit for cars altogether. At the same time, third-party insurance was made compulsory; insurance had been demanded in Sweden since 1918.[25] In 1934 a new Traffic Act reintroduced a speed limit of thirty miles per hour in "built-up areas," made mandatory a driving test, and called for pedestrian crossings. Local authorities could criminalize crossing on foot outside selected crossing points. This flurry of legislation in the decade before World War II followed the full-scale national collection of road accident statistics and data on road use in Britain, which began in 1926.

Traffic laws tried to control speeds; bit by bit they also extended the reach of the bureaucratic and panoptic state. The roles and functions of national police forces were profoundly altered by the emergence of mass automobile traffic. In Britain in the years of the twenty-mile-per-hour speed limit, police set up "speed traps." The Automobile Association was founded in 1905 partly to foil the police by employing relays of "road scouts." Police were employed to direct traffic at busy junctions before the invention of reliable traffic lights. It was partly the policemen's dislike of confronting the new masses of middle-class drivers with the news that their speeds were breaking the law which led to the abandonment of the speed limit in Britain in 1930. Between July and December 1928, for example, the British police dealt with 114,541 traffic offenses.[26] After 1937 the government instituted a corps of "courtesy cops" who were to advise rather than arrest motorists. The Department of Transport cooperated with the Automobile Association, the National Safety First Association (a private organization financed by "motoring interests"), the Pedestrians Association, and the BBC to produce educational films to drill users in proper road behavior. All these moves inserted the police more tangibly into the fabric of ordinary citizens' lives. Driving, almost more than any other activity ordinarily engaged in by the citizens of developed nations in the early twentieth century, provided multiple opportunities both for evading and for soliciting the attention of the police. The road became the arena in which the bourgeois citizen continually enacted a drama of her confrontation with the state's power, as held and exercised by the police. The state as repressive apparatus displayed itself to its bourgeoisie every day in its role as policer of traffic. Virilio, who insists that this had been the state's raison d'être since it evolved from the city-state, sees his vision come true: "the state as traffic cop."

This new visibility of the police in everyday life was lampooned in the Keystone Cops comedies and pored over more ambiguously in the thousands of police chases that punctuate newsstand thrillers and B movies. It was paralleled in all countries by a strong push for the national standardization of traffic rules and nationally mandated systems of road signage. Early in the century, locally produced signs were common, including the "horror signs" which displayed images of skulls or the grim reaper before dangerous curves on American roads. In 1925 a standardized national signage was decreed in the United States, developed by the Joint Board of Interstate Highways and approved by the secretary of agriculture. The federal highway acts of 1916, 1921, and later offered federal support to highway building and demanded in return that a national highway designation system replace the older "Trail Markings" scheme. Soon the six-pointed shield with the letters "U.S." (southern states had objected to "U.S.A.") and a number replaced route names such as Lakes to the Sea Highway, the Keystone Trail, and the White Horse Trail.[27] Throughout Europe too, systems of uniform national signage were imposed, and national codes of road conduct were enforced, often, as in Britain, against the wishes of local councils which had set up their own more stringent rules. This successful push for national uniformity in signs and rules was followed by the first stage of the building of massive concrete freeways. The first was the Autobahn system in Germany, a system of grand modernist behemoths which featured a nationally uniform system of signage, the better to direct the citizen at speed. These roads, wherever built, were unrelenting advertisements for the state's power. In the first thirty years of the motorcar, national road systems were reconfigured into a numbered system of state control where the citizen as speeder, whether as driver approaching a stop sign or as reader of a freeway exit sign, was hailed with a new relentlessness and a new intensity of interdiction, aimed at controlling the smoothness of every citizen's speed. This was a newly streamlined front for the state to display its power. And all of it was put in place in the name of preventing road accidents, curbing speeding, and making the roads and their traffic systems safer for all users.

This system marks a major front for the state's expansion of its power into the everyday lives of its citizens in the twentieth century. It was extraordinarily successful as an ideology, that is, if we take ideology, as Louis Althusser defined it, to mean the exercise of power that is so successful that it is not noticed or, when it is, appears utterly natural. In other words, the state's accession to a huge new network of traffic management has seldom in the fullest sense been considered politically. Between 1910 and 1930, every regime and political system, whether communist Russia, fascist Germany and Italy, or the Western democracies, rapidly developed national and parallel systems of traffic control. True, Mussolini's Italy even went so far as to dictate on which side of the street its citizens could walk in a given direction; yet the British government in 1939 proposed to copy this by teaching children to walk only on the left-hand side of pavement (it was opposed by the British Association of Head Teachers on the grounds that it was an attempt to "Hitlerize the British public"). Hitler's Autobahns were admired everywhere, but especially in the United States; a deputation from the American Bureau of Public Roads, one of a number of national delegations given a tour of the Reichsautobahnen by the German inspector of roads in 1937, praised the German "national public roads" as wonderful examples of the best modern road building and returned with numerous photographs that can still be seen in the U.S. National Archives. Bureaucrats were very aware of the self- and national glorification uses of Hitler's modernist engineering masterpieces, but their use in advanced traffic management was praised and acknowledged as necessary everywhere, regardless of ideology. Traffic, the car, and speed itself were to be kept out of politics.

Kept below the level of the state's politics, but ever more extensively micromanaged by national bureaucracies: this contradiction was made possible because each state could, on the traffic issue, present itself not only as the champion of smooth traffic flow but also as the preventer of "reckless driving" and hence of accidents. The state, through the police, was seen on the roads as the protector of each citizen's everyday well-being. Moreover, the state could represent itself as the assuager of each citizen's everyday fear. In the postwar years and especially since the 1960s, when social historians described the regulation of the motorcar by the state, they read this regulation as political only to the extent that in their account, the state apparatus juggled the demands of multiple competing stakeholders. These were, first, the car manufacturers, dealers, and the like who in Britain were known as the "motoring interests" and in the United States came to be known in shorthand as "Detroit"; followed by the new mass of their customers, the automobile owners, represented by groups such as the formidable Automobile Association, aided in Britain by the more aristocratic Royal Automobile Club; and last, those without cars, represented in Britain by the hapless but tenacious Pedestrians Association. Although historians differ, most agree that the extraordinary influence of the "motoring interests" in forestalling safety improvements and building more dangerous (because faster) cars effectively tied governments' hands. They take this line because it explains the central phenomenon on which they all concur: the general ineffectiveness of government safety programs. By 1909 over one thousand people had been killed by cars in Britain (by December 1909 the figure had reached 1,070); in the twenties, with many more cars now on the roads, the average death toll *every year* was 4,121; for the thirties, this figure had leaped to 6,640.[28] And hundreds of thousands were annually maimed or injured: 208,801 people were reported killed or injured on the roads of Britain in 1931.[29] Yet the stakeholder model, while accounting for the states' extreme caution in introducing national schemes of traffic management and their consequent inability to prevent or even moderate the mounting toll of death and destruction on the roads, cannot fully come to grips with the reasons why citizens (of all interests) seemed largely to accept — or taught themselves to accept — the huge numbers killed or injured.

Sean O'Connell, writing in 1998, put this problem as follows:

> In 1993 the *Guardian*'s educational supplement featured a story on the history of road safety. Its opening sentence was striking: "More than half a million people have been killed on Britain's roads this century, but that figure would be far worse were it not for the many road-safety measures that have accompanied the history of the motor car." It is difficult to imagine a half a million deaths from any other cause being treated in such a casual manner.[30]

The stakeholder model leads to the benign view of government efforts that is followed in the *Guardian* article: bureaucratic efforts are seen as Fabian reforms effected in the face of entrenched stonewallers and whining pedestrians. Underlining the overwhelming casualness of the reaction to the numbers killed, however, we might see the state's intervention instead as its nuanced response to its citizens' blasé attitude. The state, if not actually inciting people to the dangers of speed, mirrored the blasé attitude of its citizens to accidents in formulating its discourse on the new car culture. The state's discourse had as its end result, it is true, a series of interdictions relating to drivers and to all road users. To formulate these, it had to develop a sense of the dangers it would prevent. In doing so, the state came to rely on increasingly sophisticated and comprehensive ranges of figures—in short, on statistics. In other words, the state's discursive function in relation to car crashes was to see them collectively, en masse, and, in doing so, to turn them into numbers, to make of them a mass of data that could be tabulated and analyzed. It then used the findings based on this analysis to generate changes and refinements to the highway safety code, passing laws that if followed were supposed to forestall accidents. Or rather, in the language of the statistics on which they were based, their purpose was to lower the accident rates. Next, governments used their statistical findings to launch educational campaigns, aimed especially at children, to encourage road safety and prevent accidents. All of this constituted a chain of related discourses around the car crash—stretching from the policeman's initial report all the way to the road safety propaganda film—that avoided being directly about it. In seeing each accident as one of many, in collectivizing the crash, the state also ruthlessly abstracted it, failed to take into account the specificity of the particular suffering it caused, and rendered it instead as part of a numerical tabulation.

As early as 1859, John Stuart Mill had written: "By virtue of its superior intelligence gathering and information processing capacities, there is a distinct role for the central state acquired in a liberal society over and above both local and individual claims to autonomy." [31] In all the nation-states which were developing their modern form in the nineteenth century, the increasingly sophisticated collection and collation of statistics played an integral role. In Britain in particular, where the Board of Trade, which dealt with economic statistics, and the General Register Office (GRO), which dealt with social statistics, were separate entities, the use of statistical information to generate narratives which could be used for the amelioration of social problems became increasingly commonplace from 1837 onward. The GRO effectively created a national network of the hitherto independent Poor Law Unions, which had dealt with poverty in each county, in the process creating a picture of the health of the whole nation's subjects. Allied to the public health movement, under the direction of a doctor, William Farr, from 1837 to 1880, the GRO determined the national average death rate to be twenty-three per thousand and, through an 1848 public health law, demanded that districts with a rate above that number publish health tables and plan sanitation reforms. This created among Poor Law districts a national death rate competition. By the 1850s, Farr calculated that the average death rate for the healthiest regions was seventeen per thousand.[32] The GRO health tables in "classified diseases" gave precedence to endemic or epidemic illnesses that could most readily be prevented: this was statistics at the service of epidemiology, and its professed purpose was mitigation and prevention. The national register of births, marriages, and deaths, by assessing all aspects of morbidity, became, in the absence of a national policy on poverty or on health, an effective tool in arousing interest in the scandal of high morbidity rates, and thus in influencing legislation which made the proposals for mitigation into law. It was this particular paradigm of the collection, collation, and public use of national statistics, already entrenched as an essential guarantor of each citizen's identity (this was also the office which issued birth certificates) and a key component of the beneficial work of government, that was adopted once death by car crash began to show up in the morbidity tables after 1896.

This paradigm for the use of statistics, and for the generation of government policy which resulted in legislation, made for a discourse which obliquely referred to the car crash rather than representing it directly, sapping its horrific immediacy to confer on it a sense of general, national significance. "The new form of universal accountancy isolated from the tissue of events just those factors that could be judged on an impersonal, quantitative scale. Counting numbers began here and in the end numbers alone counted," wrote Lewis Mumford in *The Myth of the Machine*.[33] By rendering any given crash as a statistic, it abstracted it, turning it into a number to be tabulated and thus ignoring the particularity of the event itself and of its specific impacts on the victims. By collating the crash as a number into a specific narrative from the Victorian era, which considered morbidity statistics primarily as a tool in reformist national policymaking, it inducted that data into particular narrative assumptions of its own. In that narrative, morbidity figures collated into statistics generated numbers which then might well point up an excessive concentration of a given problem, an excess which, more or less undetectable before the numbers gathering, could now be read as scandalous, the presumption being that reforms could then be put in place to lower the figures.

When car crash morbidity numbers were fed into this system and subjected to this logic, certain strange effects ensued. The logic of the developing social science of medical epidemiology—which measured the incidence of infectious diseases—might not necessarily be that best suited to collating car crash statistics. For example, in the case of car crashes, the horror is evident, in the first instance, in the very spectacle of the crash itself and needs no numerical tabulation to read it as scandalous. Government policy documents, however, following the reformist statistical model, only read the collated numbers themselves as scandalous, so that the complaint went, for example, in British newspaper campaigns in the 1930s, that the number of deaths—seven thousand per year—was too high. This way of thinking on the part of policymakers appears so prosaic as to be inevitable; the point is not that it is defective but that, as a discourse on the car crash, it works to cover over the specific horror even as it means well, and supposes that plans will be developed to ameliorate the possibility of that horror occurring again.

To talk of car crashes in terms of statistics, to read them epidemiologically, is to fail to see how their specific horror can affect us, and moreover to assume that they can be prevented much as one prevents an infectious disease. In the early twentieth century, both sea and air traffic saw accidents whose specific horror did transfix to the point where policy was changed: consider the awe-struck sensationalism of the newspaper coverage of the *General Slocum* disaster in New York Harbor in 1904 and of the sinking of the *Titanic* in 1912. In the case of the new but soon-to-be-prosaic horror of the car crash, the statistical reading on the epidemiological model, abstracting the horror while it tries to register the cumulative force of all accidents considered as one scandal, gives us numbers which can indeed shock, but shock at the level of rational calculation rather than at that of visceral emotion. Key was the presumed impact of the rapidly expanding mass media of the period: it was as if it was assumed that no one crash could be shown as shocking enough. To describe the crash in statistical terms was to collude in this assumption that the citizen was not sensitive enough to be transfixed by a single car crash.

The effect of reading the car crash as a statistic, however, goes beyond this primary stage of abstraction. It implies that the car crash has significance only in relation to other crashes. The phenomenological valence of any single crash is eroded; it regains meaning only when crashes are seen en masse. In other words, it is only as *evidence* that the crash can be granted meaning. And this is evidence of a proposition which invariably, whether implicitly or explicitly, has been theorized in advance. Mary Poovey, in her astonishingly rich book *A History of the Modern Fact*, which is, as she describes it, a prehistory of statistics, gives much play to statistics' claim to access a pure, untheorized knowledge — after all, statistical hypotheses are ostensibly based not on ideologically tainted theories but on collated "raw" data. She demonstrates the illusory quality of such claims: both the ways in which the information is collected and the means by which it is collated to generate numbers imply the statisticians' assumptions regarding cause, pattern, and outcome.[34] In this light, the figures on car crashes turn out not to be "raw" data at all. They are apparently abstract numbers generated by assumptions implicitly held in advance, assumptions, for example, about the reasons the crash occurred. Such assumptions in turn were used to construct lists which police arriving on the crash scene were expected to tick off. The statistics-based official discourse of the crash not only abstracts the particularity of any given incident but both precedes and follows its official notation with a host of implied and unstated assumptions about the crash's meaning.

If the gift of speed in the world of consumer culture was an offer to the nominally independent democratic consumer-citizen to have access to unmediated experience, to a bodily sensation that went beyond the simulative joys of consumption, and if the crash, as a kind of degree zero and guarantee of the actuality of that experience, was the ultimate proof of its reality, then it might seem remarkable that the state's discourse of the crash is so hedged with assumptions and leavened by abstracting statistical language. Yet if consumer cultures, through the media and especially through cinema, need to teach their audiences to laugh at the crash, then the state could do no less than reassure its citizens that the phenomenon of the crash could be made to disappear through state action carried out on the lines used to tackle endemic social ills. This conveniently shifted responsibility away from drivers; most educational material on the matter of road safety in Britain, for example, was directed at pedestrians, especially at children. It allowed the driver to think of the crash as evidence of a mass phenomenon that would be dealt with at a national level, so that she would herself be free to enjoy the pleasure of the speed that might well have caused the crash, as a personal, private, and intimate thrill.

This division, which rendered speed as a private pleasure but implied that the crash was a public issue (and, in the spirit of its epidemiological reading, an "accident" like a disease one might contact), was thoroughly reinforced by another bureaucratic apparatus which grew up around the crash—that of car insurance. The earliest motoring legislation had tackled the issue of accident liability; this was soon superseded by the requirement for mandatory insurance—including so-called third-party insurance. Car insurance marked an advance in the history of insurance generally—an extremely interesting form of economic speculation—in that here more than ever what was being insured against was the potentially reckless behavior of the motorist rather than the potential damage to, or loss of, property or even life. All new technologies, especially new technologies of transportation, involve the possibility of new kinds of accidents, and new forms of insurance arise to speculate on them. The imbrication of economic speculation in technology's dangers, the insurers' insistence that a monetary value can be placed on life and limb, and the willingness to tacitly insure reckless behavior reached an intensity with car insurance such that the driver-speeder is implicitly guaranteed that he can relinquish much of a sense of personal liability for his own actions while driving, however grim the consequences. This insurance then works something like credit in the consumption economy: it ensures (if falsely) that the driver, like the consumer, can have gratification without consequences and without more than minimal payment. Insurance against the consequences of personal behavior means that one has to worry all the less as one races into the pleasures of speed. It allows the speeder to be prudent and irresponsible at once, and by placing a monetary value on human life, it offers to cover liability at a level of which consumer culture is cognizant.

The state's statistical discourse of the crash, along with its endorsement and legal requirement of insurance and thus of the mentality that accompanied it, achieved the following: it averted the driver's imagination from the possibility of crashing and assured her that if the worst happened, liability had been taken care of in advance. In effect, this discursive regime mitigated, in advance, the actuality of the crash's horror. More, it showed driving as an activity that could be imagined in the kinds of narrative terms necessary to describe gambling—except that in driving, the crash replaces the prize. Walter Benjamin has written, in "On Some Motifs in Baudelaire," on the uncanny appropriateness of gambling, and a gambling-based model of existence, for modern life.[35] Benjamin reads gambling, a characteristic behavior of nineteenth-century bourgeois life, as part of a constellation of everyday practices that range from monotonous factory work to flânerie to the reception of random shocks in the metropolis:

The latter to be sure (factory work) lacks any touch of the adventure of the mirage that lures the gambler. But it certainly does not lack the futility, the emptiness, the inability to complete something which is inherent in the activity of a wage-slave in a factory. Gambling even contains the workman's gesture that is produced by the automatic operation, for there can be no game without the quick movement of the hand by which the stake is put down or the card is picked up. The jolt in the movement of the machine is like the so-called *coup* in a game of chance.[36]

The jolt, the *coup*, the car crash. Benjamin's poignant characterization of modern gambling as a mild utopian gesture on the part of wage slaves, a doomed bid to escape the repetitive tedium of modern life, comes grimly true when the jolt of the machine turns out to be the crash of the automobile. Benjamin dreams that the Baudelairean flâneur, the modernist pedestrian, will infer the truth of the machine's jolt and its effect on the worker. But when the flâneur becomes a driver, and the jolt becomes the car crash, then the modern citizen as machine operator is a gambler without engaging in the leisured gambling of the casino or bar: she gambles through driving in a kind of Russian roulette where she bids against the odds on her own life.

Gambling as escapism gets inducted in modernity into the humdrum grind; it becomes, in Benjamin's phrase, very much the same kind of pleasure that "the worker 'experiences' at his machine."[37] When the citizen, through driving, is granted the possibility of some such experience, in a world where pleasure is more and more removed from experience and repackaged to be sold back to the consumer as simulation, and where the incitement strategies of look-but-don't-touch are increasingly present, the authenticity of fast driving as a real experience is fully guaranteed when the gambling prize becomes one's own death or a license to kill. Yet, as Benjamin explains in his meditation on gambling and machine work, the possibility of truly imagining this prize in its reality is annulled in advance because to work — or better, to drive — the machine offers experience only as a manically alert expenditure of physical energy:

There is a lithograph by Senefelder which represents a gambling club. Not one of those depicted is pursuing the game in the appropriate fashion. Each man is dominated by an emotion: one shows unrestrained joy, another, distrust of his partner, a third, dull despair, a fourth evidences belligerence; another is getting ready to depart from the world. All those modes of conduct share a concealed characteristic: the figures presented show us how the mechanism to which the participants in a game of chance entrust themselves seizes them body and soul, so that even in their private sphere, and no matter how agitated they may be, they are capable only of a reflex action.[38]

Again, one is struck by how readily Benjamin's description of gambling can be applied to fast driving. In driving, where the calibration of the reflex action is precisely what is demanded, the gambling reflex becomes, as it were, the guiding principle of action and reaction. This is machine repetitiveness, as on the assembly line, but with its monotony punctuated by the possibility of the crash, and thus the need for the user's gambling reflex, which "seizes her body and soul." Driving, like gambling, much more than factory work, whose monotony is sustained by the dependability of its repetitiveness, races forward as the characteristic behavior of late modernity. And the protocols for energy management in this behavior are reinforced — and mirrored — in the state's discourse of the car crash. With its focus on accident figures and mandatory insurance to absorb liability, the state oversees this lottery.

At the same time, reading Benjamin on gambling reminds us that the car crash, in a modern world where the driver replaced the flâneur, blew the more sedate world of leisured flânerie, along with Simmel's version of urban shock and modernist anomie, wide open. Once the anomie-ravaged milieu of Prufrock or Kafka's *The Trial* or even Woolf's *Mrs. Dalloway*, with their more or less aimless pedestrian searchers, had been superseded by the ever-alert, energy-dispensing, eye-darting, and life-gambling driver of the automobile, the old shocks that had seemed so new and unexpected to the flâneur — the jostling in the crowd, the love-at-last-sight of unexpected eye contact, the noises of the street — were now as nothing compared to the gruesome jolt of the car crash. The stakes for shock had been raised exponentially. They had now reached the point where the shock was not a jolt of limb or — as in the modernist artwork — of sensory perception but one involving the fate of a life. This shock came of a force of violence very much beyond the possibilities of human power alone. And it was this in the broadest sense to which the state reacted with its emollient discourse of statistics. The death by car crash — the ultimate guarantee that speed really was a new pleasure, that is, a new physical and emotional experience—did not need to be prevented (for its constant reappearance as horrid shock was necessary to guarantee the true experientiality of speed) but rather needed to be *turned away from* at the final moment, lest its reality prove so overpoweringly fearful that the pleasure of speed itself would be forgone. Incited to thrill to the car chase and laugh at the car crash in film, and trained by the state to think of the crash as having mostly statistical significance, the modernist subject as driver, the energized gambler, could overcome the old languors of anomie as she readied for the reflex actions that speed demanded. Modernist boredom in the face of anomie could become late-modernist adrenaline-fueled excitement as one gambled against the fatal horror of the car crash.

In this way the gambling, super-shocking culture of the crash is symptomatic of a changed logistics of the late-modernist subject. Reading Benjamin on gambling, one notes a curious turn on the matter of class, from the opening attention to the working-class "wage slave" and his experience on the assembly line (itself, note, pioneered by Henry Ford to enable mass automobile production) to the middle class, who, as Benjamin points out, took up in the nineteenth century the gambling habit that had in the eighteenth century been an aristocratic pastime. This attention to the middle class is even more apt when considering car culture. The difference between the working-class assembly line mechanic and the gambler, even when the worker feels the jolt which corresponds to the coup experienced by the gamblers, is that the bourgeois gambler has an illusion at any rate of choice of action and reaction. The gambling game, in valorizing unpredictability, offers a setting in which the behavior of the free citizen, making choices and reacting freely to unpredictable outcomes, is enacted *in parvum*. In the relation between driving and crashing, what in the case of gambling had been enacted in a faintly disreputable backroom game now got introduced into the realm of real, everyday life and the quotidian necessities of human movement. This presumption of individual freedom of action and reaction, fundamental to the human subject's relation to the machine in the case of driving a car, is associated with the growing presumption, in the twentieth century, especially in the United States, that everyone was middle-class. (This idea was often fostered, again, by figures on mass car ownership.) There is a sense, nevertheless, in which this diffident, new middle-class subject could not, in driving, have his presumption of freedom contained either by the utopian spectacle of comedy in the face of the disaster or by the state's emollient discourse of warnings, prohibitions, speed limits, and mandatory insurance. The reaches of this independence, even in the face of the fear of the crash, the fear of the possibility of dying, or the fear of killing others, begged to be explored. It is this minor, sporadic, and at times almost underground, covert exploration of the car crash, trying not necessarily to confront it directly but rather to understand its possibilities and consequences for the individuals affected by it, that we will now examine.

Crash Temptations

"Which driver is not tempted, merely by the power of his engine, to wipe out the vermin of the street, pedestrians, children and cyclists?," asks Theodor Adorno, with fearful irony, in *Minima Moralia*.[39] It was left to philosophers and novelists, it seems, to confront the ferocious quality of driving laid bare in the crash. Among others, talk of car driving and car crashing as symptomatic of an alteration in assumptions regarding late modernist subjectivity finds voice, again, in Virginia Woolf, who, as we have seen in *Mrs. Dalloway*, showed such an apprehension in the face of the ominous motorcar and its pistol shot snorting. In *Orlando*, a *jeu-d'esprit* of a novel and one of the twentieth century's most flamboyant testimonies to the capacity of the human subject to change character repeatedly, Woolf supplies one of the most vivid accounts of dangerous driving yet written:

> After twenty minutes the body and mind were like scraps of torn paper tumbling from a sack, and indeed, the process of motoring fast out of London so much resembles the chopping up small of body and mind, which precedes unconsciousness and perhaps death itself, that it is an open question in what sense Orlando can be said to have existed at the present moment.[40]

An arresting passage: starting from a presumption that driving is unsettling and dangerous, it energizes itself first with a simile of violence done to paper, and then with one of violence done to the body, as a prelude to announcing another dissipation of comprehensible subjecthood. (Notably the first violence here seems close to a violence done to a text—perhaps to the text of *Orlando* itself.) What the passage shows, as it piles on the comparisons to violence before it feels free to mention "death itself," is that the crash is imaginatively inseparable from the experience of driving, and that the violence of the presumptive possible crash imbues in advance the experience of all driving. If to drive is to gamble against the odds of dying, then this driving will inevitably be violent, and, moreover, experienced as a species of violence to the self. Woolf's wondering if, under the onslaught of this relentless violence, Orlando could be said even to exist is the counterpoint to Walter Benjamin's observation before the Senefelder lithograph of the demented gamblers who, "[seized] body and soul . . . no matter how agitated they may be, . . . are capable only of a reflex action." Capable only of reflexes, with bodies, as it were, chopped small: this driving, this experience of the only new pleasure of modernity, needs too to flirt with a death impulse. Strikingly, this extraordinarily glum anatomy of speed pleasure is couched in a tone overwrought enough that one suspects exaggeration, or at least a cool twenties flippancy about the idea of it all. It is as if here is a highbrow version of the early film comedies that laughed at the spectacle of the car crash; in neither case are the dolors of modernist anomie deemed adequate to elucidate this new and visceral horror. The anomie-laden text lamented the weight of a drab and mass-market existence; the texts of driving and crashing registered the torments and the lightness of a pleasure beyond it. For all the stress registered by a text such as that of Woolf, her driving-writing in the face of the crash is also a dream of getting beyond subjectivity as we know it, if not a dream of extinction.

In texts that drew nearer the crash, therefore, a grim lightness is almost invariably the counterpoint to a nausea-inducing terror. And this apparently involuntary comedy is again and again the symptom of a dream of the disappearance of the subject, at least as she was imagined at the time. Woolf's wondering if, after this violent motoring, Orlando can be said to "exist at all," finds its expression, in turn, in the first photographs of crashes that began to be published occasionally in newspapers. These first journalistic photographs of crashes are extraordinarily uncanny, because while they certainly render the effects of the car crash vivid in ways that, for example, the movies had never allowed, they also almost always insist on showing an empty crushed car. These are photographs of crashes without the victims — who were always, it seems, removed before the published photographs were taken. Characteristic is a photo of a collision between a train and an automobile in Branchville, Maryland, in the early 1930s, taken by a photographer for the *Baltimore Sun* (figure 21).[41] Photographs like this one, which frequently offer a side view of the shattered and crushed car and little more, may be read as the grim counterparts to standard early car advertisements,

FIGURE 21. Collision of a car and train in Branchville, early 1930s, photographed for the *Baltimore Sun*. Reproduced by permission from William Kaszynski, *The American Highway: The History and Culture of Roads in the United States* (Jefferson, N.C.: McFarland, 2000), 2.

which similarly feature only the car itself from the same angle, but with all parts shining and intact. The crash photo, echoing the advertisement for the car, thus functions in the first place as a lament for the crushed technological wonder. (These photos appeared in papers that also solicited automobile advertising.) At the same time, the side view, usually with the door falling away, meant that the photo's focus, the point most welcoming of the light of the cameraman's flashbulb, was the empty driver's seat of the car. The empty front seat, eloquent witness to the removed dead or wounded, gives us a glimpse of (possible) death as an absence of the (troublesome) human subject. The effect of this journalistic censorship, justified by concerns for victims' or readers' sensibilities, was to make one wonder whether, as in Woolf's formulation, the driver "exist[ed] at all." It is not that human subjects are refused entry to the photograph: more often than not they stand, staring at the camera, from each side of the car, framing the view. And it is these witnesses, standing inside the photo, voyeurs on our behalf, staring, however, not at the empty seat but back at us, who introduce the comedy, for often they are either awkwardly self-conscious or, as here, grotesquely eager merely to be included in the photograph. Testament to the ineffectuality of the human subject before the violent impact of the machine, their peripheral presence prevents us from reading the wrecked metal wholly tragically. Again, even in these throwaway images, the dream of the absent body and the off-key comic note are the signatures of the apparently close-up spectacle of the car crash.

If we read the most famous depiction of a crash in the fiction of the twenties, the crash which kills Myrtle Wilson in Fitzgerald's *The Great Gatsby* (1925), against the uncanny absence which bedevils these photographs, we see that what the novel achieves is to turn attention away from an absent victim and bring it around to the absent perpetrator. The moral tone of the novel, and of its representation of the crash as a significant illustration of the behavior it finds wanting, suggests that any dream of the absence of the victim is merely the inverse of the impulse to disavow the liability (and hence, by inference, the full subjectivity) of the perpetrator. In this crash it is the perpetrator, not the victim, who is absent. The extensive account of the crash is told from the point of view of the novel's narrator, who happens on the scene: it is as if one of the onlookers who so strangely frame the newspaper crash photographs described what happened. The narrator then occupies a place akin to that of the policeman who has also arrived, which reminds us that the account of this incident resembles in its narrative trajectory the police procedural, working (like much of the novel) as an apparently haphazard collation of fragments of information which it processes as circumstantial evidence. At the center of these circumstantial shards of the story of the accident there is unequivocally the body of a human subject with a name—Myrtle Wilson—and a list of telling, intimate details:

> Michaelis and this man reached her first, but when they had torn open her shirtwaist, still damp with perspiration, they saw that her left breast was swinging loose like a flap, and there was no need to listen for the heart beneath. The mouth was wide open and ripped at the corners, as though she had choked a little in giving up the tremendous vitality she had stored so long.[42]

Here the lurid note evokes the sentimental pulp thriller. Compounded on a prior mention of "her thick dark blood [mingled] with the dust," it hits its stride in the anomalous details about breast and mouth: a hint of crash pornography. These details insist on the vividness of a female subjectivity now extinguished. The novel flashes them before us with a whiff of yellow-journalism prurience: it relishes their luridness. The flapping breast—signifying what, the reader may ask?—is exposed pornographically, as if the transgressive display of Myrtle's womanhood is needed to deny the reader the impulse to hide or erase the reality of her dead, crash-smashed body. Only Gatsby himself, at that point presumably the driver of the car that hit her, shows the kind of squeamishness evidenced in contemporary crash photographs when he refuses, later, to hear the narrator's account of her injuries: "'Don't tell me, old sport.' He winced." His wince, his refusal to see the truth of the crash victim's wounds, is implicitly read as part and parcel of the overall duplicity that has led to his downfall. Detailing the particulars of Myrtle's dead body with a few nine-penny-thriller-influenced details, at a time when newspaper photographs turned away, wincing, from the horror of crash wounds, the novel effectively employs this crash as trope of the foolhardy willful deception that brings Gatsby to his end.

Further, the intense focus on the specific materiality of the victim through the pornographic eye on body parts serves as contrast to the ghostly nonpresence of the perpetrator. This figure exists as something to be grasped only at the end of a series of investigations, all lurking one beyond the other, with the "death car," implicitly driverless, in the foreground:

The "death car" as the newspapers called it, didn't stop; it came out of the gathering darkness, wavered tragically for a moment, and then disappeared around the next bend. Michaelis wasn't even sure of its color—he told the first policeman that it was light green.[43]

This "death car"—evocative of that urban myth of the driverless car that speeds around on a killing spree and even haunts Woolf's pistol shot limousine, with its ghostly passenger at the gray curtain, in *Mrs. Dalloway*—encapsulates the other dream of the crash: that it is always an accident, an incident for which no one is liable. Hidden by the "death car" is, first, the "witness" car, which stops, its driver rushing to the scene, then (after the policeman questions the narrator-sleuths) Gatsby, and then (after the narrator confronts Gatsby), none other than Daisy, who apparently was really driving the car. This all serves to fix blame, but only in a desultory and uncertain manner; for a start, Gatsby may be lying. Once we accept this possibility, then a blame game that fans out over all involved suggests itself. Gatsby, after all, is to blame too, as he and Daisy were driving drunk after their day in the city, and he certainly did not insist that they stop at the scene. Or Myrtle's husband may be to blame, as he had fought with her and locked her in a room; in rushing to escape, she had run on to the road. Or the crowded state of the road itself might be to blame, or the fact that the repair shop was so close to the roadside. The point of this ever wider distribution of possible blame is that it increasingly robs one person—Daisy, for example—of liability. Instead it vacillates to the point where the sense of responsibility for the crash remains unspoken; it will indeed be taken by all involved as an accident. What is the effect of this on the reader's sense of Daisy? Implicitly what is presented is one woman snuffing out, without any apparent concern, the life of another. The lurid particularity with which the novel displays the victim before us contrasts with the grim and funereal uncertainty that frames Daisy as she is seen after the crash. Nick Carraway, the narrator, discusses her with Gatsby, sees her through a curtained window sitting opposite Tom, her attitude unclear ("They weren't happy . . . and yet they weren't unhappy either") and a strange affectlessness hovering over it all. This is reiterated when Gatsby is described meeting Daisy again: "She had vanished into her rich house, into her rich full life, leaving Gatsby—nothing." Her refusal of her role as the perpetrator of the crash corresponds to her refusal of an interesting life with Gatsby. It marks her refusal, in the terms set by the novel, of a heroic or authentic subjecthood.

Throughout *The Great Gatsby*, as in a number of other of Fitzgerald's fictions, driving is equated with the progress of a possibly valid and authentic life. Here is the equivalence of *vif-vitesse* strewn across the framework of a novel's plotline. The road between West Egg and New York, between the glamour of the resort and the secrets and license of the city, becomes the space in the novel where truths might be expected to emerge. The yellow car becomes an extension of Gatsby, his flamboyant signature: it bespeaks the grandiloquence and vulgarity of his existence. In this glittery milieu, the hit-and-run moment, the refusal of Gatsby and Daisy to accept that they have killed another, marks a chilling denouement: a high mark of the implied code through which the novel would have us judge the characters' actions. In the murkiness of the "hit and run" may be discerned final evidence of the characters' callousness, especially that of Daisy. Nevertheless, if for Fitzgerald, *vif* equals *vitesse*, then the crash (even if it does not halt the speed at that very moment) matters less as a death (of Myrtle) than in its signification of the disintegration of the Gatsbian subjectivity that the text has taught us to love. Remember that *Gatsby*, quite as much as Woolf's *Orlando*, which was published three years later, is a novel about a succession of assumed roles and the possibility of performing them. In the case of *The Great Gatsby* the novel in fact derealizes that crash in order to subsume it to a symbolic order set up to implicitly critique a too-impudent, because too flamboyant, role-play. The crash, like the wild driving in *Orlando*, is given little meaning in itself; rather, the novel subsumes the crash's horror within an ultimately moral — say, Nietzschean — tale of the heroic endeavor of one person's will to subjectivity. Woolf approached the violence of driving; Fitzgerald gets up close to the fatal violence of the car crash. "I felt the bump," says Gatsby, of the collision. The car crash in *Gatsby* gets derealized, to be symbolic, symbolizing a kind of obliteration of subjecthood — but the subjecthood in question is that of the motorist-perpetrators. It is apt, therefore, that the perpetrator should be nebulous; the brutal body-part images of the victim, her torn, flapping breast and bloody mouth, remain gratuitous.

Closing in on speed's force and on the crash, then drawing back, both of these texts go far beyond the statistical concision generated by official government crash discourse, and both operate above (but not far above) the humor that had characterized crash depictions in the first years of motoring. It is difficult today, however, not to laugh at the vehemence of the most close-up and Nietzschean confrontation with the crash from the early days of the automobile, the famous crash wish that opens Filippo Marinetti's Futurist Manifesto. Marinetti too is in the business of subject making, but instead of reading the crash, close-up, as "the bump" of a disintegrating subjectivity, he grasps its violence as a sacramental opportunity for subjective renewal. Marinetti, like Woolf, knows the car's violence: "I stretched out in my car as a corpse on a bier, but revived under the steering wheel, a guillotine blade that threatened my stomach."[44] This revival is re-performed in his account of the inevitable crash:

> Their stupid dilemma was blocking my way—damn! Ouch! . . . . I stopped short and to my disgust rolled over into a ditch with my wheels in the air. . . . Oh maternal ditch, almost full of muddy water! Fair factory drain! I gulped down the nourishing sludge; and I remembered the blessed black breast of my Sudanese nurse. . . . When I came up—torn, filthy and stinking—from under the capsized car, I felt the white hot iron of joy pass through my heart.

Here too, twenty years before *Gatsby*, at the point of the car crash attention turns to a woman's breast. Here it spools up from the driver's memory, invoking race (the African), class (the nurse of the bourgeois household), and colonialism (Italy's interest in the Horn of Africa), as well as the psychoanalytically charged dream of an alternative motherhood (an other mother who stands for him in contrast to his own). This whole complex, as Maurizia Boscagli points out, might be expected to be the very memories that the thrusting male subject would repress to validate a narrative in Nietzschean terms. That, instead, he presents the crash as the precipitative event in an act of recovery from his unconscious shows us that Marinetti is willing to grant the crash powers of subject making not quite dreamed of by the novelists writing in English two decades later. Yet this crash, as a shock which, at the very moment it occurred, induces the kind of recollections on which Freud might have pounced, is starred in the manifesto as a whole as the key generator of public-political (even geopolitical) insight rather than private psychological revelation. The nurse and all she represents are set off against the "fair factory"—that is, the technologized West is set in contradistinction to the primitive colony. Marinetti, with his sleight of bombast over memory, wants to revive the politics which scapegoated the colonial as other. This politics, already beginning to lose its sting in much of Europe as Western imperial self-glorification declined, enjoyed a belated upswing in Italy in the period of Marinetti's notoriety. In the end, his bravura will to enjoy the car crash, his spectacular refusal to be injured by it, is an attempt to juggle the contraries of heterotopic consciousness (Western factory versus colonial "nature") together in his mind as a necessary precondition to enjoying the "hot iron of joy" (of speed, presumably) in a wholly imperial, technological-mechanical world. Marinetti's polemic intensifies the early-twentieth-century display of the crash as comedy; achieving this, he brings into the open the kinds of representational logics unspoken within that grisly comedy. It hardly needs pointing out, however, that surviving the car crash cannot be willed, so that Marinetti builds the fascinations of his manifesto on a fantasy of the crash where victims and perpetrators all emerge unscathed. This is a fantasy so foolish that it reads as comedy, and comedy can hardly sustain such grandiloquence as his. His crash account, with his survival to fight another day, has the burlesque-derived sadism of the Keystone Cops films: "speed gone mad, fandangos of disintegrating flivvers, spraying Keystone Cops to left and right, . . . a ballistic nightmare."[45]

Speed Kills

It was not until a half century later that the crash received a more intense scrutiny. From a new awareness of the carnage on the roads which followed the post–World War II automobile boom, three texts stand out. The first is Ralph Nader's famous, forceful jeremiad *Unsafe at Any Speed*, a sensation in 1965. The second: Godard's stinging, rambling film *Weekend* (1967); here I will speak only of the grandest moment of its satire on car crash culture, the famous eight-minute tracking shot of the cars on a roadway held up by a car crash. Third: J. G. Ballard's novel *Crash* (1973). All are products of the cultural moment that the poet Philip Larkin characterized as following the lifting of the "Chatterley ban," that is, the decade in which all that had shocked the readers of the earlier waves of modernism, from Baudelaire to Djuna Barnes, came to lose its sting. The sixties texts raised the barrier of shock to achieve their effects; each still persists in what had come to be seen as the modernist project. They are also complicit in the new savoir-faire, which implied that nothing shocked any longer. Still, their shock value has clung to the reputation of each, and it is the memory of this shock that we must overcome to read cogently their actual accounts of crash culture. This can be done by exploring how they deploy or overcome the predominant discourses of the car crash developed throughout the century. Coming close to the crash through comedy, through an officialese couched in statistical terms, or through an analysis of the violence of speed—through each of the crash discourses I've so far read—these texts twist earlier strategies of showing to shock us out of our speed fatigue, our apathy to speed's danger. They revamp the original, recalcitrant discourses of the car crash to thrust its reality before us. They unlock the implicit preoccupations of those discourses to unearth new anxieties and dreams about accidentality, liability, the enjoyment of violence, consumption and its relation to violence, and the subject-shattering and remaking possibilities of the crash.

In 1990 J. G. Ballard, writing annotations to his montage novel of 1969, *The Atrocity Exhibition*, notices the repeated references to Ralph Nader in his original text and decides: "His assault on the automobile clearly had me worried. . . . Looking back, one can see that Nader was the first of the eco-puritans, who proliferate now, convinced that everything is bad for us. In fact, too few things are bad for us, and one fears an uncertain future of pious bourgeois certitudes."[46] Earlier, noting that Nader, in the sixties, had "sent a seismic tremor through the mind of the U.S. consumer," Ballard suggested that "every car crash seemed a prayer to Ralph Nader."[47] Ballard's "like a prayer" here is eloquent. What Nader does in *Unsafe at Any Speed* is foster worry and then allay it by showing that it can be transformed into productive outrage. His book is a fascinating intervention in the twentieth-century discussion of the car crash partly because it interweaves the two key discursive modes that had been used up to that point to characterize the crash. In the first place, the book periodically interrupts its argument to offer direct and vivid narratives of crashes. These fit in the genre of direct crash representation, which, as we have seen, in early-twentieth-century versions often turned comic or, in the hands of the more serious modernists, could become the site for a rethinking of subjectivity. In Nader these narratives are delivered with a deadpan factuality intended to induce anxiety and a muted shock. This discursive strand is complemented by the principal, lawyerlike argumentative strand. Here the full apparatus of statistical, official discourse is deployed to generate our outrage. This outrage, predictably, is imagined not as that of the victims of the accidents described but as that of the consumer whose object of consumption—the purchased automobile—has been built with obvious defects. Nader thus hews unceasingly to the logic that, as I've shown, meant that car crashes would invariably be comic rather than tragic in the early films: that is, he sees the car crash as a betrayal of good consumerism. The effect of pitching his discourse of outrage at this level is a kind of chilly realism: it is as if the modern subject would only effectively be addressed as a buyer, not as a potential victim of shocking violence. It means, however, that the discourse which hopes to put before us the reality of a series of car crashes is always a thesis discourse rather than an attempt at a new realism: the crashes described in the text were always really test crashes to prove the ineffectiveness of the victims' automobiles. The victims are the victims of bad commodities, the perpetrators, the purveyors of those commodities and the enemy, a badly calibrated consumer culture. Nader's vision of an ideal consumerist polis, where the commodity would be optimally safe, all anxiety allayed and all outrage unnecessary, again derealizes the gruesome nature of the crash by rendering its significance in such consumerist terms. But he goes further: he also places the civic discourse of car crashes—the statistical record of crashes, reasons for them, and liabilities, which is centered on the "death rate" or deaths per thousands of miles driven—under the aegis of a consumer imperative. Appropriately, his book's title mimics, and inverts, the sort of phrase that might have been used as an advertising slogan; by paying consumer culture the compliment of blaming it for car crashes, he makes safety marketable; that is, he implies that we can buy our way out of the reality of the car crash. Nader's focus on safety as a commodity attribute is completely justifiable in pragmatic and tactical terms: if the pleasure of speed has been from the start sold, through the sale of the most characteristic of twentieth-century commodities, the automobile, then it is only by articulating a simple ethics of consumer rights that the complacency of the consumer could be punctured and a more demanding kind of buying advocated. Yet this pragmatism succeeds precisely by never allowing the crash to speak for itself. The crashes of *Unsafe at Any Speed* echo the crashes of early Hollywood, and their narratives teeter on the brink of comedy because they still work as quasi advertisements for automobiles and so still comply with the discursive conventions of such advertisements.

It is to shock us out of the assumptions and consumerist dreams underlying these conventions that Godard stages his famous tracking shot in the film *Weekend*. In a movie whose title promises an anatomy of the vaunted "free time" of the bourgeois consumer class, this famous drawn-out shot employs every protocol that film had used to that point to showcase car culture. Instead of the still camera straining to catch the moving car, or racing to represent the thrilling pleasure of the speeded-up car chase, here a moving camera pans an endless line of stopped cars on a highway. This is repetitive, and boring, even if the occupants of each car behave differently in their common activity: waiting. With this shot, we have returned, with a difference, to *Heart of Darkness* and the relentless dreariness, in a speeded-up daily life, of the wait. This time around, however, impatience is denuded of misty phenomenological distinction; in a speed world where to move pleasurably fast is equated even with life itself, the waiting is merely sordid, an aggravation which generates not even the semblance of insight or contemplation but rather a dull petulance. Inevitably, Godard's trolling camera invites us to read this petulance as comedy. The comedy, however, is now satirical, for we laugh at these complaining stalled characters while we, who see through the tracking camera's eye, move smoothly on. (In fact, we are seeing from the perspective of a sports car driver who has insolently taken to the road's verge.)

Then Godard, without warning, shocks us with the sight of the cause of the stoppage: a horrific car crash. Suddenly (although, of course, we guessed all along) our satirical laughter freezes, and we adjust from jeering at the impatience of the stopped cars' occupants to realizing that we are ourselves now participating in the callous gaze of the sports car occupants as they slide by and then pick up speed again on the open road. The futility of the waiting is brought up against the wrecked bodies of the crash, both part of a failed dream of leisured ease and consumerist plenty. As the sports car speeds on into this antipastoral, we are left to remember those bodies and scorched chrome shards as a moment when a conventional sense of detachment from consumer dreams, based on some presumed sense of our own privileged viewpoint, is horribly insufficient to face the horror of the car crash itself. This crash remains a represented but unreadable moment in the film, casting a long shadow over the rest. In showing all the stopped cars, Godard has stalled the old movie comedy of the car chase, freezing it into satire. In the repetition, showing car after car, he touches on the state's discourse of the car accident as a statistical matter. By placing the mangled automobiles of victims and perpetrators of the crash before us, and leaving us to coldly look, and by showing the crash as an interruption of speed culture, he lays down an uncompromising challenge. Still, our eyes as viewers move onward along with those of the sports car's occupants, and we are only made somewhat aware of our own rubbernecking callousness.

A decade later, Ballard's *Crash*, taking such callousness as a given, sets out to investigate the precise sentiments generated by the sight and sensation of the car crash, and decides, in the manner of much early-seventies moralizing, that they involve a perverse sexuality. Much of the argument that has arisen about this willfully and mischievously shocking text has concerned the issue of whether the versions of perverse sexuality at the interface of libido and crushed mechanics are so interesting that Ballard is in fact sadistically celebrating the car crash, or whether he is more properly offering us a horror story which makes us attend to the crash's peculiar terror. In the responses to a celebrated commentary by Jean Baudrillard on the novel, for example, published in English in 1991, N. Katherine Hayles takes Baudrillard to task for "arguing that there is no moral point to *Crash*,"[48] while Vivian Sobchack decides that Baudrillard reads *Crash* "obscenely ... [because] where Ballard is cautionary and his prose (as Baudrillard recognizes) is technical, Baudrillard is celebratory and his own prose impassioned."[49] Ballard himself may be said to have carefully orchestrated this order of response, even from the period before he wrote the novel, for his interest in car crashes and people's responses to them dates at least to the exhibition of crashed cars which he staged in London in 1973. Even then, he focused carefully on inciting and manipulating his audience's reaction:

> Scouring the wrecker's yard around London, I was unable to find a crashed Lincoln, perhaps fortunately. As it was, the audience reaction to the telescoped Pontiac, Mini and Austin Cambridge verged on nervous hysteria, though had the cars been parked in the street outside the gallery no one would have given them a glance or devoted a moment's thought to the injured occupants. In a calculated test of the spectators, I hired a topless girl to interview the guests.[50]

This calculated conditioning of the audience continued in the subsequent novel and particularly in his introduction to the French edition of 1974. Treat with caution also, therefore, the apparent openness of his annotations to the revised edition of *The Atrocity Exhibition* in 1990, from which his reflections just cited were taken. Note that they direct our attention toward the degree to which the audience might be shocked by Ballard's forthrightness in his representation of car crashes. To effectively read the novel decades after its publication, however, we need to go beyond debates over matters that are now moot. Rather, we should ask if Ballard has recast the older discourses of the crash in ways that generate genuinely new insights. If, as the novel's critics to date agree, *Crash* is a perverse novel, it needs to be read perversely: that is, thoroughly against the grain of the reading toward which the author has successfully steered critics up to now.

Crash is an extremely literary novel, even pretentious in its literary claims. By this I do not mean that it must be lodged, in one critical leap of faith, in some *soi-disant* literary pantheon, but rather that it works to transport into high writerly art an area of contemporary experience — driving, and the car crash — that had previously been, with a few exceptions, largely outside it. (The exceptions include the texts we have considered already and some we have not: Huxley's thoughts on driving as a new modus of tourism in *Along the Road* [1925], some works by E. M. Forster and by William Faulkner, the road novels of Kerouac, Thompson, and others.)[51] The first tip-off the reader gets to the novel's self-conscious literary quality is the constant stream of similes. "The crashed bodies of package tourists, like a hemorrhage of the sun," begins the novel's fourth sentence, announcing boldly what will be a sustained grandiloquence of literary flourishes as a signature of *Crash*'s textual feel.[52] Reiterated similification, however, brings a gaudy and overdressed look to the text: the mechanics of the high literary are almost willfully on show. This is so, I suggest, because the author's task is to transfer to the literary — with a considerable twist — material that has previously flown only through more mundane discursive channels. *Crash*, along with all of Ballard's science fiction work, might best be compared to the novels two centuries earlier of Daniel Defoe, who, in *Robinson Crusoe*, for example, similarly employs a slightly mannered, all-too-technical prose to bring into the emerging literary genre of the fictitious memoir realms of existence known to bourgeois business and colonist fantasy heretofore below the horizon of literary discourse. Ballard, however, does not simply transform the technical vocabulary of the automobile assembly line worker, the traffic engineer, and the tow truck operator into serviceable literary prose. More comprehensively, his novel, so openly laying down from the start its literary claims, may be said to engage in transforming all previous discourses on cars and especially car crashes into novel idioms. *Transformation* is key here: the novel's achievement as literature, and also as shock text in the most compelling sense, is to take the earlier discourses and hand them over to other registers altogether, as a defamiliarizing ploy.

As we have seen, two main strands of discourse had developed to represent the car crash, that of the state and quasi-statist officialdom, which was based on statistical knowledge and tended toward concepts like accident rates and the necessity for insurance, and the more concrete discourse that attempted to get closer to the crash itself, which often emerged as comedy or, in more ambitious instances, devolved into meditations on the disintegration of the modernist human subject. What occurs in *Crash* is that, first, the generalized statist discourse on the crash gets transmuted into a more particularized description (which is nevertheless pervasive throughout the novel) of the lonely, alienating, featureless non-place world of freeways, airports, overpasses, junkyards, office buildings, multistory parking garages, and apartment complexes. Ballard here refashions the state's discourse on the crash, which provides an ambient, cautionary noise behind the punctum of the accident, into a matter of setting. This is not Augé's "non-place": it is much too glamorous for that. Out of its sensibility, Ballard brilliantly fashions a late modern antipastoral. The novel's constant monotonal hymn to the cool precision of traffic engineering in concrete becomes its base note. It is entirely familiar to the reader of high literature: this is a postwar reworking, to describe an infinitely more alienating terrain, of the anomie-inflected urban landscapes of Kafka, Eliot, and Musil. By introducing this antipastoral of cruel months and unreal cities into car discourse, Ballard carries Godard's critique in *Weekend* much further. He gives us, in the lurid colors made possible by his literariness, a series of tropes for representing freeways and traffic management that, watered down, would, in the following decades, become the lingua franca of urban planners as they discussed the horrors of commuting. Despite *Crash*'s evocation of the slick glamour and the freedom conferred by anonymity that such a blank landscape evokes, the point, constantly emphasized, is that here is a world — the crash's context — where alienation is so mind-bogglingly pervasive as to be, for those who use these concrete routeways, a psychological imperative. Ballard's achievement is to evoke a new imagination of lived space, neither "place" nor "non-place," and certainly neither home nor heterotopia, but one whose anonymity reaches a feverish intensity. How does this evocation of a new kind of blank terrain rewrite the statist statistical version of the car crash? By actualizing (an appropriately seventies term) its abstractions as landscape, it seems to transform the notion of accidentality into inevitability: Ballard's is not a *civitas* where one can by chance fall into an accident but rather a concrete-scape where the crash becomes, by authorial fiat, the truth of the landscape itself.

In reworking the second discursive strand that has up to this point been used to characterize the car crash and in various ways aimed to get a close-

up view of the actuality of the crash itself, Ballard overrides the earlier discursive protocols of humor or discussions on the degeneration of subjecthood and instead allows his literary eye to discern one element only: sex.
This is what has shocked his (puritan) critics, mainly because they are used
to literature treating sex and the erotic in pastoral terms, terms to which the
world of technology (which has been treated in literature mostly as clinical,
mechanical, and so on) seems opposed. *Crash* enjoys itself being a literary
text that probes the foolishness of this old cultural dichotomy: it sets up a
rigorous metaphoric scheme which opposes the rigidity of technological
metal (heavy metal) to the liquidity of the body and its fluids, and then proceeds to shuffle and destabilize this distinction. On the techno side, his key
word is "chromium," a word sounding a note of sour chemical modernity
that echoes like a bell on every few pages of the text. On the soft, fleshy
side the key word is "semen," emerging and oozing on page after page.
Pitting human corporeal liquidity against the brittle hardness of shiny modern metals leaves the bodies seeming pathetic, even when the text merrily
confuses the terms of the dichotomy in presenting Vaughan's body as a
hard, heavy metal one and Catherine's scheming as tough and hard likewise. What we need to keep in mind to read this novel against the grain,
however, to counter it with a criticism that is as tough as the text itself, is
that like the "topless girl" (Ballard's term) whom the author employed as
an interviewer during the exhibition of crashed cars which gave rise to the
subsequent novel, the sex in *Crash* is to a large extent an afterthought, a
striking and baroque decorative detail that allures us as voyeurs into the
text but is not integral to its central concern, which is the phenomenon of
the car crash.

The great enabling idea around which the plot of *Crash* develops is that
the car crash unleashes in the individual involved an extraordinary preoccupation with sex. The narrator, after his first crash described in the novel, is
surprised with how thoroughly sex has come to obsess him—until he encounters, first, Stella Remington, the survivor of the crash in which he, the
narrator, killed her husband, and finds that she too is sex obsessed, and, second, until he begins to know and understand Vaughan, for whom an obsession with sex that needs car crashes to be unleashed has reached truly manic
proportions. Now if, following multiple authorial pointers in the text, we
get diverted to thinking that perverse and rabid sexuality is what matters
here, we can indeed be led into numerous post-Freudian speculations on

the relations between sadomasochism, sex, violence, and our awareness of our impending deaths. As the narrator works to explain in the opening pages of the novel what Vaughan meant to him, this is where the novel would have us go, noting sententiously that "for him these wounds were the keys to a new sexuality, born from a perverse technology." I submit that it is a mistake born of utopian dreams to imagine that Ballard is articulating the parameters of a new sexuality here; this sadomasochistic, fatalist discourse of sexuality has a long history, the matter of an extensive tradition that in the era of modernity stretches from Sade to Georges Bataille. (The other successor to this tradition from the era of *Crash* itself is Pier Paolo Pasolini's revision of Sade in *Salò, or the 120 Days of Sodom* [1975].) If anything, what Ballard (like Pasolini) might be marking with his avid representation of the sex-torture matrix is the beginning of the end of this tradition as a *sexuality* in Foucault's terms, that is, as a way of conceptualizing and articulating the relation of sex to various forms of power. Rather, what is new here is that the novel attends to sex *alone* once it faces up to the reality of the car crash. This strategy resembles *Robinson Crusoe*'s having its hero attend only to the careful husbanding of possessions at the moment when he finds himself marooned on his island. The question, then, is what the function and effect are of this monological and monotonous attention in the crash representation to this single area of subjective experience.

Rather in the spirit in which, as Ballard admits in 1990, he had hired the "topless girl" to pose questions at the 1969 crashed-cars exhibition ("she had originally agreed to appear naked but on seeing the cars informed me that she would only appear topless"),[53] this concentration on sex seems a calculated test of his readers. By now, it is this constant return to exotically perverse sex that seems most dated about the novel. Yet it is also a means by which the author reminds us of the comedy and the strange jollity that had attended the first popular representations of the car crash, especially in film. What Ballard manages to do in his novel is to turn the long and varied association of sex and cars in popular culture into a veritable orgy. The whole panoply of texts and images that have associated cars and sex, from the days when car advertisers showed buxom suffragette drivers in their advertisements as a means to attract the attention of male buyers, to the lovers' lane and drive-in fantasies of back-seat sexual license, to the starlet displays of mechanics shop calendars and car shows (from which Ballard no doubt took the idea for the topless girl at his exhibition), offered the author a pop-cultural carnival which showed off the car as site and symbol of male heterosexual desire. The relentless sex fixation of *Crash* gives him an opportunity both to festively celebrate this phenomenon and to send it up.

In addition, the focus in *Crash* on sexuality gives the author the opportunity to string out his novel as a narrative of a love triangle; in the characteristic deceit-and-desire shuttling of such plots, it professes to focus on the desire of the hero-narrator for the heroine while foregrounding the more urgent matter of the relationship between the men. The narrator, Catherine, and Vaughan form the triangle, while the sole developed human relation in the novel is that between the narrator and Vaughan. Here, certainly, the author is simply repeating, not quite wholeheartedly, thoroughly tested formulas: we might, tracing the conventionality of this plot, take *Crash* as a rewriting even of *The Great Gatsby*, where the triangle of Gatsby, Daisy, and the narrator, Nick Carraway, follows the same formula. Again, we might sense that this strand of pop-cultural desire (the avid attention to sex) and the use of a plot formula from high fiction (the love triangle) are being iterated in *Crash* to better celebrate their demise: by turning both into a tumult of semen, chrome, and wounded bodies, *Crash* seems to be strikingly open about its derision for each. In *Crash*'s morass of alien — and, by now, dated — porn (it is "the first pornographic novel based on technology," the author claims with a wicked pride [6]), we are being tested to see, rather, how we might imagine not a new perversity of an old pleasure (sexuality) but rather the perversity of the only new pleasure (speed).

This is to say that sex in *Crash* is a simulation, a gigantic con game, in which the perverse variations of the oldest pleasure, sexuality, are manipulated to proffer a test case for the possible perversions of the newest pleasure, speed — perversions that have only been hinted at, up to now, in the violent and unanswerable punctum of the crash. Ballard incites us to read the sex in *Crash* as an allegorical discourse. Our culture possesses a massive vocabulary for describing sexuality in its multifarious variations, but we have almost no vocabulary yet for the various pleasures of speed: why not confront these two pleasures with each other in the moment of crisis in the latter to see if one can discern on the template of the extensively developed vocabulary of sex a cartography of the potential pleasures of speed?

There is something to be said for reading Ballard as the last Futurist, or as a post-Futurist elaborator of science fiction dystopias. That is, we might see *Crash* as beginning where the hyperbolic account of the car crash at the opening of Marinetti's Futurist Manifesto leaves off, and imagine that Ballard is giving us in Vaughan, and by extension in Vaughan's acolyte the narrator, a blueprint of a new subjectivity, a properly outfitted subjectivity for the era of technology. In this vein, we can see the novel's obsession with sexuality as a means of showing its characters' responses to the car crash as an attempt to constitute a new model of the human subject's desire. As sexuality might seem the most raw and elemental of human desires, then the coming cyborg subject must have that desire elaborated before all else, and *Crash*, in the brutal honesty of its sexual technics, begins this construction of a new logics of affect. Such a reading is plausible, yet, as one reads on, unconvincing: all that is achieved in these terms in the novel is a breaching of the heterosexist norms of the so-called sexual revolution of the 1970s, when the narrator and Vaughan, in a few paragraphs that are remarkably tender by the text's standards (200–203), finally make love. Since, predictably, Vaughan is killed in a car crash soon afterward (trying to make contact with the camp icon Elizabeth Taylor by crashing into her limousine), we need not think that even the slightest turn from the norms of heterosexist sexualities is really being championed here. No, *Crash*'s sex is all experimental, all a matter of slumming variations on an old story (that of the possibilities of juggling sex and power) to discern the pattern of a new narrative. And this pattern has not per se to do with further variations on the pleasures of sexuality (stories too often told already elsewhere) or, worse, with the possible pleasures of crashing cars (the novel is, pace Ballard, a cautionary tale), but, much more ambitiously, with the possible pleasures of speed.

Here is a typical paragraph from *Crash*, its slightly straining poetry rising in a fine peroration. It is also, I want to claim, the passage which marks the very heart of the novel, offering in a beautifully maintained balance the forces which mostly get offset in the text:

> We had entered an immense traffic jam. From the junction of the motorway and Western Avenue to the ascent ramp of the flyover the traffic lanes were packed with vehicles, windshields leaching out the colors of the sun setting over the western suburbs of London. Brake-lights flared in the evening air, glowing in the huge pool of cellulosed bodies. Vaughan sat with one arm out of the passenger window. He slapped the door impatiently, pounding the panel with his fist. To the right the high wall of a double-decker airline coach formed a cliff of faces. The passengers at the windows resembled rows of the dead looking down at us from the galleries of a columbarium. The enormous energy of the

twentieth century, enough to drive the planet into a new orbit around a happier star, was being expended to maintain this immense motionless pause. (151)

In this extraordinary, moving paragraph, Ballard's full panoply of poetic effects is all on show: the evening setting, the sententious, classical image of the columbarium, the exponential opening of the field of vision from the immense traffic jam to the cold, touching immensity of the universe which holds "a happier star." Such grandiloquence is in proportion, however, because it is here, in the grand sweep of the final sentence, that the forces that menace the novel and all within it are put on show: "the enormous energy of the twentieth century" versus the traffic jam's enforcement of "this immense motionless pause." This is Godard's panning shot of the stopped cars once more, but now orchestrated on an epic scale. It attends to those who wait, the impatient—that is, those (through their cars) used to movement, to flow, for whom, therefore, the wait is the exceptional and unacceptable interruption. We have returned to Conrad and the unbearable heaviness of the wait in *Heart of Darkness*, except that whereas Conrad's story, told to while away the wait, was a tale that marked the end of the heterotopic imagination, *Crash*, three-quarters of a century later, marks a stop in the ceaseless flow of speed that is the chief pleasure to be enjoyed in coming to terms with the featureless postheterotopic world displayed in this text. The most valued entity in this new order of pleasure is celebrated here: "energy." Yet at times all this energy—"the enormous energy of the twentieth century"—can be orchestrated to coalesce into a pause. What has caused the particular pause described in this passage is, as we can guess, a horrific car accident; we learn this as the sirens wail through the next paragraph. What Ballard has given us here, however, is a definition of the traffic accident in the terms that matter: immense energy contorted into a pause.

As the sirens wail and the rubberneckers gather, the novel swivels its thoughts to sexuality: "Clearly the most vivid erotic fantasies would be moving through our minds, of imagining acts of intercourse performed with enormous decorum and solicitude upon the blood-stained loins of this young woman as she lay within her car. . . ." (156). And the novel's incessant and relentless sexual turn at the moment of the crash is again enacted. For the critic to claim that this sex is merely allegorical might seem to offer a reading of the novel's joys based merely on puritanism; one appears to deny in advance the validity of the pleasure in its own terms. But this would mean underrating the possibilities of the allegory involved: that is, how the pleasure of rampant sexuality and the pleasure of excessive speed might fit one upon the other, replicate one another's patterns, and share, or not, the same signifiers of what might in the first place come under the rubric of pleasure. What I've suggested is that the sexual pleasure suggested here is only a secondary concern of the text, and that, granted textual attention at the moment of the crash, it really substitutes for the pleasure which preoccupies the text, that of speed.

Thus on the one hand we can say that the older pleasure, sexuality, has a rich and varied vocabulary to describe it, and that this vocabulary might be useful in understanding any other pleasure. The two pleasures may also, it is worth speculating, have much in common, and one may fade into and intermingle with the other, in the sense that all pleasurable sensations experienced by the human subject get registered in ways that are scarcely separable into wholly different experiential realms. On the other hand, notice that the discourse of sexuality in the book takes off at the moment of the crash: that is, the moment, in Ballard's own terms, when all the world's energy is orchestrated into a pause. As such, sex is a pleasure practiced now as an alternative to speed's pleasure; it is the pleasure practiced while one, frustrated, waits; it is *Crash*'s alternative to the storytelling practiced by the slightly less impatient Marlow in Conrad's novel. In this light, sex gets to be speed's other, what is practiced as a compensation when speed stops. Worse, both of these contesting relations between sexuality and speed can be true at once, so that if sex is the baroque decoration in *Crash* as postmodern text, then the complexity of the sex-speed allegory renders that aesthetic symbiosis baroque too. Probing among the complex interstices of this baroque allegorical relation, what can Ballard teach us about the new pleasures of speed? Clinically carrying his elaboration of the old pleasure, sexuality, to its limits, does he get to offer any kind of taxonomy of the pleasures of the new? What I've suggested is that the turn to sexuality in itself gives Ballard the opportunity to retread some of the oldest narratives of sexual desire (the love triangle, love between acolyte and teacher) in a new and hence exotic setting. What we need to look for, then, as we begin to elaborate a language for speed's pleasure, is what in Ballard's account of sex might be novel if it were applied to speed.

Reading the novel's pleasure textuality in this way, one is led firmly away from any presumed glamour that may be thought to inhere in the mechanistic. Instead one is guided to concentrate on decidedly humanistic values:

community attachment, the nucleus and origin of a kind of politics. By choosing the most ancient of pleasures, sex, to work as allegory for the new one, speed, Ballard is performing an aesthetic of willful archaism. He is truly looking backward to intuit the future. In doing so, he articulates a jeremiad in advance on speed's pleasure: speed as pleasure must not try to break away from all that is valuable in the older forms of human satisfaction. When it does so, he warns, speed will turn on us and kill us.

Overdrive

Are we having, today, *another*, a different experience of speed? Is our relation to motion and time qualitatively different? Or must we speak prudently of an extraordinary — although qualitatively homogenous — acceleration of the same experience?
— Jacques Derrida, "No Apocalypse, Not Now (Full Speed Ahead, Seven Missiles, Seven Missives)"

I got no car and it's breaking my heart, but I found a driver, and that's a start.
— The Beatles, "Baby You Can Drive My Car"

"Speed? There is a fascination about it that all feel, whether they admit it or not, for there is nothing in the animal world that would not go faster if it could," wrote W. J. Gordon in 1910.[1] But Gordon is wrong: speed's delight is not merely instinctual. Rather, the fascination with speed has fluctuated; it has a history, and a very long one, that waxed and waned since the invention of the stirrup and the wheel, through the long history of the breeding of faster and stronger horses, to the development and perfection of carriage springs and the building of railway locomotives. Already in 1849 Thomas de Quincey could rhapsodize about "the glory of motion" in *The English Mail Coach*.[2] In fact, the pioneers of the motorcar did very little: they attached a new, lighter engine to a carriage. Nevertheless, they unleashed a fascination with speed that has been unprecedented in modernity: a speed madness that lasted from roughly 1900 to 1930 — the era of modernism. It is a history of this fascination in that moment — how it was incited, how it showed itself, and how it was policed, the energies that it unleashed and its aftershocks — that I've outlined here.

It was this enthusiasm for speed which incited Aldous Huxley to his audacious claim that speed is the only new pleasure invented by modernity. Confronted with numerous accounts of modernism and technology cast as measured praise of utilitarian progress, I was struck to discover instead a commentator who focused on the importance of pleasure. (The intellectual lodestar here is Roland Barthes, not only in *The Pleasure of the Text* but in all his writing; in a grim twist of fate, he died after being struck by a car while crossing a Paris street.) Texts that map a dance between technology and culture are often torn between a base note of techno-boosterism and a tendency to decry the horrors wrought by technology's advance. It is tough, when surveying what car culture has wrought, not to play the Luddite: think of the massive pollution caused by the petrol engine, the concrete grimness of freeways, the isolating effect on drivers, the frustration of jammed traffic, the gutting of city centers, the millions of crash deaths and horrific injuries enacted in public view. All of this has transformed the everyday fabric of modern life for the worse. People's persistence with this technology in the face of such brutality implies a kind of fascination (if, by now, a taken-for-granted one) with what the car offers: personal speed as pleasure. It is as if the desire for personal speed, granted as the gift of a prosthetic technology, is so intense that we are content to ruin our planet to experience it.

By now, driving seems such a mundane habit, however, that speed's celebration has surfaced only in the obscure pages of uncataloged car magazines, the unregarded showstopper sequences of B movies, in the video games of bored adolescents: in all the backroom, lowbrow purlieus of the modern, hidden from the shockingly clarifying light of high culture. On second look, however, speed's pleasure, like Poe's infamous postcard, is hidden in plain sight everywhere in high art: even Eliot's *The Waste Land* speaks of "the human engine . . . Like a taxi throbbing waiting." One task of this book has been to notate these surfacings of speed as metaphor and actuality in high culture and to read them symptomatically as the very throb of a modernist base note.

The speed thrills of modernism: of what can they be a symptom? Speed matters utterly to modernism, I have argued, not because it suggests any great change in the average Western subject's relation to time: modernity's enforced and incited seesaw regimen of rushing, waiting, scheduling, timekeeping, clocking-in, and boiling with impatience had been gathering momentum for centuries before, say, 1910. Rather, speed thrills are symptomatic of a revolution in the modernist citizen's concept of space and place. These speed appearances mark changes in the way the subject inhabited space in the world. Derrida, quoted in the epigraph, is right: we can acknowledge a change in the modernist time sense but must prudently label it no more than "an extraordinary acceleration of the same experience." What Derrida forgoes in his characterization of speed as "our relation to motion and time" is any consideration of the subject's relation to space. The new twentieth-century car speed was open now to vast numbers of ordinary people, whereas even the means of most rapid movement of an earlier era, horse speed, had been restricted to the upper classes. This new speed was pleasurable not to the degree to which it "saved time," opening up a time for the dubious new leisure and the delicious ennui of boredom, but rather in the way it covered space and plowed on at a fantastic rate over actual territory. The new speed, in other words, offered to people as a pleasure what the latest stage of modernity developed as the best way of being: movement.

When people have asked me why as a literary scholar I'm writing about speed, I've told them that it was a means to understand modernist representations of space. I began this work by considering how novels such as Joyce's *Ulysses* and Robert Musil's *The Man without Qualities* created a sense of the urban settings and spaces they portrayed, and by comparing the clean lines of Le Corbusier's Villa Savoye and Eileen Gray's E-1027 with the tangled textuality of, for example, Gertrude Stein's *Tender Buttons*. Pursuing that work, I came upon all the modernist architects who had designed cars: Le Corbusier's own wood-framed Voiture Minimum, the sleek design of Gropius, and Buckminster Fuller's Dymaxion. Then I came to the page in *Vers un architecture* where Le Corbusier counterposes on the same page a photo of the Parthenon with one of a 1921 Delage Grand Sport automobile (figure 22). The Delage was a twentieth-century classic design, he implied, not only because its form followed function but because it was design in the service of movement. It signified what was implicit in the work of each of these architects who designed cars: the dream of an architecture freed from stasis and from fixity: design for movement. Speed, then, gets to be the secret of modernist space, for speed is the measure of movement, and movement is the trope for the management of space in modernity.

It is easy to see that movement was everywhere in the era of modernism. This was the time of the height of the European diasporas, when millions moved to new continents and the masses, on Ellis Island or the docks

Paestum, de 600 à 550 av. J.-C.

Cliché Albert Morancé.   Parthénon, de 447 à 434 av. J.-C.

Le Parthénon est un produit de sélection appliquée à un standart établi. Depuis un siècle déjà, le temple grec était organisé dans tous ses éléments.

Lorsqu'un standart est établi, le jeu de la concurrence immédiate et violente s'exerce. C'est le match; pour gagner, il faut faire mieux que l'adversaire *dans toutes les parties*, dans la ligne d'ensemble et dans tous les détails. C'est alors l'étude poussée des parties. Progrès.

Le standart est une nécessité d'ordre apporté dans le travail humain.

Le standart s'établit sur des bases certaines, non pas arbi-

Cliché de *La Vie Automobile*.   Humbert, 1907.   Delage, Grand-Sport, 1921.

FIGURE 22. Le Corbusier, *Vers un architecture* (Paris, 1923), 106, 107.
Courtesy of the artist's estate.

of Bremen, exchanged the static worldview that equated identity with a knowledge of belonging to a home place with dreams of the possibilities offered by mobility and movement. It was the time when the rush from countryside to cities had given rise to those broad spaces still marked by a void of identification, the suburbs. It was the time of the detective story and cafe culture, of literature and art that glorified the scene of circulation and traffic, the street. It was the period when a new angst about the newly vast urban crowds prompted a civic desire to keep the crowd's members moving; there arose whole civil service divisions, even scientific disciplines, designed to ease circulation and improve transport. This was the time when the idea of traffic became a common currency. It was also the moment of the resurrected Olympic games, at which the movement of the human body could be celebrated as a global event. At the same time, the repetitive, ritualized movements of the factory worker fascinated everyone from Walter Benjamin to the proponents of Taylorism. Human movement was a prime concern of the moment of modernism.

Yet none of this was new: the history of refugees, traders, pilgrims, and migrant labor, even of athletics, is a long one. And art had always celebrated movement, from the *Odyssey* to the picaresque and latterly the flâneur novel. What was unprecedented, once movement was generalized rather than exceptional, was that the notion of home, and of place — as a setting that corresponded to a long-lasting community which granted identity — was more or less surrendered. Movement occurred from a place; speed was experienced in a space (that is to say, in a non-place, a place which has been abstracted and departicularized to the extent that all local flavor which cast it as a locus of identification has been leached from it). The world as a collection of unique and distinct places was abstracted into one efficient space; the comforts and the culture of place are given up; the newly invented leisure industry invented tourism to offer to people a simulacrum of the sense of place they used to know. Instead — for a brief moment, the modernist moment of movement — people were offered the possibility of movement as pleasure for its own sake. They were offered speed. Speed, then, is not just the friction and the inconvenience of going faster, or of "killing time"; it is the idea that movement, instead of being a plotted leap from the pleasures of one identifiable place to the potential pleasures of another, would be a pleasure in itself, a pleasure that represents an escape from the horrific stasis of place and instead gets to be a physical sensation, a new kind of arousal experienced not as emotion but more viscerally, as an incitement imprinted on one's body. The old, emotional ties of place were lost to speed, to the thrill of a rush of adrenaline. The moderns, speeding, could experience modernity in their bones.

To historicize this phenomenon, and to consider its global reach, is to begin to imagine that it might have political implications. Modernism's spatial turn might be said to have been inaugurated with Halford Mackinder's essay "The Geographical Pivot of History" (1904), when the learned head of the Royal Geographical Society pointed out the cultural implications of the fact that now at last the whole of the exotic world available for empire had been mapped: there were now no more foreign places to conquer and colonize. At that moment, it became impossible to imagine empire as it had been successfully imagined for centuries: that is, as an exotic other place, a heterotopia — the repository of Western fantasies of power and excess. The colonial locale had long been cast in Western imaginations as a wildly distorted mirror image of the home place; now, just as the place at home was being abstracted, being shorn of its imaginative possibilities in the service of efficiency, it turned out that the colonial other place, fully mapped and known to bureaucracy, and removed from the realm of place-as-fantasy, was up for abstraction too. It is the trauma occasioned by this discovery that is charted in the drear slowness which effects everything African in Conrad's *Heart of Darkness*. At this early-twentieth-century moment, the home place was to be deserted, and the colonial other places of the earth were also mapped and taken. With global space fully abstracted or about to be, both nostalgia for home and the old tropes of exploration were rendered obsolete. In their place, traversing the abstracted landscape, it was only movement itself that might satisfy. It was through speed that satisfaction in movement was made manifest.

To understand how this intrusion of actual experience was short-lived, consider what occurred after the moment of modernist speed fascination. If the modernist speed moment after 1904 was in part a response to the end of heterotopic imaginings of exotic spaces, then it was also an interlude before the new technological imagining of entirely simulated fantasy places that postmodernism, through technology, has granted us with cyberspace. As the real geographic spaces of empire were colonized and abstracted, and so removed from the realm of imaginative possibilities, technologies of the spectacle entered the scene to provide a store of imagined worlds to Western imaginations. Film, the modernist medium par excellence, began this trend, but it was only with the invention of television (already mentioned, perhaps for the first time in high literature, in Joyce's *Finnegans Wake* [1939]),[3] and soon the computer screen, that cyberspace as completely simulated other world became an option for culture. The moment of movement, and its physical sensation in speed, comes between these two. For about thirty years, between the death of the fantasy of ideal space as either home or other and the invention of technologies that could represent virtual other spaces of fantasy, there was an unlikely hiatus, an opportunity to savor a new sensation. It was as if, for a short time, technology had not yet taken up the cultural slack presented by historical developments in what is now termed globalization. For a moment, utopian longing failed to work as the basis for the Western imagining of the subject's relation to space and place. Instead, movement mattered, and speed was not so much movement's measurement as its pleasure.

Don't, however, rush to see this as a moment of "realism" in the truest sense, that is, as a window of consciousness where the subject's relation to space was not mediated or misled by dreams of adventure of escapism. Note

that the possibility of experiencing pleasure in speed was even more intensively controlled and mediated, in this modernist interlude, by the twin
engines of modernity, technology and consumerism. Simply, the Western
subject was soon convinced that the most vivid experience of speed could
be achieved only by sharing one's bodily power with a prosthesis powered
by technology. This subject could be a projectile, but at a price. This price
was literal: the technology, wrapped in commodity allure, had to be bought
and paid for. Speed was presented to the subject in commodity form. From
the beginning, the automobile was sold as the most alluring commodity
in the glittery carnival of consumer products. This experience of speed,
and the deployment of technology that let one enjoy speed, had been subsumed into the exchange protocols of consumption and commodity fetishism. In this way movement itself, as tangible effort and affect, as well as the
use of technology as prosthesis, was subordinated to consumption: it was
made a form of consumption. However, as commodity fetishism became
the governing form of more and more aspects of human activity, it too was
forced into further complexities and strategies of enticement and reward.
Commodification itself was transformed. What was bought and sold in this
latest expanded form of commodity exchange was not only the glittering
commodity per se but, flaunted within it, its accelerative power, its ability
to physically move you with a force not felt before. The commodity embodied the power to generate the pleasure of an experience, a tangible effect
that went far beyond the commodity's standard pleasure, that of ownership.

Here was a commodity selling itself as a service; this was part of the
development of the modern service economy. The implication was three-
fold: that experience from now on was not possible without prior commodification, that commodification was powerfully heterogeneous as well
as hegemonic — that is, it could cater to all needs, even ones that it would
itself invent and invite consumers to sample — and that commodification
would colonize and reorganize science and technology to the point where
the results of their researches could be enjoyed only via the protocols of
consumption. (Thus the 1890s were the great era of inventions, which were
scientific and technological innovations instantly grasped as consumer
products.) What this techno-commodification implies is that the new experience of speed needs to be grasped not as the realization of a neoroman-
tic dream of contact with nature and a truly educative organicity but as
a thoroughly modern, and merely modern, accession to affect, gratifying

and pleasurable wholly within modernist parameters. It was a version of experience in parentheses. In this version, experience is shot through by the protocols of consumption, which are always now preconditions of that experience. It is a version, moreover, where consumption's superficial affect is sharpened and enhanced by prostheticizing technologies, in which powerful machines insist on the modern subject's comparative powerlessness at the same time as they grant her a terrific and thrilling sense of this new consumption- and technology-enhanced personal power.

This nexus of an intensified new stage of commodity consumption and the co-optation of technology as consumer durable to effect a new personal sensation marks a new stage in the multileveled interpellation of the modernist subject and, in compensation, offers her a new affect, this new thrill of speed, a tangible pleasure to be sensed in one's body. This experience is compensatory in the sense that the onerous quality of modernity's speeded-up regime of timekeeping—the clocking in, the rush of the assembly line, even the popularization of the wristwatch—could become a delicious thrill, instead, when speed was cast as a matter of conquering space. Because it was to be carried out under the sign of consumption, speed was to be a leisure activity. Because it was a form of consumption which purchased not only the glittering object but the physical thrill which went with it, it was an excessive expenditure of human and mechanical energy. Practiced in the time of leisure, the part-time that could be snatched clear of the nine-to-five regime of time regimentation, it was a form of unproductive, excessive expenditure. Speed was glorious wasted effort and a thrill without a goal. It was thrilling only when it was acceleration for its own sake. It is in this sheer excessiveness that we can glimpse the shadow of a possibility of this speed thrill as teaching us something new about the modernist interplay of technology, commodification, and subjectivity. In this excessiveness, in the fullest sense of the term, it might be political.

Any activity that offered the possibility of intense physical sensation, at the historical moment when the regimes of the spectacle and the spectacular (as in film) and later the virtual (as in cyberspace) were being invented, might in itself be felt to have political implications. Modern mass sports, which were also developed in this very period, offered the same wildly popular possibility of physicality at a moment when "just looking" was becoming the mantra of a contented existence, and were at once organized in terms of national and regional affiliations, to be played under the aegis of national organizations. If speeding in a car offered the driver a more thoroughly modernist sensation in its melding of consumption, technology, and the prostheticized body, this new thrill was to have the potential to be universal, even as each state rushed to control it. Like most modernist innovations, and all commodification, it further alienated the individual from any sense of community affiliation, concentrating on her as a figure alone. It seems wishful, therefore, to draw a line from the figure of the speeding driver to any notion of political action. If for modernism's first figurative trope of the subject in movement, the flâneur, there corresponded, in the political realm, the demonstration, the march through the streets, the barricade — and hence the possibility that urban walking could be transformed into popular political action — for later modernism's more occasional trope of movement, the car, there corresponds only the armored car or the tank, anonymous conveyances resolutely in the hands of national armies and those in power. Still, in all these movie car chase scenes, the cheers are for the breakneck bank robber, not the police: the thrill of speed becomes the thrill of escape from the state's law. But these are scenes, not speed thrills themselves, experienced only at the secondhand of representation, wherein lies the lesson: that even if, in the moment of high modernism, speed seemed for a while to trump representation, and literary representation most of all, it turns out that it is only through representations, when the new thrill of speed is granted a context, that a politics of speed might even be imagined. Speed, as modernity's single new experience, may have been for a moment too strange even for modernist obscurities to handle; but speed, in the end, needs representation if it is to be meaningful and if that meaning is to have political significance — if, in short, it is to matter in the world.

Speed, then, cannot represent itself; it must be represented. This book has charted the wayward, episodic, minor representations of speed in modernist novels, photography, art, and some film, and the effect of these representations, the records of the one new sensation, to suggest how speed matters in the world. From the hyperbole of the Futurists to the self-conscious brilliance of J. G. Ballard's *Crash*, speed and literature have not suited each other all that well, and most of the literature of speed consists of flashes in the panoramas of larger fictions, from Fitzgerald's *The Great Gatsby* to Woolf's *Orlando*. Perhaps, if speed's experience was truly tangible only for the brief modernist moment of the first thirty years or so of the twentieth century, then the time to represent speed as vivid physical sensation — a sensation with specific, assignable meanings and significances — is past.

But speed persists, and with it the need to represent it. From its inception, speed has been so thoroughly the subject of many of the new modernist art forms—the comic book, the cartoon, film itself, the arcade game, the video game, and virtual reality—that it is as if they had been invented to show speed. With speed their mainstay, they aimed to incorporate speed into their own enabling forms (consider, for example, rolling film stock): they were developed to *be* speed to perfectly replicate, as well as represent, velocity. All these forms, like speed itself in the roller coaster, had their origins in the fairground and the penny arcade and still, with the exception of film, carry the stigma of mass popular genres even as they revel in the technological possibilities of modernity much more enthusiastically than did any of the masterworks of high culture. For high culture, initial resistance to the modishness and popularity of speed transformed itself soon into intense anxiety about the price—and the possible tragic consequences—of speed culture. In the second half of the century, texts like Ballard's unnerving *Crash* and films such as Godard's maligned *Weekend* bear testimony to the depth charge that this anxiety continued to generate, even as speed as not-quite-new pleasure still excited and aroused. Respectable high culture has been in all senses, then, reactionary to speed: disreputable low culture's embrace of it might seem to prove high culture's point. This cultural class divide regarding speed has helped cut off the possibility of any broad-scale politics of speed from emerging.

Speed, to gain a politics, any politics, needs to be represented, but representation preempts the reality of the new experience, which is what is so tangible and provocative about speed in the first place. In the modernist moment, speed was raw, experiential—and little represented. It suits the sellers of technology that we become blasé to, and hence comfortable with, the effects of speed. As we do so, speed representations come to matter more: they take us out of our dream world and remind us of the necessity of the tangible. For critics of culture, it is tempting to see technology as the enabler, merely, of better and better machineries of representation: from the phonograph to the movie screen to the virtual reality studio. In the meantime, technology is content to merely serve us "behind the scenes." Lurking behind its spectacles, it gives us speed that we can never sense, by performing functions faster—speeding to defeat time. In this process, it robs us, with the excuse of convenience, even of the tangibility of affect that we term impatience. Precisely because of this unseen, unsensed infiltration of the technological, technology needs to be the subject matter of culture.

Speed needs to matter to the most serious forms of culture, to be dealt with not just as the invisibility principle of technology as it delivers more dazzling media and cultural forms. To think speed is to overcome the acceptance of technology as an invisible instrumentality, the efficient mechanical hand of modern service. For this to occur, we must be able to sense technological force as palpable sensation, as affect that breaks through the comfort of the apparently instantaneous service and dazzling representations that technology, as mirage, appears to promise. The best case of this in the last hundred years has been the seemingly mundane experience of speeding. Speed's delivery vehicle, the automobile, therefore counts as modernism's most stunning and most characteristic artifact. As speed shocks and horrifies, as it excites and thrills, it—and its representations—gives us, in a technologically mediated and mediatized world, a sensation in modernity of the possibilities of the material world and of the possibilities of the interaction of each of us with it. For this, speed matters. With so much of our lives controlled and so much of our experience mediated, speed is not only modernity's sole new pleasure but one of the few that remain available to us. In the dreamscape of the society of the spectacle, only the intervention of real experience can arouse us. We need speed.

NOTES

Introduction

1. L. Harding et al., "The car was doing 121 mph—and the driver was drunk: Shock new details of Diana's death," *Guardian* (London), September 2, 1997. See also the *International Herald Tribune* (Paris), headline of September 2: "Diana's Driver Was Legally Drunk; Cyclists Surrounded Speeding Car."

2. Jameson also speaks in some detail of what he calls "the embodiment of new forms of the psychic subject on the physical sensorium" in relation to the "cinematographic perception" possible from a speeding train, as it is described in E. M. Forster's *Howards End*, in "Modernism and Imperialism," 44.

3. The term comes from Virilio, *Speed and Politics*, esp. part 3, "Dromocratic Society," 66–132.

4. On the distancing involved in the split between subject and other as key to what she terms foundational consciousness, and the relation of this formation to the refusal of the energy stored in nature, see Brennan's eloquent work in *Exhausting Modernity*, where she outlines a thesis that she elaborates further in *The Transmission of Affect*.

CHAPTER 1. *Speed Theory*

1. Aldous Huxley, "Wanted, a New Pleasure," in *Aldous Huxley: Complete Essays*, vol. 3, *1930–1935*, ed. Robert S. Baker and James Sexton (Chicago: Ivan R. Dee, 2001), 263–64. For a broad-ranging discussion of Huxley's attitude to science and technology, see Robert S. Baker, "Science and Modernity in Aldous Huxley's Inter-war Essays and Novels," in *Aldous Huxley between East and West*, ed. C. C. Barfoot (Amsterdam: Radopi, 2001), 35–58.

2. Simmel, "The Metropolis and Mental Life," reprinted in *Images of Man: The Classical Tradition of Sociological Thinking*, ed. C. Wright Mills (New York: George Braziller, 1960).

3. Elfriede Jelinek, "A Gloom of Her Own," interview with Elfriede Jelinek by Deborah Solomon, *New York Times Magazine*, November 24, 2004, 6.

4. Quoted in Harvey Levenstein, *Seductive Journey: American Tourists in France*

from Jefferson to the Jazz Age (Chicago: University of Chicago Press, 1998), 135. Levenstein notes that Gordon Bennett was the publisher of the *Paris Herald*.

5. Manfredo Tafuri, *Theory of the Avant Garde* (Cambridge, Mass.: MIT Press, 1973).

6. Fredric Jameson, "Cognitive Mapping," in *Marxism and the Interpretation of Culture*, ed. Cary Nelson and Lawrence Grossberg (Urbana: University of Illinois Press, 1988), 347–60.

7. Jameson, *The Political Unconscious*.

8. Marx, *Capital*, 539.

9. Foucault, "Of Other Spaces," 22.

10. Ibid., 23 (italics mine).

11. Bachelard, *The Poetics of Space*.

12. Donlyn Lyndon and Charles Moore, *Chambers for a Memory Palace* (Cambridge, Mass.: MIT Press, 1994).

13. Foucault, "Of Other Spaces," 25.

14. Jameson, *Postmodernism*, 44; hereafter cited in the text.

15. See Tafuri, *Theory of the Avant Garde*; and Aldo Rossi, *The Architecture of the City*, ed. Diane Ghiorardo and Joan Ockman (Cambridge, Mass.: MIT Press, 1982). For a short introduction and samples of their work, including "Territory and Architecture" (1985), see Vitorrio Gregotti, "The School of Venice," in *Theorizing Architecture: An Anthology of Architectural Theory, 1965–1996*, ed. Kate Nesbitt (New York: Princeton Architectural Press, 1996), 338–69. See also Massimo Caracci, *Architecture and Nihilism: On the Philosophy of Modern Architecture*, ed. Stephen Sartarelli (New Haven, Conn.: Yale University Press, 1993).

16. Tafuri, *Theory of the Avant Garde*, 81.

17. Fredric Jameson, "Is Space Political?" in *Anyplace*, ed. Cynthia C. Davidson (Cambridge, Mass.: MIT Press, 1995), 192–205.

18. For a meditation on dispensable buildings and Los Angeles, see Norman M. Klein, *The History of Forgetting: Los Angeles and the Erasure of Memory* (London: Verso, 1997).

19. See Ernest Mandel, *Late Capitalism* (London: Verso, 1978).

20. Kevin Lynch, *The Image of the City* (Cambridge, Mass.: MIT Press, 1960).

21. See Mark Wigley, *The Architecture of Deconstruction: Derrida's Haunt* (Cambridge, Mass.: MIT Press, 1993); Vidler, *The Architectural Uncanny*; and Colomina, *Sexuality and Space*.

22. Tschumi, *Architecture and Disjunction*, 121; hereafter cited in the text.

23. Lefebvre, *The Production of Space*, 343; hereafter cited in the text.

24. Debord, "Situationist Theses on Traffic," quoted in Ross, *Fast Cars, Clean Bodies*, 26.

25. Harvey, "The Geopolitics of Capitalism," 145.

26. Ibid.

27. Halford J. Mackinder, "The Geographical Pivot of History," *Geographical Journal* 23 (1904): 421–37.

28. Joyce, "Proteus," episode 3 of *Ulysses*, 36.

29. Virilio, *Speed and Politics*.

30. Ibid.

31. Virilio, *Speed and Politics*, 134.

32. On this tradition, see Brewer, *Marxist Theories of Imperialism*.

33. An exemplary text here is Said, *Culture and Imperialism*.

34. See Frantz Fanon, *The Wretched of the Earth*, trans. Constance Farrington (New York: Grove Press, 1968).

35. See, for example, Williams, *Autogeddon*: "The fuhrer kept a signed photograph of Ford on his desk in the Reich Chancellery, and in August 1938 awarded him the Grand Cross of the German Eagle, a decoration for distinguished and helpful foreigners" (30).

36. Flink, *The Automobile Age*, 5.

37. Stevenson, *British Society, 1914–45*, 111.

38. Dimmenberg, "The Will to Motorization," 98.

39. On French dominance of the early automobile industry, see Flink, *The Automobile Age*, 15–19.

40. Wigley, *Architecture of Deconstruction*; Martin Heidegger, "Being, Dwelling, Thinking," in *Poetry, Language, Thought*, trans. Albert Hofstader (New York: Harper and Row, 1971).

41. Quoted in Kern, *Culture of Time and Space*, 119.

42. Ehrenburg, *Life of the Automobile*, 24.

43. Banham, *Los Angeles*.

44. Kern, *Culture of Time and Space*, 109–30. Octave Uzanne's book was originally published by Paul Ollendorff as *La locomotion à travers l'histoire et les moeurs* (Paris, 1900).

45. Cecelia Tichi, *Shifting Gears: Technology, Literature, Culture in Modernist America* (Chapel Hill: University of North Carolina Press, 1987).

46. Marinetti, "Founding Manifesto of Futurism," 41.

47. Kern, *Culture of Time and Space*, 135–36. In his book *Relativity* (1916), Einstein explained: "We entirely shun the vague word 'space' of which, we must honestly acknowledge, we cannot form the slightest conception and we replace it by 'motion relative to a practically rigid body of reference.'" Quoted in Kern, *Culture of Time and Space*, 136.

48. See Rhode, *History of the Cinema*, 23–24. Note too that cars were not the only machines displayed in early films. See, for example, Cowan, "The Heart Machine."

49. Eliot, *Collected Essays*, 485.

1. The first citation for the word in the *Oxford English Dictionary* is from 1889; the first to use it to describe the literary genre ("full-blown detectives—the sort you read of in the thrillers") is taken from the *Pall Mall Magazine*, no. 380 (November 1896).

2. See Kyriazi, *Great American Amusement Parks*, 34. Kyriazi notes that the "Oriental Scenic Railway" was the "first fully developed roller coaster." It was preceded by Thompson's "Switchback Railway" at Coney Island, a "simple affair" of 1884. The famous Cyclone was built at Coney Island in 1928. Ibid., 34–35. There are also Russian, French, and British precursors; Thompson himself had many competitors, and was inspired by scenic train ride attractions.

3. Benjamin, "On Some Motifs in Baudelaire," 166–67.

4. Traffic was equally light in Paris: when the photographer Nadar was photographed by George Eastman in the Place de l'Opera in Paris in 1890, there are a few pedestrians in view, but not a single wheeled vehicle in sight in the whole sweep of the Place. Camille Pissarro's *Boulevard des Italiens, Morning, Sunlight* (1897) shows a street relatively filled with carriages and horse-drawn omnibuses, but few enough that pedestrians can cross the wide street wherever and whenever they wish. See John Russell, *Paris* (New York: Harry N. Abrams, 1993), 114, 102–3.

5. See Eric Hobsbawm, *The Age of Empire, 1875–1914* (New York: Vintage Books, 1989), 21.

6. Simmel, "Metropolis and Mental Life," 438, 440–41.

7. In "On Some Motifs in Baudelaire," Benjamin notes how Engels was one of the first in this modern tradition (155–200).

8. A. Conan Doyle, "The Adventure of the Blue Carbuncle," in *The Sherlock Holmes Omnibus: A Facsimile of the Original "Strand" Magazine Stories, 1891–1893* (New York: Bramhall House, 1975), 85.

9. Tschumi, *Architecture and Disjunction*.

10. James M. Cain, *Double Indemnity* (New York: Vintage, 1978), 7. The book was originally published in 1936.

11. R. L. Stevenson, *Dr. Jekyll and Mr. Hyde* (Hertfordshire: Wordsworth Classics, 1995), 4.

12. See, for example, Ruth Rendell, *Live Flesh* (New York: Ballantine Books, 1986).

13. Augé, *Non-Places*, 42; hereafter cited in the text.

14. See C. Kaplan, *Questions of Travel*.

15. Foucault, "Of Other Spaces."

16. Conan Doyle, "A Case of Identity," 85.

17. Conan Doyle, "The Engineer's Thumb," 193; hereafter cited in the text.

18. Garreau, *Edge City*.
19. Simmel, "Metropolis and Mental Life," 441.
20. Harbison, *The Built, the Unbuilt*, 78–80. Harbison calls Castle Drago an "unnervingly sleek building, in an abstract sense Lutyens's most modern, because it is able to concentrate as few of his others can on pure wall and pure perforation of it."
21. See Colomina, "The Split Wall," 88–90.
22. Ibid., 103.
23. Ibid.
24. On invasion narratives, see Brantlinger, *Bread and Circuses*.
25. Chinua Achebe, "An Image of Africa," on Conrad. See also GoGwilt, *Invention of the West*.
26. On Conrad and imperial space see Con Coroneos's excellent *Space, Conrad and Modernity*, 109.
27. Conrad, *Heart of Darkness*, 11–12; hereafter cited in the text.
28. See C. Kaplan, *Questions of Travel*.
29. Fredric Jameson brilliantly analyzes the effectiveness of Conrad's use of impressionist technique in "Romance and Reification in Joseph Conrad," the final chapter of *The Political Unconscious* (206–80), chiefly in relation to *Nostromo*. *Nostromo* might be said to defer some of the stark discoveries about abstracted and instrumentalized spaces that in *Heart of Darkness* are much more openly sited in the reader's field of vision.
30. Obviously, the image is most common in representations of shipwrecks and their aftermath. All kinds of images that confound the ship's place with contrasts between land and sea, however, have this uncanniness. See Brueghel's *Icarus*, for example, and W. H. Auden's poem about it, "Musee de Beaux Arts," written 1938, published 1940.
31. Foucault, "Of Other Spaces," 27.
32. On the Kaffir Krall and its fascinating hero Peter Lobengula, see Boscagli, *Eye on the Flesh*, 178–83.
33. On Casement's Congo reports and Conrad's interest in them, see Reid, *Lives of Roger Casement*, 20–66. A letter from Conrad to Casement is quoted on pages 54–56.
34. Bhabha, "Signs Taken for Wonders," 104.
35. See Fussell, "The Passport Nuisance," 24–31.
36. Georges Bataille, writing about the Bastille, quoted in Hollier, *Against Architecture*, 47.
37. Gartman, *Auto-Opium*, 123–26.
38. See Shand, "The *Reichsautobahn*."
39. Virilio, *Speed and Politics*, 21.
40. For an excellent discussion of the relation of meaning-loss in the metropole to

the colonial imaginary, and the relation of this to British modernism, see Jed Esty, *A Shrinking Island: Modernism and National culture in England* (Princeton: Princeton University Press, 2003), esp. 23–28.

41. Quoted in Jay and Neve, *Fin-de-Siècle Reader*, 50.
42. Kyriazi, *Great American Amusement Parks*, 34, 38.
43. Roller coasters continued to be made faster and more exciting throughout the twentieth century. The famous Coney Island Cyclone was built only in 1928.
44. See Richards, *Commodity Culture*.
45. Kyriazi, *Great American Amusement Parks*, 39.
46. On early automobile design and the roughness of the machine aesthetic, see, for example, Stern, *Pictorial History of the Automobile*.

CHAPTER 3. *Gaining Speed*

1. Sandra Dawson, "Dangerous Desires: Gender, Bumper Cars, and the Popular Imagination in Interwar Britain," unpublished paper, Department of History, UC Santa Barbara. She notes that the patent was taken out by Max and Harold Stoehrer, "Amusement Device," Patent Specification 177,395, Leeds Patent Office, UK, 1921.
2. Marx, *Capital*, 533.
3. Flink, *The Automobile Age*, 25.
4. Ibid., 11, 4, 17.
5. Nigel Gosling, *Paris, 1900–1914* (New York: William Morrow, 1978), 14.
6. W. J. Curtis, *Modern Architecture since 1900*, 3rd ed. (London: Phaidon Press, 1966), 50–51.
7. Debord, *Society of the Spectacle*.
8. Jean Baudrillard, *Symbolic Exchange and Death*, quoted in Beckmann, *The Virtual Dimension*, xv.
9. Wicke, "Who's She When She's at Home," 177.
10. Marx, *Capital*, 163.
11. Ibid., 178. Here Marx shows himself to be thinking of the commodity in the same way that an imperialist thought of territories; for Marx, as for the Victorian consumer, the political and consumer systems could be envisioned in parallel terms.
12. See Welsh, *The City of Dickens*.
13. Hardy, *Tess of the d'Urbervilles*, 54; hereafter cited in the text.
14. Flink, *The Automobile Age*, 11.
15. Ibid., 19. By 1912 the United States was producing 378,000 cars per year.
16. Marsh and Collet, *Driving Passion*, 29.
17. Stern, *Pictorial History*, 211.
18. Marsh and Collet, *Driving Passion*, 20.

19. Flink, *The Automobile Age*, 15.
20. Gartman, *Auto-Opium*, 33.
21. Ibid., 34.
22. For one account of this accident, see Brottman, *Car Crash Culture*, xvi.
23. Bishop, *Age of the Automobile*, 41n.
24. See Netter, *Automobile*, 21.
25. Monestier, *Les conquerants de'Olympe*.
26. Bishop, *Age of the Automobile*.
27. James Joyce, "After the Race," in *Dubliners*, 43.
28. Ellmann, *James Joyce*, 170. Ellmann makes the startling claim that in this story Joyce may have had in mind W. B. Yeats's mythic tale of Red Hanrahan, which had appeared in 1903. "After the Race" was published in the *Irish Homestead*, December 17, 1904.
29. Marsh and Collet, *Driving Passion*, 151.
30. Flink, *The Automobile Age*, 30.
31. Nolan, *Barney Oldfield*, 124.
32. Gartman, *Auto-Opium*, 36.
33. Flink, *The Automobile Age*, 18.
34. Ibid., 33.
35. Wolf, *Car Mania*, 70, 72.
36. Flink, *The Automobile Age*, 37–80.
37. Gartman, *Auto-Opium*, 58.
38. Ibid., 46.
39. Ibid.
40. Wolf, *Car Mania*, 73.
41. Ford, *My Life and Work*, 73, 105.
42. Ehrenburg, *Life of the Automobile*, 17, quoted in Wolf, *Car Mania*, 72.
43. Wolf, *Car Mania*, 72.
44. Grahame, *The Wind in the Willows*, 40–41; hereafter cited in the text.
45. Evelyn Waugh, *Remote People*, 73–137.
46. Joyce, *Ulysses*, 188.
47. See Duffy, *The Subaltern Ulysses*, 53–92.
48. Woolf, *Mrs. Dalloway*, 19; hereafter cited in the text.
49. See S. Kaplan, *L.A. Lost and Found*, 114–15, for a discussion of the design of Bullocks Wiltshire Dept. Store, and the new emphasis on the importance of parking in encouraging mass consumption.
50. Gilette, "Evolution of the Planned Shopping Center," 449–60.
51. For information on the film *A Runaway Match* (1903, dir. Alf Collins), see Varaces: The Movie Car Chase Database, http://www.varaces.com.

1. See Tubbs, *Art and the Automobile*, 56–57.
2. See Herman Glaser et al., *Das Automobil in der Kunst, 1886–1986* (Munich: Haus der Kunst, 1986), 75 [exhibition catalogue], especially on how this work allowed Matisse to develop his interest in the juxtaposition of interior and exterior spaces.
3. Joyce, "After the Race," 44.
4. Wolfgang Schivelbusch, *The Railway Journey: Trains and Travel in the Nineteenth Century*, trans. Anselm Hollo (New York: Urizen, 1977), esp. chap. 4, "Panoramic Travel," 57–72.
5. Quoted in *Das Automobil in der Kunst*, 5.
6. Merleau-Ponty, quoted in Virilio, *The Vision Machine*, 7.
7. See Jacques Derrida, "Différance," in *Margins of Philosophy*, trans. Alan Bass (Chicago: University of Chicago Press, 1982), 13.
8. Simmel, "Metropolis and Mental Life," 409–10.
9. Guy Debord, *Society of the Spectacle*, quoted in David Lloyd and Paul Thomas, *Culture and the State* (New York: Routledge, 1998), 31.
10. Walter Benjamin, "On Surrealism," quoted in Buck-Morss, "Dream World of Mass-Culture," 309–38, 324.
11. It is worth comparing the use of the term "abstract space" in the work of Bergson to its use in that of Lefebvre almost three-quarters of a century later. To a considerable degree, their usages are similar. For Bergson, "abstract space" is a mirage of infinitude produced by the regime of rationality; for Lefebvre, it is the dream, possibly destined to be fulfilled, of the universe's known territory rationally allocated to uses best suited to the maximization of profit.
12. Bergson, *Matter and Memory*, 206.
13. See Grosz, "Towards an Architecture," 242–52, 246.
14. Ibid., 248n12. See also Deleuze, *Bergsonism*.
15. Grosz, "Towards an Architecture," 247.
16. Deleuze, *Cinema I*, 104, 107; hereafter cited in the text.
17. Virilio, *Art of the Motor*, 92.
18. Banham, *Theory and Design*, 100.
19. F. T. Marinetti, "The Founding Manifesto of Futurism," quoted in Banham, *Theory and Design*, 101. For the complete text, see Umbro Apollonio, ed., *Futurist Manifestos* (New York, 1973).
20. Banham, *Theory and Design*, 122.
21. Rosso's relief sculpture is shown in Banham, *Theory and Design*, 113.
22. For a series of reproductions of both these works, see Martin, *Futurist Art and Theory*, figs. 162–67.
23. For a short account of this text, see Kern, *Culture of Time and Space*, 120–22.
24. On Rodin's interest in movement, see Virilio, *The Vision Machine*, 1–3.

25. Lewis, "The Romance of War," 115.

26. Quoted in Buck-Morss, *The Dialectics of Seeing*, 313.

27. Glaser et al., *Das Automobil in der Kunst*, 51.

28. Pettifer and Turner, *Automania*, 240–41.

29. Tubbs, *Art and the Automobile*, 88.

30. On Vincent's career, see Tubbs, *Art and the Automobile*, 98.

31. See Von Reimar, *Automobil*, 82.

32. Ibid., 67.

33. See the frontispiece to Tubbs, *Art and the Automobile*, for a good reproduction of this startling image. Similar materials from German fascist male pop culture and technoculture are reproduced in Klaus Theweleit, *Male Fantasies*.

34. Brodsky, "Guide to a Renamed City," quoted in Michael Bell and Sze Tsung Leong, eds., *Slow Space* (New York: Montacelli Press, 1998), 27.

35. Crary, *Techniques of the Observer*, 19. For a review of Crary's place in recent U.S. art criticism, see Jay, "Returning the Gaze."

36. Ibid., 123.

37. See Avant, "Vision in the Ganzfeld." This is quoted in Wamble, "Parsing of the Eye."

38. For discourses of the kinesthetic body, torque, and so on during this period, see Schwartz, "Torque."

39. Ibid., 104.

CHAPTER 5. *Crash Culture*

1. See Williams, *Autogeddon*, 57.

2. Hubert Juin, *Le livre de Paris, 1900* (Paris: Belfond, 1977), 105.

3. Katie Alvord, *Divorce Your Car* (Gabriola Island, Canada: New Society Publishers, 2000), 114–15.

4. Ballard, introduction to *Crash*, 6.

5. For a definition of ideology in the sense the term is used here, see Louis Althusser, "Ideology and Ideological State Apparatuses," in *Lenin and Philosophy and Other Essays* (New York: Monthly Review Press, 1971).

6. Virilio, *Speed and Politics*, 48.

7. Theodor Adorno, *The Jargon of Authenticity*, trans. Knut Tarnowski and Frederic Will (Evanston: Northwestern University Press, 1973).

8. For this quote and a reading of the film by Marcel Carné, *Les tricheurs*, see Ross, *Fast Cars, Clean Bodies*, 46. See also François Truffaut, "Feu James Dean," *Arts*, September 26, 1956, 4.

9. Here I follow the terminology of Andrew Feenberg in *Transforming Technology: A Critical Theory Revisited* (New York: Oxford University Press, 2002).

10. Paul Virilio and Sylvere Lotringer, *Pure War*, trans. Mark Polizotti (New York: Semiotext(e), 1983).

11. Ibid., 133–35.

12. Regarding the "framework," see Bergson, *Matter and Memory*.

13. The "Belisha Beacon," a flashing orange globe on a pole to mark a zebra (pedestrian) crossing, is named after Leslie Hore-Belisha, British minister of transport, who introduced the device in 1934.

14. On early British speed limits, see Richardson, *The British Motor Industry*, 179–82.

15. For a selection of the best *Punch* motoring cartoons, see Hammerton, *Mr. Punch Awheel*. For the cartoons I describe see pp. 191 and 148.

16. For examples of advertising that catered to motor travelers, see Stern, *Pictorial History of the Automobile*, 75–77. For example, there is an advertisement from Saks and Co. for a raccoon coat as "Automobile Apparel."

17. See Tubbs, *Art and the Automobile*, 16.

18. For "trick pictures" and their role in showing cars in early movies, see Smith, "A Runaway Match," 179–192, esp. 181.

19. See Harding and Popple, *Kingdom of the Shadows*, 96–99. This book offers an extract from Talbot, *Moving Pictures* (211–15).

20. For Talbot, see Harding and Popple, *Kingdom of the Shadows*, 97.

21. Harding and Popple, 99.

22. See Marsh and Collett, *Driving Passion*, 151. The accident is reported in the *Times* (London), August 21, 1896, and August 26, 1896.

23. Foley, *The Pace That Kills*, 1–2.

24. On the complex history of the assertion of these interests and how they played out in British politics, see Plowden, *Motor Car and Politics*.

25. For this and much more discussion on traffic legislation in Britain during this period, see O'Connell, *Car in British Society*, 112–49.

26. Ibid., 124.

27. See Kaszynski, *The American Highway*, 40 (on trail markings) and 56–62 (on the introduction of uniform signage).

28. O'Connell, *Car in British Society*, 115–16.

29. Richardson, *British Motor Industry*, 178.

30. O'Connell, *Car in British Society*, 114.

31. J. S. Mill, *Representative Government*, quoted in Szreter, "GRO and the Government Health Movement," 439.

32. See Desrosiers, *Politics of Large Numbers*, 166–72.

33. Mumford, *Myth of the Machine*, 212.

34. Poovey, *History of the Modern Fact*, esp. xi–xv and 307–28.

35. Benjamin, "On Some Motifs in Baudelaire," 176–80.

36. Ibid., 177.

37. Ibid., 176. The quotation marks are Benjamin's.

38. Ibid., 178–79.

39. Adorno, *Minima Moralia*, quoted in Williams, *Autogeddon*, 90.

40. Woolf, *Orlando*, 309.
41. Reproduced in Kaszynski, *The American Highway*, 114.
42. Fitzgerald, *The Great Gatsby*, 119.
43. Ibid., 119.
44. Filippo T. Marinetti, *Marinetti, Selected Writings*, ed. R. W. Flint (New York: Farrar, Straus and Giroux, 1971), 41, quoted in Boscagli, *Eye on the Flesh*, 135. Boscagli points up the strange tropes in the text thrown up by Marinetti's anxiety about masculine mastery.
45. Durgnat, *The Crazy Mirror*, 69.
46. Ballard, *The Atrocity Exhibition*, annotation on 77. Nader is one of the figures from the sixties referred to continually in Ballard's book.
47. Ibid., 23. Here Ballard is commenting on a scene in which Talbot, looking down on Dealey Plaza in Dallas, Texas, and experiencing "the Annunciation," is heard to murmur, "Ralph Nader."
48. Hayles, "The Borders of Madness," 321–23.
49. Sobchack, "Baudrillard's Obscenity," 327.
50. Ballard, *The Atrocity Exhibition*, note on 24–25.
51. See Huxley, *Along the Road*, esp. part 1, sec. 3, "The Traveler's Eye View," 31–42.
52. Ballard, *Crash*, 7.
53. Ballard, *The Atrocity Exhibition*, note on 25.

Epilogue

1. Gordon, *Our Home Railways*, 1.3.
2. For a discussion of the role of de Quincey's essay in the history of interest in speed and vision, see Pichois, *Vitesse et vision*, 74.
3. See Joyce, *Finnegans Wake*, 348–50: "He blocks his oggles because he confesses to all his tellavicious nieces" (349), and 52: "Television kills telephony in brothers' broil."

BIBLIOGRAPHY

Achebe, Chinua. "An Image of Africa: Racism in Conrad's *Heart of Darkness*." *Massachusetts Review* 8, no. 4 (winter 1977): 782–94.

Adorno, Theodor. *Minima Moralia*. Trans. E. F. N. Jephcott. London: Verso, 1978.

Agamben, Giorgio. "Notes on Gesture." In *Means without End: Notes on Politics*, trans. Vincenzo Binetti and Cesare Casarino. Minneapolis: University of Minnesota Press, 2000.

Althusser, Louis. *Lenin and Philosophy and Other Essays*, trans. Ben Brewster. New York: Monthly Review Press, 1971.

Apollonio, Umbro, ed. *Futurist Manifestos*. New York: Viking, 1973.

Auge, Marc. *Non-Places: Towards an Anthropology of Supermodernity*. London: Verso, 1995.

Avant, Lloyd. "Vision in the Ganzfeld." *Psychological Bulletin* 64, no. 4 (1965): 248–58.

Bachelard, Gaston. *The Poetics of Space*. Boston: Beacon, 1969. Originally published as *La poétique de l'espace*. Paris: Presses Universitaires de France, 1958.

Ballard, J. G. *The Atrocity Exhibition*. New rev. edn. San Francisco: Re/Search, 1990.

——. *Crash*. New York: Farrar, Straus and Giroux, 1994. Originally published 1973.

Banham, Rayner. *Los Angeles: The Architecture of the Four Ecologies*. London: Penguin, 1971.

——. *Theory and Design in the First Machine Age*. 2nd edn. New York: Praeger, 1967.

Beard, George M. *A Practical Treatise on Nervous Exhaustion (Neurasthenia): Its Symptoms, Nature, Sequences, and Treatment*. New York: E. B. Trent, 1905. New York: Kraus Reprint, 1971.

Beckmann, John, ed. *The Virtual Dimension*. New York: Princeton Architectural Press, 1998.

Benjamin, Walter. "On Some Motifs in Baudelaire." In *Illuminations*, ed. Hannah Arendt, trans. Harry Zohn. New York: Schocken, 1969.

Bergson, Henri. *Matter and Memory*, trans. N. M. Paul and W. S. Palmer. New York: Zone Books, 1988. Originally published 1896.

Bhabha, Homi. "Signs Taken for Wonders: Questions of Ambivalence and Authority under a Tree outside Delhi, May 1817." In *The Location of Culture*, by Homi Bhabha. London: Routledge, 1994.

Bishop, George. *The Age of the Automobile*. London: Hamlyn, 1977.

Boscagli, Maurizia. *The Eye on the Flesh: Fashions of Masculinity in the Early Twentieth Century*. Boulder: Westview, 1996.

Brantlinger, Patrick. *Bread and Circuses: Theories of Mass Culture as Social Decay*. Ithaca: Cornell University Press, 1983.

Brennan, Theresa. *Exhausting Modernity*. London: Routledge, 2000.

———. *The Transmission of Affect*. Ithaca: Cornell University Press, 2004.

Brewer, Derek. *Marxist Theories of Imperialism*. London: Routledge and Kegan Paul, 1980.

Brodsky, Joseph. "A Guide to a Renamed City." In *Less than One: Selected Essays*. New York: Farrar, Straus and Giroux, 1987.

Brottman, Mikita. Introduction to *Car Crash Culture*, ed. Mikita Brottman. New York: Palgrave, 2002.

Buck-Morss, Susan. *The Dialectics of Seeing: Walter Benjamin and the Arcades Project*. Cambridge: MIT Press, 1991.

———. "Dream World of Mass-Culture." In *Modernity and the Hegemony of Vision*, ed. David. M. Levit. Berkeley: University of California Press, 1993.

Caujolle, J. H., et al. *J. H. Lartigue*. Milan: Fabri, 1982.

Colomina, Beatrice, ed. *Sexuality and Space*. New York: Princeton Architectural Press, 1993.

———. "The Split Wall: Domestic Voyeurism." In *Sexuality and Space*, ed. Beatriz Colomina, 88–90. New York: Princeton Architectural Press, 1992.

Conrad, Joseph. *Heart of Darkness*. London: Penguin, 1994.

Coroneos, Con. *Space, Conrad and Modernity*. New York: Oxford University Press, 2002.

Cowan, Michael. "The Heart Machine: 'Rhythm' and the Body in Weimar Film and Fritz Lang's *Metropolis*." *Modernism/Modernity* 14, no. 2 (April 2007): 225–48.

Crary, Jonathan. *Techniques of the Observer: On Vision and Modernity in the Nineteenth Century*. Cambridge: MIT Press, 1990.

Crary, Jonathan, and Sanford Kwinter, eds. *Zone 6: Incorporations*. New York: Urzone, 1992.

Debord, Guy. *Society of the Spectacle*. Detroit: Black and Red, 1983. Originally published as *La société du spectacle*. Paris: Buchet-Chastel, 1967.

Deleuze, Gilles. *Bergsonism*, trans. H. Tomlinson and Barbara Habberjam. New York: Zone, 1988.

———. *Cinema I: The Movement Image*. Minneapolis: University of Minnesota Press, 1986.

Derrida, Jacques, Catherine Porter, and Philip Lewis. "No Apocalypse, Not Now

(Full Speed Ahead, Seven Missiles, Seven Minutes)." *Diacritics* 14, no. 2 (summer 1984): 20–31.

Desrosiers, Alain. *The Politics of Large Numbers: A History of Statistical Reasoning*. Trans. Camille Nash. Cambridge: Harvard University Press, 1998.

Dimmenberg, Edward. "The Will to Motorization: Cinemas, Highways, and Modernity." *October* 73 (summer 1995): 91–137.

Donovan, Frank. *Wheels for a Nation*. London: Thomas Y. Crowell, 1965.

Doyle, A. Conan. "The Engineer's Thumb." In *The Adventures of Sherlock Holmes*. Oxford: Oxford World Classics, 1989. Originally published 1892.

Duffy, Enda. *The Subaltern Ulysses*. Minneapolis: University of Minnesota Press, 1994.

Durgnat, Raymond. *The Crazy Mirror: Hollywood Comedy and the American Image*. New York: Horizon, 1980.

Ehrenburg, Ilya. *The Life of the Automobile*. Trans. Joachim Neugroschel. London: Pluto, 1976. Originally published in Russian by Petropolis, Berlin, 1929.

Eksteins, Modris. *Rites of Spring*. New York: Doubleday Anchor, 1990.

Eliot, T. S. *Collected Essays*. London: Faber and Faber, 1953.

Ellmann, Richard. *James Joyce*. Oxford: Oxford University Press, 1959.

Esparza, Richard, and Howard Spencer. *Auto Exotica: The Automobile in Art*. Reno: Reno Art Museum, 1992.

Esty, Jed. *A Shrinking Island: Modernism and National Culture in England*. Princeton: Princeton University Press, 2003.

Featherstone, Mike, Nigel Thrift, and John Urry, eds. *Automobilities*. London: Sage, 2005.

Feenberg, Andrew. *Transforming Technology: A Critical Theory Revisited*. New York: Oxford University Press, 2002.

Fitzgerald, F. Scott. *The Great Gatsby*. New York: Scribe Classics, 1992. Originally published 1925.

Flink, James. *The Automobile Age*. Cambridge: MIT Press, 1988.

Foley, T. C. *The Pace That Kills: Speed as a Factor in Motor Accidents*. London: Public Affairs News Service, 1934.

Ford, Henry. *My Life and Work*. In collaboration with Samuel Crowther. New York: Doubleday, Page, 1923.

Foucault, Michel. "Of Other Spaces." *Diacritics* 16 (spring 1986): 22–27.

Fussell, Paul. "The Passport Nuisance." In *Abroad: British Literary Travelling between the Wars*. Oxford: Oxford University Press, 1980.

Garreau, Joel. *Edge City: Life on the New Frontier*. New York: Anchor, 1992.

Gartman, David. *Auto-Opium: A Social History of American Automobile Design*. London: Routledge, 1994.

Gilette, Howard J., Jr. "The Evolution of the Planned Shopping Center in Suburb and City." *Journal of the American Planning Association* 51, no. 4 (1985): 449–60.

GoGwilt, Christopher L. *The Invention of the West: Joseph Conrad and the Double-Mapping of Europe and Empire*. Stanford: Stanford University Press, 1995.

Gordon, W. J. *Our Home Railways: How They Began and How They Are Worked*. London: Frederick Warne, 1910.

Grahame, Kenneth. *The Wind in the Willows*. London: Aladdin Classics, 1999.

Grosz, Elizabeth. *The Nick of Time: Politics, Evolution, and the Untimely*. Durham: Duke University Press, 2004.

———. "Towards an Architecture of Invention." In *Anyhow*, ed. Cynthia C. Davidson. Cambridge: MIT Press, 1998.

Hammerton, J. A., ed. *Mr. Punch Awheel: The Humors of Motoring*. London: Educational Book Company, 1908.

Harbison, Robert. *The Built, the Unbuilt, and the Unbuildable: In Pursuit of Architectural Meaning*. Cambridge: MIT Press, 1991.

Harding, Colin, and Simon Popple. *In the Kingdom of the Shadows: A Companion to Early Cinema*. Teaneck, N.J.: Fairleigh Dickinson University Press, 1996.

Harding, L., et al. "The car was doing 121 mph — and the driver was drunk: Shock new details of Diana's death." *Guardian* (London), September 2, 1997.

Hardy, Thomas. *Tess of the d'Urbervilles*. London: Penguin Classics, 1998. Originally published 1891.

Harvey, David. "The Geopolitics of Capitalism." In *Social Relations and Spatial Structures*, ed. Derek Gregory and John Urry. New York: St. Martin's, 1985.

Hayles, N. Katherine. "The Borders of Madness." *Science Fiction Studies* 18, no. 3 (1991): 321–23.

Hollier, Denis. *Against Architecture: The Writings of Georges Bataille*. Cambridge: MIT Press, 1995.

Huxley, Aldous. *Along the Road: Notes and Essays of a Tourist*. New York: Ecco Press, 1952. Originally published 1925.

Jameson, Fredric. "Modernism and Imperialism." In *Nationalism, Colonialism, and Imperialism*, ed. Terry Eagleton, Fredric Jameson, and Edward Said, 43–66. Minneapolis: University of Minnesota Press, 1990.

———. *The Political Unconscious: Narrative as a Socially Symbolic Act*. Ithaca: Cornell University Press, 1981.

———. *Postmodernism, or, The Cultural Logic of Late Capitalism*. Durham: Duke University Press, 1991.

———. "Romance and Reification in Joseph Conrad." In *The Political Unconscious: Narrative as a Socially Symbolic Act*, by Fredric Jameson, 206–80. Ithaca: Cornell University Press, 1981.

Jay, Martin. *Downcast Eyes*. Berkeley: University of California Press, 1993.

———. "Returning the Gaze: The American Response to the French Critique of Occularcentrism." In *Traveling Theory: France and the U.S.*, ed. Irene Van der Poel and Sophie Bertho, 114–33. Madison, N.J.: Fairleigh Dickinson University Press, 1999.

Jay, Mike, and Michael Neve, eds. *1900: A Fin-de-Siecle Reader*. London: Penguin, 1999.

Joyce, James. "After the Race." In *Dubliners*. London: Penguin, 1967. Originally published 1914.

————. *Finnegans Wake*. New York: Viking, 1958. Originally published 1939.

————. *Ulysses*. New York: Vintage, 1986. Originally published 1922.

Kaplan, Caren. *Questions of Travel: Postmodern Discourses of Displacement*. Durham: Duke University Press, 1996.

Kaplan, Sam. *L.A Lost and Found: An Architectural History of Los Angeles*. New York: Crown, 1987.

Kaszynski, William. *The American Highway: The History and Culture of Roads in the United States*. Jefferson, N.C.: McFarland, 2000.

Kern, Stephen. *A Cultural History of Causality: Science, Murder Novels, and Systems of Thought*. Princeton: Princeton University Press, 2006.

————. *The Culture of Time and Space, 1880–1918*. Cambridge: Harvard University Press, 1978.

Kyriazi, Gary. *The Great American Amusement Parks*. Secaucus, N.J.: Castle, 1976.

Lartigue, J. H. *J. H. Lartigue*. London: Thames and Hudson, 1993.

Le Corbusier. *Towards a New Architecture*. New York: Dover, 1985.

Lefebvre, Henri. *The Production of Space*. Trans. Donald Nicholson-Smith. Oxford: Blackwell, 1984.

Lewis, Wyndham. "The Romance of War." In *Blasting and Bombardeering*. Berkeley: University of California Press, 1967. Originally published 1937.

MacKenzie, Adrian. *Transductions: Bodies and Machines at Speed*. London: Continuum, 2002.

Mackinder, Halford J. "The Geographical Pivot of History." *Geographical Journal* 23 (1904): 421–37.

Marinetti, Filippo T. "The Founding Manifesto of Futurism." *Le Figaro*, February 20, 1909. In F. T. Marinetti, *Selected Writings*, ed. R. W. Flint. New York: Farrar, Straus and Giroux, 1971.

Marsh, P., and P. Collett. *Driving Passion: The Psychology of the Car*. Boston: Faber and Faber, 1987.

Martin, Marianne W. *Futurist Art and Theory*. Oxford: Clarendon, 1968.

Marx, Karl. *Capital*. Vol. 1. Trans. Ben Fowkes. New York: Vintage, 1977.

Massumi, Brian. *Parables for the Virtual: Movement, Affect, Sensation*. Durham: Duke University Press, 2002.

McCannell, Dean. *The Tourist: A New Theory of the Leisure Class*. Berkeley: University of California Press, 1999.

Monestier, Alain. *Les conquérants de'Olympe: Naissance du sport moderne*. Paris: Albain Michel, 1996.

Mumford, Lewis. *The Myth of the Machine*. New York: Harcourt, Brace and World, 1966.

————. *Technics and Civilization*. New York: Harcourt, Brace, 1934.

Nader, Ralph. *Unsafe at Any Speed: The Designed-In Dangers of the American Automobile*. Expanded edn. New York: Grossman, 1972.

Netter, Marc. *Automobile*. Paris: Editions D'Art Somogy / Cité des Sciences et de l'Industrie, 1996.

Nolan, William F. *Barney Oldfield: The Life and Times of America's Legendary Speed King*. Carpinteria, Calif.: Brown Fox, 2002.

O'Connell, Sean. *The Car in British Society: Class, Gender, and Motoring, 1896–1939*. Manchester: Manchester University Press, 1989.

Pettifer, Julian, and Nigel Turner. *Automania: Man and the Motor Car*. London: Collins, 1984.

Pichois, Claude. *Vitesse et vision du monde*. Neuchatel: La Baconniere, 1973.

Plowden, William. *The Motor Car and Politics in Britain*. Harmondsworth: Pelican, 1973.

Poovey, Mary. *A History of the Modern Fact: Problems of Knowledge in the Sciences of Wealth and Society*. Chicago: University of Chicago Press, 1998.

Reid, L. B. *The Lives of Roger Casement*. New Haven: Yale University Press, 1976.

Rhode, Eric. *A History of the Cinema from Its Origins to 1970*. London: Penguin, 1976.

Richards, Thomas. *The Commodity Culture of Victorian England*. Stanford: Stanford University Press, 1992.

Richardson, Kenneth. *The British Motor Industry, 1896–1939*. London: Archon, 1977.

Rodner, S. *J. M. W. Turner, Romantic Painter for the Industrial Revolution*. Berkeley: University of California Press, 1997.

Ross, Kristin. *Fast Cars, Clean Bodies: Decolonization and the Reordering of French Culture*. Cambridge: MIT Press, 1995.

Said, Edward. *Culture and Imperialism*. New York: Vintage, 1994.

Schnapp, Jeffrey. "Crash (Speed as Engine of Individuation)." *Modernism/Modernity* 6, no. 1 (January 1999): 1–49.

Schnapp, Jeffrey, et al., eds. *Crowds*. Stanford: Stanford University Press, 2006.

Schwartz, Hillel. "Torque: The New Kinaesthetic of the Twentieth Century." In *Zone 6: Incorporations*, ed. Jonathan Crary and Sanford Kwinter. New York: Urzone, 1992.

Shand, James D. "The *Reichsautobahn*: Symbol of the Third Reich." *Journal of Contemporary History* 19 (1984): 189–200.

Simmel, Georg. "The Metropolis and Mental Life." In *Images of Man: The Classical Tradition of Sociological Thinking*, ed. C. Wright Mills. New York: George Braziller, 1960.

Smith, Julian. "A Runaway Match: The Automobile in Early American Film, 1900–1920." In *The Automobile and American Culture*, ed. David A. Lewis and Lawrence Goldstein, 179–92. Ann Arbor: University of Michigan Press, 1980.

Sobchack, Vivian. "Baudrillard's Obscenity." *Science Fiction Studies* 18, no. 3 (November 1991): 327–29.

Stern, Philip Van Doren. *A Pictorial History of the Automobile, as Seen in Motor Magazine, 1903–1953*. New York: Viking, 1953.

Stevenson, John. *British Society, 1914–45*. London: Penguin, 1984.

Szreter, S. "The GRO and the Government Health Movement in Britain, 1837–1914." *Social History of Medicine* 4, no. 3 (December 1991): 435–63.

Talbot, Fredrick A. *Moving Pictures: How They Are Made and Worked*. London: Heinemann, 1912.

Taussig, Michael. *The Nervous System*. Routledge: New York, 1992.

Theweleit, Klaus. *Male Fantasies*. Vol. 1, *Women, Floods, Bodies, History*. Minneapolis: University of Minnesota Press, 1988.

Tichi, Cecelia. *Shifting Gears: Technology, Literature, Culture in Modernist America*. Chapel Hill: University of North Carolina Press, 1987.

Tison, Christophe. *L'Ere du vite*. Paris: Balland, 1989.

Tschumi, Bernard. *Architecture and Disjunction*. Cambridge: MIT Press, 1994.

Tubbs, D. B. *Art and the Automobile*. New York: Grosset and Dunlap, 1978.

Vidler, Anthony. *The Architectural Uncanny*. Cambridge: MIT Press, 1992.

Virilio, Paul. *The Art of the Motor*. Trans. Julie Rose. Minneapolis: University of Minnesota Press, 1995.

———. *Bunker Archeology*. Trans. Paul Collins. New York: Princeton Architectural Press, 1994. Originally published in French as an exhibition catalogue, 1975.

———. *Open Sky*, trans. Julie Rose. London: Verso, 1997.

———. *Speed and Politics: An Essay on Dromology*. Trans. Mark Polizzotti. New York: Semiotext(e), 1986. Originally published as *Vitesse et politique*, Paris: Galilee, 1977.

———. *The Vision Machine*. Bloomington: Indiana University Press, 1994.

———. *War and Cinema*. Trans. Patrick Camiller. London: Verso, 1989. Originally published in French 1984.

Von Reimar, Zellar. *Automobil: Das Magische Objekt in der Kunst*. Frankfurt: Insel, 1985.

Wamble, Mark. "The Parsing of the Eye." In *Slow Space*, ed. Michael Bell and Sze Tsung Leong. New York: Monacelli, 1998.

Waugh, Evelyn. *Remote People*. Reprinted as "A Coronation," in *When the Going Was Good*. London: Penguin, 1973.

Welsh, Alexander. *The City of Dickens*. Oxford: Clarendon, 1971.

Wharton, Edith. *A Motor-Flight through France*. New York: Charles Scribner's Sons, 1909.

Wicke, Jennifer. "Who's She When She's at Home: Molly Bloom and the Work of Consumption." In *Molly Blooms: A Polylogue on Penelope*, ed. David Pierce, 174–95. Madison: University of Wisconsin Press, 1994.

Williams, Heathcote. *Autogeddon*. New York: Little, Brown, 1991.

Wolf, Winfried. *Car Mania: A Critical History of Transport*. Trans. Gus Fagan. London: Pluto, 1986.

Woolf, Virginia. *Mrs. Dalloway*. New York: Harcourt, Brace and World, 1925.

————. *Orlando*. New York: Harcourt, Brace and World, 1928.

Yeats, W. B. *Selected Poems and Four Plays*. New York: Scribner, 1996.

INDEX

Defamiliarization, 5, 9

Defence of the Realm Act (DORA), 97

Defoe, Daniel, 19, 253, 256

Delange Grand Sport, 265–66

Delaunay, Robert: *Homage to Berliot*, 185; *The Red Tower*, 158; and Sonia, 180

de Lempicka, Tamara, 186–88

Deleuze, Gilles, 48, 167, 169, 189; *Cinema I: The Movement Image*, 157, 169–72

Department store, 114, 206

De Quincey, Thomas, 263

Derrida, Jacques, 32, 164; "Force and Signification," 48; "No Apocalypse, Not Now (Full Speed Ahead, Seven missiles, Seven Missives)," 263, 265

Detective fiction, 60, 64, 68–70, 74; *Dial M for Murder*, 55. *See also* Doyle, Arthur Conan

Detroit, 231

Dial M for Murder (film), 55

Diana, Princess of Wales, 2, 3

Dickens, Charles, 199; *Great Expectations*, 81; *Pickwick Papers*, 118–19; Staplehurst disaster and, 119

Discipline and Punish (Foucault), 192

Distance, 9

Dix, Otto, 64

Djinnis, Camille, 126

Dodgem car, 111–13, 135

Double Indemnity (Cain), 68

Doyle, Arthur Conan, 61, 72, 92, 100, 105; "The Engineer's Thumb," 75–82

Dracula (Stoker), 65, 77

Driscoll, Bridget, 128, 199

Driver's license, 7

Driving, 6, 132; goggles, 13

Dr. Jekyll and Mr. Hyde (Stevenson), 61, 68, 77

Dublin, 39, 62, 102

Duchamp, Marcel, 48, 49

Duncan, Isadora, 3, 56, 125

Dunlop, John Boyd, 113

Dynamism, 6

Economist (magazine), 47

Ehrenburg, Ilya, 48, 54; *Life of the Automobile*, 111, 139

Einstein, Albert, 22, 52, 167

Ekstein, Modris, 1

Electric chair, 49

Electric taxi, 199

Electrification, mass, 18, 117

Eliot, T. S., 238, 254; *Love Song of J. Alfred Prufrock*, 7, 21, 47, 50, 55, 60, 63, 102, 140; *The Wasteland*, 264

Ellis Island, 265

Ellul, Jacques, 205

Empire, Age of, 8, 19, 87, 116

Endocolonization, 9, 44, 45, 49

Energy, 5, 6; human, 206; as Victorian topic, 215, 238, 259

Engineering, mechanical: in *Heart of Darkness*, 95; traffic and, 22, 62

"Engineer's Thumb, The" (Doyle), 75–82

English Mail Coach (De Quincey), 263

Epidemiology, 233–34

Espansione spiraliza de muscoli in movimento (Boccioni), 172

Esther Waters (G. Moore), 127

Euclidean perspective, 36, 37

Experience, 4, 104, 130; driving and, 134–35, 160, 202–4, 268; pleasure and, 117–18

Exposition Universelle (Paris), 49, 113

Fairgrounds, 60, 104

Fanon, Frantz, 45

Fascism, Italian, 170

Faulkner, William, 253

Fear, 59, 61, 106; of car crash, 203–4, 240

Enda Duffy is a professor of English at the
University of California, Santa Barbara. He is
the author of *The Subaltern Ulysses* (1994).

➤

Library of Congress Cataloging-in-Publication Data
Duffy, Enda.
The speed handbook : velocity, pleasure, modernism /
Enda Duffy.
p. cm. — (Post-contemporary interventions)
Includes bibliographical references and index.
ISBN 978-0-8223-4430-8 (cloth : alk. paper)
ISBN 978-0-8223-4442-1 (pbk. : alk. paper)
1. Speed — Social aspects. 2. Time — Social aspects.
3. Civilization, Modern — 20th century.
I. Title. II. Series: Post-contemporary interventions.
HM656.D84 2009
304.2'37 — dc22   2009003270